Content

CONTRIBUTIONS AND CREDITS

© Churbarry Enterprises Ltd.
CONTACT, PUBLISHER AND EDITOR
Anthony Churchill, 7 Craven Hill, London W2 3EN.
Phone +44 20 7402 2247. Fax +44 20 7402 1919. E-Mail churbarry@aol.com
CO-ORDINATOR Linda Miller.
PRODUCTION CONTROLLER Cesar Rocha.
DESIGNER AND ARTIST Christopher Howson.
EDITORIAL RESEARCHERS Monika Kludas John Hamilton Holly Hollins Guy Pearse Woods Gleason.
FRONT COVER PHOTOS Main picture Nigel Pert. Top left Cutty Sark Scots Whisky, the other two Beken of Cowes.
SAFETY CONSULTANT Frank Scott MA, FNI, Marine Consultant.

PHOTOGRAPHERS

Our thanks to our superb photographers. The main sources are the ships themselves, and Beken of Cowes. Others include Janka Bielak, Jack Brockway, William Churchill, Cutty Sark Scots Whisky, 'Max', Marius Pedersen of Luftpost, Nigel Pert, Perestroika Sailing, Den Phillips, Jonathan Wills, and many others, with our full listing on page 239.

ISBN: 0 948337 05 2

If you want to go sailing to adventure...
especially in a group of ships with youth aboard, or maybe in a *Cutty Sark Tall Ships' Race.*

*THE SHIPS AND NEW CREWS ARRIVE IN PORT
*PREPARATION FOR THE VOYAGE
*TO THE START LINE
*AT SEA, THE STORM BEGINS
*CALMER WEATHER, AND DOLPHINS
*LAND AHOY AND THE SHIPS TIE UP
*THE PARTIES ASHORE AND SHIP VISITS
*GOOD BYE. UNTIL NEXT YEAR.

FOR COPIES OF THIS VIDEO send cheques to Churbarry Enterprises, 7 Craven Hill, London W2 3EN, £16.00 plus £2.00 post and packaging (or equivalent in foreign currency). Pix Cutty Sark Scots Whisky, and Beken of Cowes. © Ocean Brunswick.

SAIL TO ADVENTURE

SAIL TO ADVENTURE
The excitement in Port......and then at Sea... find out what Sail Training is all about...with coverage of
THE CUTTY SARK TALL SHIPS' RACES
THE CUTTY SARK TALL SHIPS' RACES ARE SPONSORED BY CUTTY SARK SCOTS WHISKY AND ORGANISED BY THE INTERNATIONAL SAIL TRAINING ASSOCIATION.
price £16.00

A COMPANION BOOK 'SAIL A TALL SHIP' a small 'SHIP' the official ISTA Guide, gives details on over 100 ships, large and small, with costs, what you'll expect, voyage lengths, who to contact, what to take, in 182 pages at £18.00 plus £2.00 p and p, from Churbarry Enterprises Ltd, 7 Craven Hill, London W2 3EN. Phone (UK) 0171 402 2247 Fax (UK) 0171 402 1919

OFFICIAL VIDEO OF THE INTERNATIONAL SAIL TRAINING ASSOCIATION

First buy our video...

...which'll show you the excitement.

This is the first video, named an official video of the International Sail Training Association.

Write to us giving your name and address, and enclose (at a special rate) £14.00 + £2.00 post and packaging (by cheque, money order, bankers draft, eurocheque, in sterling) and send to: Churbarry Enterprises, 7 Craven Hill, London W2 3EN. (If you don't like the video, return it within 10 days and we'll refund the £14.00).

Forewords

From Anthony Churchill, Editor.

SAILING TO ADVENTURE - on a sail training ship, on an adventure ship, or charter ship, is for the old, not so old, and young. For learners. And the skilled. In our pages you will find details of the sail training fleet, offering voyages for all of us. You will find round the world yachts, holiday cruisers, racers, regatta boats, day sailers. A varied world for those who love the sea, and wish to learn about it......we hope each of you will find your 'at sea' wishes from these pages.

The International Sail Training Association
from Peter Newell, Race Director.

For many years the tradition of sail training and all that it espoused, in providing opportunities for youth development, has been growing throughout the world. New sail training organisations have been and are being formed all the time, as more people come to understand the value of the challenge that the sea presents. The Annual Cutty Sark Tall Ships' Races, organised by the International Sail Training Association each year since 1956, and the successful operation of the two STA sail training ships Sir Winston Churchill and Malcolm Miller have done much to foster and develop this tradition. Proof of this, if proof were needed, is evident by the number of new sail training ships that are being built and brought into the sail training 'family'.

But how does a youngster, or anyone else, find out how they can become involved with the sea? How can they get on board and experience the challenge? The answers are all to be found in this excellent and long-awaited Guide.

The details of over 200 sail training vessels are here in one publication. It has taken a long time to compile but it has been well worth the effort. It will quickly become the definitive reference book both for those in the sail training fraternity as well as for those wishing to start. I am sure that all those who read this book will find it immensely helpful and I hope that they take up the challenge offered by sail training.

The Association of Sea Training Organisations
from John Hamilton, Chairman.

ASTO is a national body, Anthony Churchill's splendid book is international, however I do not find this a problem! Both the Association and the author have a similar aim, namely to bring these wonderful sailing ships to the attention of as many people as possible, not just in Britain, but throughout the world.

Now, for both young and old, to sail as a crew-member in one of these ships is most certainly an adventure. It is a most memorable experience and one that usually has lasting results. For it will not just be a voyage from one port to another, it will also be a voyage of self discovery. You will not be forced to work aloft among the spars and rigging of a giant wind-jammer, you will not be forced onto the foredeck of a yacht bouncing about in a seaway, to change a headsail. But if you do go you will find that it is not the life-threatening experience you thought it would be. You will do the job, and many other jobs, and feel a huge glow of satisfaction. You will have worked as part of a team - as one of your watch - and you will have achieved things that you never thought you could possibly have achieved.

You will be asked to steer, possibly a thousand tons of sail-driven ship with a hundred souls on board, all in your hands for the hour's trick. At first you'll be sure you can't do it. But you can and do and again the feeling when you are relieved from the wheel will be one of self-satisfaction.

Within the covers of this book, Anthony Churchill has given you the chance to learn about the ships, to know in which ones it is possible to sail and how to arrange a voyage in those which take volunteer crew.

For those new to the world of "Tall Ships" this book could be your gateway to the adventure of a lifetime. For those who have discovered the ships already, here is information on others which you may well not have known about.

Young or Old, Novice or Knowledgeable...

.....you can with certainty find a place on board a ship or yacht to suit your needs. Our Guide will tell you about the alternatives. We list the ships, tell you where each ship goes to, her size, philosophy, how to contact her owners, and what you can expect from a voyage. We also include an idea on costs.

The Ships

In this Guide, we are mainly interested in ships based near, or regularly sailing through the North Sea, the North Atlantic, Baltic and Mediterranean, and we have also covered ships which are harder to get aboard, either because they are based further afield - thus in America, Australia, Japan - or because their chosen tasks do not allow you easy access to them.

We'll try to tell you about the different kinds of vessel, from the largest four masted square rigged ships to sleek single mast ocean racers, or gentle elderly cruising yachts. Most of our information is given by the ships themselves. So, one warning. It is up to you to check before a voyage, and when you join, that the ship of your choice has up to date safety certificates and sufficient insurance for your needs.

So what will you get from a voyage?

We hope you will be rewarded with a widening of your horizons. On board you will learn the skills of seamanship and the ways of the sea, and yet we also believe it is more important if you can learn something new about yourself, and your fellows. You'll benefit, whether you are a loner, or sociable. Maybe you'll discover the sea isn't for you, in which case an adventure voyage is a good way of finding out. But beware, many who come find they cannot leave the sea afterwards. There's a lure, a love, a learning to be had, and a way of life that levels, inspires and improves. Even if you have no previous experience, accept the challenge of a voyage. The adventure and teamwork will test you to the limit, and you'll have an experience you'll never forget.

Our Contents

Most of our book details the ships that are available, with addresses, phone and fax numbers, E-Mail and Web sites. Contact them for information about the voyages they undertake. If you have any queries, the International Sail Training Association and affiliated National Associations will try and help. They are listed on page 17.

Publisher's Note

And one thought, dear reader. This is our first attempt to put together all the information you'll need in a Guide. If you come across a gremlin, please tell us. All suggestions for when we reprint, are welcome. Should other ships be in the book? What extra information would you like ? Please write, fax or E-Mail to me: see details of contact points on page 3.

by Anthony Churchill

16 superb official posters of Tall Ships

Size A2 (610mm x 420mm, 24 x 16.5 inches),
Christian Radich - Sedov
Dar Mlodziezy -Gloria - Sagres II

Size A3 (420 x 297mm, 16.5 x 11.5 inches),
Juan Sebastian de Elcano - Mir - Sagres II
Pallada - Iskra - Shabab Oman
Alexander von Humboldt
Tovarisch - Captain Miranda
Zawisza Czarny - Cuauhtemoc.

Payment (from the UK) by UK Cheques and postal orders, or (from elsewhere) by Sterling

'Sail to adventure'

So what do you expect from joining an Adventure Ship? Here's a fivesome for you to consider: teamwork, excitement, concern about others, danger, and fun.

Many believe that "Sailing to Adventure" takes place only on large, multimasted ships. They are a part of the scene, and very important, but the 'big ones' are outnumbered by many more of moderate size. At the top end are the giant 'Tall Ships' of maybe 100 metres (328 feet) long, but as an Australian coined the phrase "you don't have to be big to be tall". Most of the fleet is made up of smaller vessels, down to a length as little as 9.1 metres (30 feet). We've illustrated the sizes on the front cover of our Guide. Besides the large Portuguese Sagres II, we show a medium sized ship, the UK's Sir Winston Churchill, and Italy's modern Stella Polare represents the smaller ship. We hope to give a good indication of the various types and sizes that may satisfy you.

The character of each ship differs, but the intention of Sail Training does not. It teaches you about the sea, for sure, and you'll learn much about 'the ropes' of being on the ocean waves, at night and by day. Indeed a voyage may be the gateway for you into the wide world of sailing. But more important is that you will embark on a voyage of discovery. You may feel that in to-day's 'safe society' you are not being stretched, you are not challenged, either in facing up to immediate adversity, or in getting to know and understand your fellows, whether they be from different walks of life, regions, religions or nationalities.

Older people take part in some voyages, but usually it is the young who come on board. In the Cutty Sark Tall Ships' Races, for instance, half the crew have to be between 15 and 25.

YOU'LL FIND ...
Adventure
There is too little adventure in our everyday lives, too little getting out and finding what else lies outside a cosy indoors. If you want to get a broader view of life, then the challenge of the sea will widen your horizon and you may discover you have greater abilities and strengths than you thought possible, and which are often not revealed by a 'normal' lifestyle.

Adversity
It takes courage to set out on a sea voyage when you have no experience other than some stories you've heard, especially when some of these are about adversity. The knowledge that the ship has to be sailed round the clock, irrespective of weather or mishap, and that the only immediate first aid, fire brigade, or sail repairer is 'you' and the crew, dawns on all who realise that they may be outside the range of the normal emergency services that are so much a part of life today. It is a kind of Outward Bound with the added spice of being at sea. The close living space means that each member of the crew becomes familiar with practically all of their comrades' habits and traits, be they endearing or unfortunate. This should lead to tolerance in your attitude and approach to others. The world (and the people in it) is more varied than you'd think.

Danger
Dangers are real and perceived. Conditions can change rapidly at sea, and you and your fellows will face problems which need a quick change of mental 'gear', and a togetherness approach to find a solution. You may be on a gentle sail, and quickly have to face, within a minute perhaps, any number of 'sea changes'. The wind can rise quickly and you may have to manoeuvre swiftly out of a dangerous situation, or to recover a sail that's suddenly 'blown out'. You must always be prepared for the making of a quick response to danger, for instance in the unlikely situation of someone falling overboard. That's part of the challenge .

Fun
Here is the key. The adversity and danger must be considered, but it's not only the voyage at sea, and the satisfactory dealing with difficulties in your path, but the 'run ashore' in a foreign port, the parties and the friendships, the contrasts and the people.

Teamwork
Opportunities are created by placing you as part of a team where a spirit of co-operation is essential and which is of a quite different quality than that needed - for instance - in land based activities or structured games. A crew quickly become aware of their interdependence when, for example, they need to sleep while the others are trusted to sail the ship safely through the night.

Leadership
A skill which many young people have little opportunity to attempt, let alone practice, in unfamiliar surroundings. The command structure of a ship at sea is a necessity. And there are always a number of situations where new crew members can be placed in leadership roles whilst at the same time being supervised. Maybe leadership is not your game, but at sea everyone is part of the team and has to rely on others for a successful voyage.

Your choice
Which voyage suits you? Maybe you prefer a small ship on her own. You can get a more intense pleasure, maybe, with only a few shipmates around you and no other ships nearby. At the other end of the scale is the International Sail Training Association's annual gathering, the Cutty Sark Tall Ships' Races, when as many as 100 ships from many countries race and cruise together, and you can join for a week or five weeks if you wish. The Races are important, and are the subject of a later article in this Guide.

Preparation for a voyage

what to take, and not to take on board...

When you go aboard a Sail Training Ship, what should you take with you? And what don't you take? Some of you may shy away from a voyage if you think you haven't got the right gear. In the final analysis, ships have their own rules, and each will tell you, or send you a comprehensive list of what they require. Usually bedding, and foul weather gear is provided, but - for instance - a large Russian ship may ask for sleeping bags. If the ship is large, it may not be so fussy at cutting down on your personal items. There might be room for suitcases, for instance, but a small ship may limit your luggage. So here are some ideas which you may wish to confirm with the ship of your choice.

NORMAL WEAR

How many underclothes, shirts, trousers, socks are needed. Summer nights can be colder than you'd think. Some ships ask for gloves, (wool is best) to keep hands warm. some sailors have them with the fingers cut out so you can easily 'work ship' (help with ropes, etc) in them. And a hat - wool again is best. Trendy gear may get in the way of your movement about the ship. Jeans are fine. Remember a ship has many a corner to bump your ankles or elbows. Track suits can be recommended.

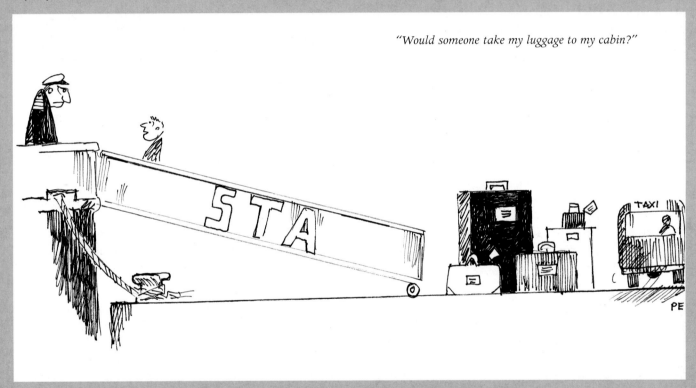

"Would someone take my luggage to my cabin?"

SLEEPING
A good sleep in the warm makes you a more useful crew member when you're called on deck. Do you have to bring sleeping bag, blankets, pillows, sheets? And are towels provided?

HYGIENE
Well, you have to bring washing things. Remember the shampoo and soap, and other disposables as on most of the ships (except maybe the largest) there won't be a shop on board.

MEDICAL
Each ship will have first aid kit, but do you bring sea sickness tablets, personal first aid (elastoplast, bandages).
Remember, the sun's rays reflected off the sea are stronger than you think, and there's windburn which can make your skin additionally uncomfortable. So what about sunhats, sunglasses, suncreams, lipbalm?

SHORE GOING GEAR
Most people are informal and its 'in' to wear sailing clothes ashore. Many ships won't have enough room for a snazzy set of clothes.

SUITCASES
Ask if suitcases are acceptable They are difficult to stow away, so collapsible bags are better, or backpacks (without frames). If you bring some plastic bags with you, put your clothes in them to keep them dry in case of heavy weather. Seawater has an annoying habit of finding a way to drip in the most inconvenient places, usually on your clothes and nobody else's.

FOOTWEAR
Shiny 'city' shoes are out; trainers or gym shoes are fine. But how many pairs do you bring? A dose of seawater on deck and you may need a second pair. Sea boots are often provided.

FOUL WEATHER

If the wind blows a gale, you'll want to be protected. So what does the ship provide, and what must you bring? Usually heavy weather oilskins are provided to keep out the waves, and also 'wellies', but not always. And ask if there's a benefit to bring other gear. For instance a towel cut in half lengthwise becomes a neck towel to pull in tight around the neck, to stop the drips getting through. What about a second pair of socks, larger than your usual, to make a layer of two of them?

FOOD AND DRINK

Three meals a day (and probably all-times hot drinks) should be provided. What about soft drinks? Can you purchase anything on board? Or can you bring extra? What is the attitude to alcohol? (Be prepared to inform the ship if you are taking any medication or suffer from any disabling diseases such as asthma, epilepsy, diabetes, etc. These are not necessarily a bar to your participating in a voyage.)

CASH

Is there a shop on board? Probably not. But you may need money for your 'run ashore' in a foreign port. So do you bring cash, or foreign cash. And how much? And credit cards?

GOING FOREIGN

If you are going to other countries, do you need a passport, 'jabs' (inoculations) before you go?

WHAT YOU MAY CONSIDER NOT BRINGING

Smart shore going gear (is there room on board); jewellery which can get in the way of your 'working ship'. What about watches (unless waterproof). Personal stereos, phones and radios; the ship will have a policy on these, so ask if they're allowed. Remember, mechanical things and seawater make bad bedfellows.

PLEASE BRING

Musical instruments - if you can play. A mouth organ, tin whistle or guitar are usually most welcome. Larger instruments may be a problem of storage space on board, so ask.

WHAT YOU MAY BRING, FOR YOURSELF

Food, probably sweets, chocolates, books. Binoculars, to enjoy the view; and a camera (and film) to remember the best adventure you'll ever have.

SOME THOUGHTS

If you wear glasses or have contact lenses, take a spare set with you just in case. And for those glasses, you may want string (or cheap cord) bought from a chemist or oculist, tied behind the head so they can drop from your nose to your chest, and not overboard. Some ships (medium to large) ask if you can bring a torch, to keep in your pocket. And what about a notebook and pen?

WARNING

Before you join, ask if there are any conditions before your acceptance. Some sail training groups insist you must be able to swim - 50 metres is one ship's requirement. If you have a medical condition, or are disabled, ask before you book. Some ships cater specifically for the disabled - such as the Lord Nelson. Others have a number of voyages for the handicapped, and for those with special needs.

FINALLY

Why not send a photocopy of these pages to your intended ship, to see what they have to say. Any of their (or your) comments would be most welcome to us, to help us in any future reprints of this book. Each ship may well have a firm view of its own, so let us hear from you.

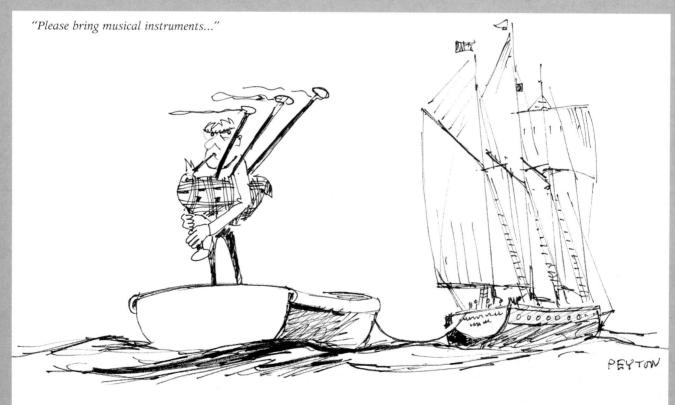

"Please bring musical instruments..."

'Sea Terms'

When you get on board, the assumption is that you haven't been to sea before. But knowing something about the sea and its language before you get on board can be an advantage - and then the professional crew can spend more time with those with less knowledge than you. It may also help you if you know a few basic knots, shown below.

BOW.	The front end of the ship.
BULKHEAD	Wall
STERN.	The back end of the ship.
DECK.	The floor.
DECKHEAD	Ceiling
PORT.	The left hand side looking forward.
STARBOARD.	The right hand side looking forward
go FORARD.	Go to the front end of the ship.
go AFT.	Go to the back end of the ship.
GALLEY.	The kitchen.
CHARTROOM.	The navigation area.
HEADS.	The lavatories.
HALYARD.	Rope for hoisting a sail.
SHEET.	Rope for controlling a sail, in and out.
DOWNHAUL.	Rope for pulling down a sail.
STAY.	Wire that supports a mast.
SHROUDS.	Group of wires supporting a mast.
KNOTS.	has two meanings. 'Going at 20 knots' means the ship is progressing at 20 sea miles per hour. And, of course, knots are ties in ropes - see below.

A WATCH.	Normally, a 4 hour period on duty.
DOG-WATCH.	2 two hour periods between 1600 and 2000 hrs to rotate the watch routine.
STAND BY.	Get ready.
AVAST.	Stop pulling a rope but don't let go.
SLACKAWAY.	Ease out a rope.
MAKE FAST.	Secure a rope.
BELAY THAT.	Stop carrying out the last order.
COMPANIONWAY.	Ladder or stairs between the deck and the ship's interior.
CHAIN LOCKER.	Enclosed area near the bow where the anchor chain is kept (stowed).
STOW.	To put away safely or keep.
BINNACLE.	The housing for the steering compass.
HELM	The steering wheel or tiller

WORDS IN THIS BOOK WHICH YOU MAY NOT UNDERSTAND.

AFTERGUARD.	Collective term to describe professional crew, or officers.
BOSUN.	The same as boatswain, the person responsible for maintenance of ship and its rig.
WINDWARD.	The side of the ship towards which the wind is blowing (the uphill side).
LEEWARD.	The side of the ship further from the wind.
LEE SHORE.	The shore on to which the wind blows.

KNOTS

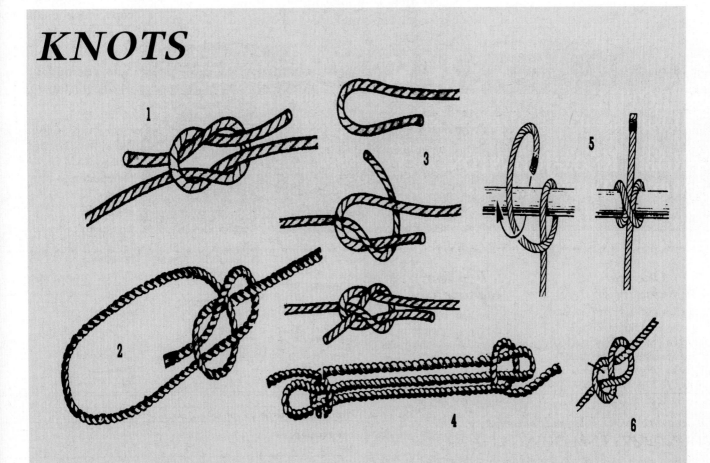

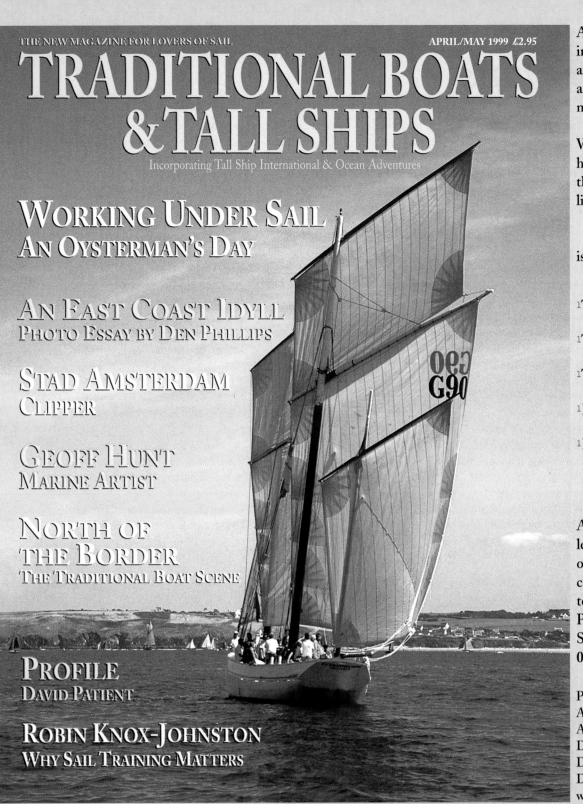

THE NEW MAGAZINE FOR LOVERS OF SAIL

APRIL/MAY 1999 £2.95

TRADITIONAL BOATS & TALL SHIPS

Incorporating Tall Ship International & Ocean Adventures

WORKING UNDER SAIL
AN OYSTERMAN'S DAY

AN EAST COAST IDYLL
PHOTO ESSAY BY DEN PHILLIPS

STAD AMSTERDAM
CLIPPER

GEOFF HUNT
MARINE ARTIST

NORTH OF THE BORDER
THE TRADITIONAL BOAT SCENE

PROFILE
DAVID PATIENT

ROBIN KNOX-JOHNSTON
WHY SAIL TRAINING MATTERS

A magazine for everyone interested in tall ships and traditional sail. It a magazine for a maritime nation.

What greater tradition has Britain than that o the sea and sail? It is a living, vibrant tradition *Traditional Boats & Tall Ships* is its splendid champio

[1] Tall ships - past, present and future
[1] Traditional boats - past, present and fut
[1] The men and women who sail them
[1] Exploration & discovery under sail
[1] Profiles of maritime artists, writers & photographers

Available from all leading newsagents, or to be assured of you copy why not subscribe to the magazine on the Poundbury Publishing Subscription Hotline: 01305 266360.

Poundbury Publishing Lt
Agriculture House,
Acland Road,
Dorchester,
Dorset.
DTI IEF
www.poundbury.co.uk

One Year Subscription
Save over 20%
on the Subscription Price
and receive 6 bi-monthly issues
of *Traditional Boats & Tall Ships*,
a glorious full colour magazine.
Just £17.00 *(UK delivery only)*
instead of £21.50

Two Year Subscription
Save over 25%
on the Subscription Price
and receive 12 bi-monthly issues
of *Traditional Boats & Tall Ships*.
Subscribe now.
Just £32.50 *(UK delivery only)*
instead of £43.50

Or send a cheque or P/O made payable to:
POUNDBURY PUBLISHING LTD
Please send your details to: Poundbury Publishing Ltd,
Agriculture House, Acland Road, Dorchester, Dorset DTI IEF

SUBSCRIPTION HOTLINE ORDERS
01305 266360 *(Mon - Fri 9am-5.30pm)*

	UK	Europe & Eire	Rest of World
Post paid			*Air mail*
One Year	£21.50	£23.00	£28.00
Special offer £17.00			
Two Year	£43.50	£45.00	£54.00
Special offer £32.50			

Please charge my Credit Card ❑ Visa ❑ Mastercard

Card No: _____ Expiry date: _____

Amount: _____ Date: _____

Signature: _____

Please start the subscription with the _____ issue

PLEASE PRINT
Name: _____
Address: _____
Postcode: _____
Tel No: _____ Email: _____

Please tick one of the following
❑ 1 year subscription   ❑ 2 year subscription

Safety

Good sail training demands an environment that is both safe and challenging. Whilst nothing at sea can be entirely safe, these two requirements are in no way mutually exclusive, as witnessed by the excellent record of the regular sail training vessels.

The most important element in running a safe ship is not equipment or her certificates of inspection. It is the human factor. A ship has to be run safely, and to achieve that, some measure of discipline is vital. The degree and formality of discipline is open to wide interpretation, but it is always there. The sea does not forgive carelessness or neglect, and as regards safety there are no passengers or trainees. Everyone is involved.

Training

Safety requires training, and each ship should run information sessions for new crew that covers all the safety equipment, action required in the event of an emergency, and the emergency alarms used on board. This is all additional to being trained on how to sail the ship. Larger ships will have posters on display that show the layout of all safety and firefighting equipment, and designated crew stations for emergencies.

Government Inspections

Those vessels of greater than 24 metres (79 feet) are covered by a considerable body of national and international legislation such as SOLAS (Safety of life at Sea), IMO (International Maritime Organisation), etc. In order to ensure compliance with these regulations these ships are not only subject to inspection by their own state inspectors (Flag State Inspection), but also by state inspectors in any country that they visit (Port State Inspection). In addition these vessels are subject to inspection by the various classification societies, such as the famous Lloyds Register. This is the origin of the term A1, though strictly speaking it should be 100A1+ for an ocean going vessel. All these inspections are very thorough (some even require the ship to be in a dry dock), and any critical shortcomings can result in the vessel being formally detained and large fines levied.

Before paying out good money to sail on a vessel it is important to ensure that she meets some form of recognised standard (national or international), and that all her legal paperwork is 'in date'. Smaller vessels are usually subject to some form of Code of Practice.

ISTA Inspections

These are totally separate from any state inspections that may take place, and they are only in force for the period of the Cutty Sark Tall Ships' Races. The wide variety of vessels and nations involved in the Tall Ships fleet could lead to people trying to dodge expensive safety requirements, and there is a need for a common standard. It is important to appreciate that the ISTA do not have the power to detain a vessel, only to disqualify her from competing in the race. For larger ships ISTA checks for legal compliance with international rules (while not usurping Flag/Port or State functions), and covers special race requirements that are not covered by national or international legislation. Smaller vessels are often outside the scope of legislation and government inspections, and for them the ISTA inspection teams often find themselves performing the dual function of inspecting and advising. Their aim is always to assist where necessary to bring a vessel up to the common standard before the race, rather than simply to disqualify outright. Captain Terry Hughes,

FNI, FRIN, who is a very experienced Master Mariner, is in charge of this side of affairs, and ensures that ISTA regulations always keep up with the latest developments in safety standards.

ISTA REGULATIONS

These are published as part of the racing and sailing rules and cover a wide variety of points. A sample of the more obvious ones is as below:

Lifelines

The rules require the vessel to have lifelines (preferably wire), or solid bulwarks, around the sides of the ship, to help prevent you falling overboard. These have to be at least 610 mm high.

Safety Net
All bowsprits must have a safety net underneath.

Lifejackets
All vessels must have lifejackets for all crew members, each fitted with a light & whistle. Buoyancy aids, whilst legal for some nations, do not meet ISTA race standards, and such vessels wishing to race have to upgrade to genuine lifejackets.

Liferafts
Inflatable liferafts have to be carried in all vessels, and in larger vessels these have to be mounted to "float free" in the event of an accident. Each raft has its capacity clearly marked, and the rafts must be able to carry all the crew (normally there is a large over-capacity). Each raft is surveyed at regular intervals (normally annually), and the expiry date should be clearly marked.

Lifebuoys
These solid floating rings have to be kept on deck, and the minimum carried starts at two, and rise with the size of ship. Your ship should have at least one with a buoyant automatic light attached.

Safety harnesses
The ship should have a safety harness for everyone on board. These should have a snaphook, in good working condition. ISTA recommends that all harnesses are professionally made to an established safety standard, and prefers those designs that spread the load over the body in the event of a fall.

Pyrotechnics
This is a generic term for rockets and flares, which have a limited shelf life (normally three years), and the expiry date is always clearly marked on each item. The materials used in manufacture deteriorate with age and become unstable, so no out of date 'pyros' should be kept on board. The race rules specify a minimum of these items, and this is much more than the average family yacht would carry.

Radios
All vessels have to have short range VHF radio for communicating with the race 'guard ship'. For longer ocean races a longer range MF radio is required. However these are equipment minima, and most vessels carry well above it. A good sign in a small yacht is when additional handheld VHF is carried, and that it is a modern waterproof model capable of being taken into the liferaft in an emergency. Many vessels now have satellite communications, these are not an ISTA requirement, yet.

GMDSS
You may hear of this acronym, which stands for Global Maritime Distress & Safety System. It is an integrated electronic distress system that becomes mandatory for the larger vessels from 1999. Its full remit does not involve the bulk of the ISTA fleet, but as will be seen some elements of it are ISTA requirements for all vessels, even the smaller ones.

EPIRB
It means Electronic Position Indicator Radio Beacon. It is a very important piece of safety equipment and has been the cause of many rescues world wide. If your ship gets into trouble (or a person falls overboard), then the EPIRB is activated. The lower frequency is that used specifically for homing and uses an aircraft frequency, so when activated, aircraft can pinpoint your position. The upper frequency is specifically designed for Satellite reception, so that the satellite records your position and alerts the correct rescue services. In technical terms, the two main types of EPIRB used by GMDSS to provide ocean coverage are: (a) 406 MHZ (with 121.5/243 MHZ Homer)(satellite doppler shift CPA fix on 406 frequency). and (b) Inmarsat E (1.6 GHz)(fixing by built-in GPS)(Homer and some have SART). Both of the above are individually hand-coded to identify the unit in distress. There are some personal locator beacons (PLBS) which are largely restricted to racing yachts, and some older models, both of which only operate on 121.5/243 MHZ, and give a less accurate fix, have less coverage, and do not identify the unit in distress. In Round the World Races, when the rules state that the loss of a man overboard leads to disqualification of the yacht from that race, personal EPIRBS are carried and can locate a person overboard, even in the southern oceans. There is also a VHF Channel 70 model, whose limited coverage does not greatly encourage its use. ISTA rules now require all Tall Ship race entrants to carry an EPIRB providing GMDSS ocean coverage (406 MHZ or Inmarsat-E).

SARTS
Search And Rescue Radar Transponders. These are triggered by navigational radars to provide a return that is electronically enhanced and highlighted to assist ships in locating liferafts in a SAR (Search and Rescue) scenario. They are only required for vessels over 300 tons by SOLAS, but some national rules (such as those in the UK) are more rigorous. Although ISTA does not yet require SARTS as a rule, the better vessels already have one.

Fire Fighting
You will see fire fighting gear onboard, most obviously in larger ships which have the works - firehoses, foam, fire resistant clothing, compressed air breathing apparatus, and trained firefighters. However even smaller yachts must meet a minimum standard, and a particularly important issue for ISTA is that they should have the ability to shut off fuel to the engine, and fight the fire without having to open the engine compartment.

Navigation
It should go without saying that a vessel should have the necessary charts, but ISTA do check along with compass, echo sounder, distance log, and other books and equipment. Larger vessels have to have radar and in these days even the smallest yacht normally has a satellite navigation system. You should be very dubious indeed if you cannot see any obvious electronic navaids. Always ask.

General
If you are ever in any doubt about conditions in your vessel try to seek advice from someone with professional qualifications. This is relatively easy in the races as the officials are easily identified, and there are many other ships around, but it is less easy if you are abroad, and do not speak the local language. The majority of ships are extremely well run, but as in all walks of life there are rogues operating on the legal margins (well away from inspectors). The choice is yours. Do not stay if you believe the vessel to be unsafe.

Who to ask for advice?

The International Sail Training Association.

5 Mumby Road, Gosport, Hants PO12 1AA Phone +44 (0)2392 586367. Fax +44 (0)2392 584661
e mail:raceoffice@ista.co.uk Web http://www.ista.co.uk

NATIONAL SAIL TRAINING ASSOCIATIONS AFFILIATED TO THE ISTA.

American Sail Training Association,
P O Box 1459,
Newport, RI 02840, USA.
phone +1 401 846 1775.
fax +1 401 849 5400.
e mail asta@sailtraining.org
web http://www.tallships.sailtraining.org

Aporvela,
Centro de Operacoes,
Doca do Terreiro do Trigo,
P - 1100 Lisboa,
Portugal.
phone +351 1 887 6854.
fax +351 1 887 3885.

Australian STA,
P O Box 196,
Crows Nest,
NSW 2065,
Australia.
phone +61 2 9906 1277.
fax +61 2 9906 1030.
e mail auboz@ozemail.com.au

STA Belgium,
Grote Singel 6,
B-2900 Schoten,
Belgium.
phone +323 658 0006.
fax +323 237 1138.
e mail gvdd.advo@glo.be

Danish Sail Training Association,
Lodsvœnget 12,
DK-6710 Esbjerg V,
Denmark.
phone +45 7511 7581.
fax +45 7614 3686.
e mail chh@ave.dk

STA Finland,
c/o Pekka Toumisalo,
PO Box 62,
FIN-04201 Kervotka,
Finland.
phone +358 9 685 26 16.
fax. +358 9 685 26 15.
e mail: purjelaivasaatio@pp.kolumbus.fi
Web http://www.koti.kolumbus.fi

STA France
France-Voiles-Equipages,
8 rue Jean Delalande,
35400 Saint-Malo,
France.
phone +33 99 82 35 33.
fax +33 99 82 27 47.

STA Germany,
Hafenhaus,
Columbusbahnhof,
D - 27568 Bremerhaven.
Phone +49 471 945880.
Fax +49 471 9458845.

STA Indonesia
Mabesal, Gilangkap, PO Box 7334, Jakarta
TMII 13560 A, Indonesia.
phone +62 21 872 3162.
fax +62 21 871 1858.

STA Italy,
c/o Yacht Club Italiano,
Porticciolo Duca degli Abruzzi,
1-16128 Genova,
Italia.
phone + 39 010 254 3652.
fax +39 010 254 6168.

STA Japan,
Memorial Park Tower A,
2-1-1 Minato-Mirai, Nishi-ku,
Yokohama,
Kanagawa 220-0012,

Japan.
phone +81 45 680 5222.
fax +81 45 680 5221.
e mail: LDD00622@nifty.ne.jp

STA Netherlands,
Postbus 55,
N - 2340 AB Oegstgeest,
Netherlands.
phone +31 71 5153013.
fax +31 71 5153013.

STA Poland,
PO Box 113,
81-963 Gdynia 1,
Poland.
phone +48 58 620 62 25.

STA Russia,
Head of St. Petersburg Engineering,
Marine College,
Kosaya Linia 15a,
Ru-199026 St. Petersburg,
Russia.
phone +7 812 217 1934.
fax +7 812 356 60 69.

STA Sweden,
MKV, Box 5155,
S-426 05 V Flölunda,
Sweden.
phone +46 31 692000.
fax +46 31 691681.
mobile +46 70569 2147.
e mail ragnar.westblad@swipnet.se

OTHER NATIONAL REPRESENTATIVES, WHO CAN BE CONTACTED THROUGH THE ISTA:
Ireland
Norway
Spain
Ukraine

OTHER SAIL TRAINING ORGANISATIONS

STA Tall Ships,
2a The Hard,
Portsmouth,
PO1 3PT.
phone +44 2392 832055.
fax +44 2392 815769.
e mail:tallships@sta.org.uk

ASTO (Association of Sea Training
Organisations),
c/o RYA, RYA House,

Romsey Road,
Eastleigh,
Hampshire SO5 4XA.
phone +44 2380 627 400.
fax +44 2380 629 924..

Canadian STA,
PO Box 21067, Ottawa South RPO,
Ottawa,
Ontario K1S 5N2, Canada.
phone +1 613 730 3243.
fax +1 613 730 2224.

STA of South Africa,
PO Box 1804,
New Germany,
Kwa Zulu Natal,
South Africa 3620.
phone.+27 31 361 7986.
fax +27 31 361 7972.

STA of Western Australia,
PO Box 1100,
Fremantle 6160, Western Australia,
Australia.
phone +61 9 430 105.
fax +61 9 430 4494.

If you are ringing a country from outside its boundaries, where + is indicated, prefix with 00 from most European countries, but use 07 (from Spain) 095 (Norway) and 009 (Sweden). Other major Sail Training Countries' prefixes are 001 (USA) 0011 (Australia) Canada (001) Finland (990) Japan (001) Poland (0) Russia (810) Brazil (00) Mexico (98) etc. If phoning from a country and to a country, leave out the first group (+44, +1, +7, etc) and prefix the other groups with a 0.

Lifejackets and Buoyancy Aids

Top left
50 Newton
buoyancy aid

Top right
100 Newton
lifejacket

Middle left
150 Newton
lifejacket
uninflated

Middle right
275 Newton
lifejacket
uninflated

Bottom left
150 Newton lifejacket
inflated

Bottom right
275 Newton
lifejacket
inflated

The equipment
is courtesy of
Crewsaver
Ltd

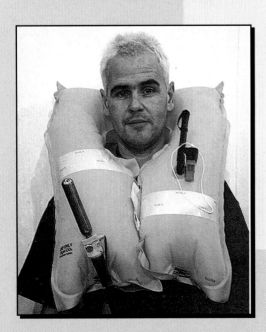

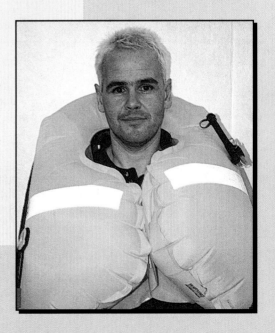

Insurance, first aid, jackets

INSURANCE

It is now generally accepted that before going abroad for a holiday it is essential to have adequate insurance. There are many ways of securing this, either as part of the holiday package or on an individual basis.

Exactly the same applies with regard to a Sail Training Voyage and as part of making a booking, you MUST check on what personal insurance, if any, is provided as part of the fee. Sometimes there is a separate and mandatory insurance scheme shown as an additional fee to each voyage. However if there is no personal insurance cover built in, or required, then you should make alternative arrangements. If insurance is provided, then you must satisfy yourself that it is adequate for you. Remember, you may want to go aloft.

Although some details of individual ship's insurance are covered in the ship details section of this Guide they should always be checked and verified by you when making a booking.

You should also check what safety certificates are held by the ship. This should normally be fully certificated by the country in which the vessel is registered. You should also be particularly careful when a ship is registered outside the European Union.

The largest European group of Sail Training ships, the Ocean Youth Trust, offers the following cover, within the 'charter' fee. This is generous compared with the majority of sail training ships, but might give you a benchmark against which you can measure other ships' policies.

Liability to members of the public	£5m
Liability for products	£5m
Liability to third parties	£5m
Liability to passengers	£5m

Medical expenses when abroad	£500,000 per person
Personal accident	£2,000 per person
Death	£20,000 per person
Personal effects	£500 per person
Cash	£100 per person

FIRST AID

Most Sail Training Ships will carry equipment in accordance with Merchant Ships' Regulations. Some have on board permanent skilled medical staff. It is, like insurance, something you should question when making a booking.

SAFETY JACKETS

In ISTA Races "All vessels must have lifejackets...Buoyancy aids, whilst legal for some nations, do not meet ISTA race standards". In the CE 'The Community European', a manufacturer can only sell lifejackets, buoyancy aids and safety harnesses tested to CEN European Specifications, and they must carry the signs below. The 275, 150, 100 and 50 are Newtons. A Newton is a unit of force with 10 Newtons approximately equivalent to 1 kilo (2.2 lbs) of buoyancy. The higher the Newton, the higher the buoyancy ratings, which is shown for adult sizes only. Smaller sizes will have proportionally less buoyancy.

In general, the 275 Newton lifejacket is suitable for non-swimmers, suitable offshore and in severe conditions when maximum protection is required and heavy waterproof clothing is worn. It is not guaranteed to self right an unconscious wearer, though it should in the majority of cases. The 150 Newton jacket is suitable for non swimmers, for use in all but the most severe conditions. It may not immediately right an unconscious user wearing heavy waterproof clothing. It is equivalent to previous British BSI approved lifejackets. The 100 Newton lifejacket is only suitable for swimmers, and is not guaranteed to self right an unconscious user wearing waterproof clothing and should not be expected to protect the airway of an unconscious person in rough water. The 50 Newton buoyancy aid is only suitable for competent swimmers, in sheltered waters where help is close at hand, and it only provides support to a conscious person who can help themselves.

HARNESSES

The CEN standard for harnesses (a rope from the lifejacket with clip on at its end) is based on these reasons; the need to secure the wearer when on deck, to prevent him/her falling into the water, and to help recovery back onto the deck. They are not intended to prevent falls from a height. When a lifejacket is combined with a safety harness, both must have separate CEN approval.

We thank Crewsaver of Gosport Hant, England for information on safety jackets and harnesses, and for permission to use photographs of their products.

Sails of the largest ships in the sail training fleet

1. Flying Jib
2. Outer Jib
3. Inner Jib
4. Fore Staysail
5. Fore Course
6. Fore Lower Topsail
7. Fore Upper Topsail
8. Fore Lower Topgallant
9. Fore Upper Topgallant
10. Fore Royal
11. Main Staysail
12. Main Topmast Staysail
13. Main Topgallant Staysail
14. Main Course
15. Main Lower Topsail
16. Main Upper Topsail
17. Main Lower Topgallant
18. Main Upper Topgallant
19. Main Royal
20. Mizzen Staysail
21. Mizzen Topmast Staysail
22. Mizzen Topgallant Staysail
23. Crossjack
24. Mizzen Lower Topsail
25. Mizzen Upper Topsail
26. Mizzen Lower Topgallant.
27. Mizzen Upper Topgallant
28. Mizzen Royal
29. Jigger Staysail
30. Jigger Topmast Staysail
31. Jigger Topgallant Staysail
32. Spanker
33. Spanker Topsail
34. Bowsprit
35. Foremast
36. Fore topmast
37. Fore Topgallant
38. Fore Royal Mast
39. Fore Royal Mast
40. Mainmast
41. Main Topmast
42. Main Topgallantmast
43. Main Royal Mast
44. Mizzenmast
45. Mizzen Topmast
46. Mizzen Topgallantmast
47. Mizzen Royal
48. Jigger Mast
49. Jigger Topmast
50. Spanker Boom
51. Spanker Gaff

Rigs

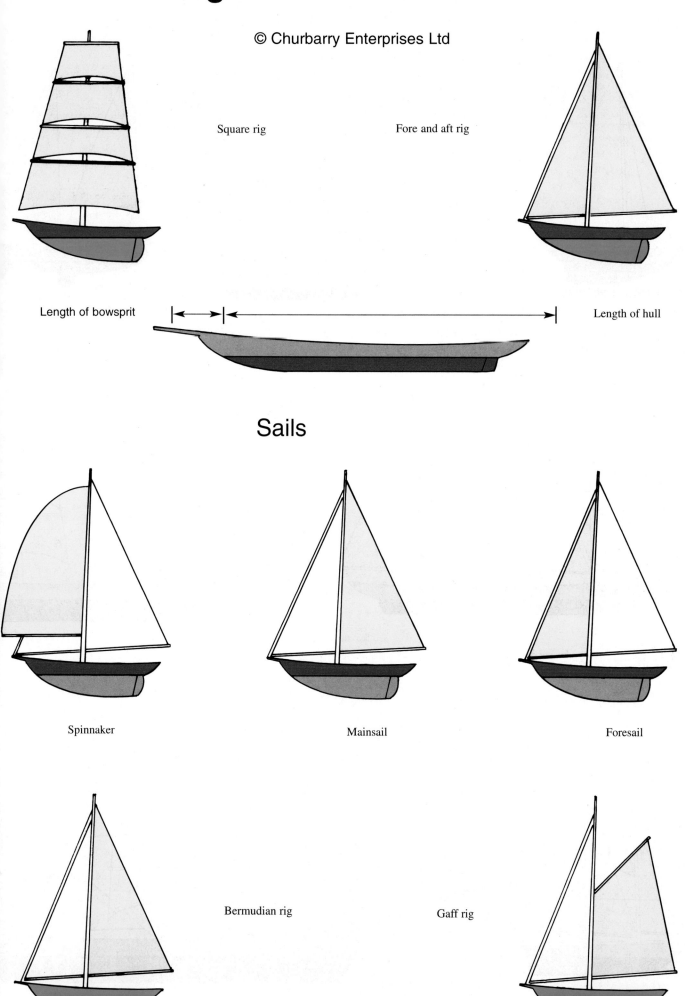

© Churbarry Enterprises Ltd

Square rig

Fore and aft rig

Length of bowsprit

Length of hull

Sails

Spinnaker

Mainsail

Foresail

Bermudian rig

Gaff rig

Rigs

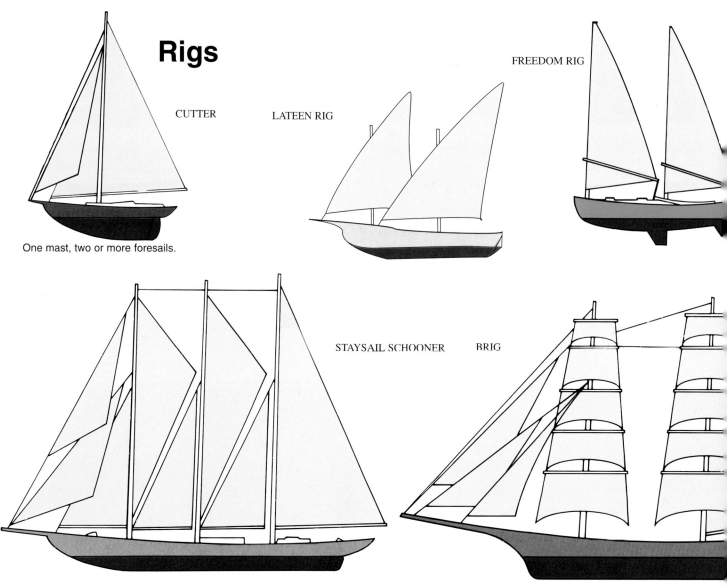

CUTTER

One mast, two or more foresails.

LATEEN RIG

FREEDOM RIG

STAYSAIL SCHOONER

BRIG

Two masts, square sails on both masts.

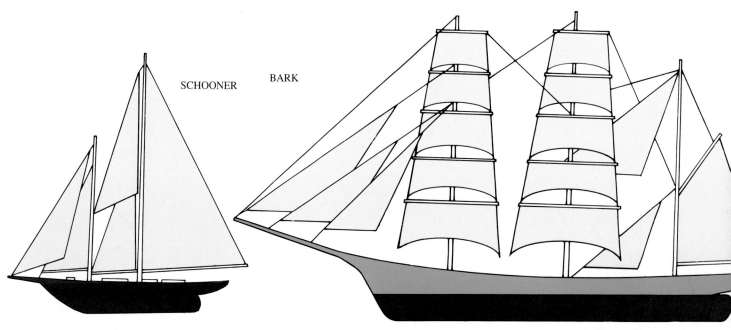

SCHOONER

BARK

Two or more masts of equal size, or the last one is higher, with no square sails.

Three or more masts, with square sails, but not on the last mast.

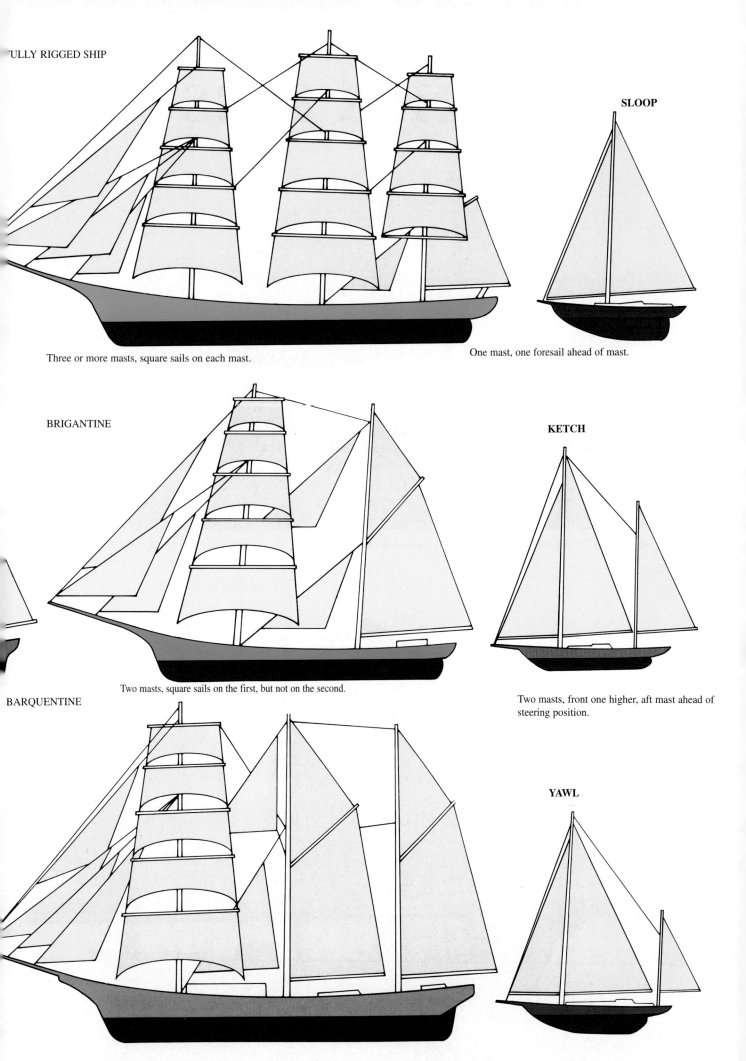

ULLY RIGGED SHIP

Three or more masts, square sails on each mast.

SLOOP

One mast, one foresail ahead of mast.

BRIGANTINE

Two masts, square sails on the first, but not on the second.

KETCH

Two masts, front one higher, aft mast ahead of steering position.

BARQUENTINE

Three or more masts, with square sails only on the front mast.

YAWL

Two masts, front one higher, aftmast behind steering position.

OTHER RIGS

A popular French fishing rig, from Brittany and Normandy (above)

A Chinese Junk rig (below)

The Cutty Sark Tall Ships' Races now to 2004

by Peter Newell, Race Director of ISTA (the International Sail Training Association), organiser of the races.

Has 'sail training' or as many call it these days, 'sailing to adventure' caught your imagination? You may choose a trip on a variety of ships, each with its own agenda. One ship might prefer to sail off on voyages on her own. Or she may prefer sailing in tandem with another. There is a third alternative, of sailing in company with many ships. For instance, each year we, at the ISTA, arrange the world's largest gathering of sail training ships, with our Cutty Sark Tall Ships' Races, and between 80 and 120 ships may decide to join in, and race and cruise with us, during the months of July and August. On this page (and the next) we map the races' chosen routes until the year 2002. They show that we vary the races each year, with our spotlight switching, from the Baltic, to the

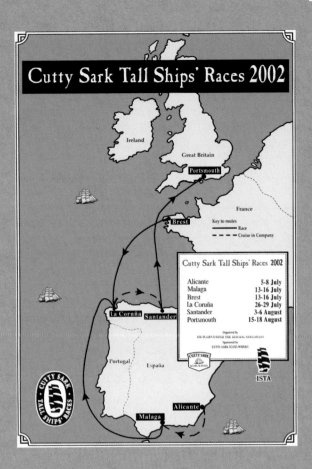

Cutty Sark Tall Ships' Races 2002

Alicante	5-8 July
Malaga	13-16 July
Brest	13-16 July
La Coruña	26-29 July
Santander	3-6 August
Portsmouth	15-18 August

Organised by
THE INTERNATIONAL SAIL TRAINING ASSOCIATION
Sponsored by
CUTTY SARK SCOTS WHISKY

Cutty Sark Tall Ships' Races 1999

SAINT-MALO	20-23 JULY
GREENOCK	30 JULY - 2 AUGUST
LERWICK	9-12 AUGUST
AALBORG	18-21 AUGUST

Organised by
THE INTERNATIONAL SAIL TRAINING ASSOCIATION
Sponsored by
CUTTY SARK SCOTS WHISKY

Cutty Sark Tall Ships' Races 2000

Gdansk	5-8 July
Helsinki	14-17 July
Mariehamn	21-24 July
Stockholm	26-29 July
Flensburg	4-7 August

Organised by
THE INTERNATIONAL SAIL TRAINING ASSOCIATION
Sponsored by
CUTTY SARK SCOTS WHISKY

Cutty Sark Tall Ships' Races 2001

Antwerp	5-8 July
Ålesund	18-21 July
Bergen	27-30 July
Esbjerg	4-7 August

Organised by
THE INTERNATIONAL SAIL TRAINING ASSOCIATION
Sponsored by
CUTTY SARK SCOTS WHISKY

North Atlantic, to Round Britain. Usually we only have one series of Races in each year, but in 1996 we had two - a Mediterranean Race and a Baltic Race, an experiment repeated in the Year 2000 with a Baltic Race, and also "*Tall Ships 2000*®" with ships headed from Europe across the Atlantic to the Americas, and back. In a normal year, we gather at one port, where new crews, many of them quite unused to sailing, join up and are 'shown the ropes'. During a few days in harbour, the ships are examined by ISTA officers, to see that safety equipment comes up to scratch. Our ISTA regulations are rather harsher than are demanded by the national authorities, which monitor sail training ships with their own rules.

Each ship in our Races has to conform to other of our requirements - for instance they must have half the number on board between the ages of 15 and 25. After three or so days in port, the ships depart under motor, or sail if possible, in a Parade of Sail, a sail past to thank the local host port and its population. Ships then head for a start line, sometimes far out to sea if there are nearby hazards. After the start gun, the fleet sets off into the wide ocean, far from the comfort of dry land, on an exhilarating experience where you may learn a lot about sailing, but even more about yourself and your fellows. The word 'race' means that you may pick out a rival ship of similar size, and see if you can sail faster. Sir Winston Churchill may have English boys on board, and her sistership Malcolm Miller may have Scottish girls. The Russian Mir may wish to outdo her sistership, the Polish Dar Mlodziezy. Royalist (Sea Scouts from the UK), and Asgard II (Ireland), are much of a size, and will watch each other's manoeuvres. Ships old and new, large and small, take part. We have a secret 'handicap' system for the whole fleet, so we can see how well each has done, and we publish race results at the end of each 'leg'. The finish line is passed and the ships enter harbour for another few days ashore, with parties and games, and a time for reflection and sightseeing. We encourage crews to change ships, so if you are a Norwegian or German, you may find yourself on a Scottish or Russian ship for the next leg of the voyage. After another Parade of Sail, the ships cruise to a third port, maybe anchoring in Norwegian fjords or port-hopping along the coasts of France, Spain and Portugal. Once more the ships reach a harbour, have a few days ashore, and then race to a final port.

For tens of thousands at each port, the sight of the fleet is a spectacle which they may be able to enjoy only once in a decade. On their behalf, we insist that there is no charge for anyone to enter a port area and see the fleet. And there is no charge to go on board a ship. Each ship may be 'open' or closed, as it wishes, but many ships are anxious for the public to admire them, and they will display 'time of opening' notices by their ships' gangways.

To find out more, just write to us - for the adventure of a lifetime. Our address is on page 17.

The Future? Most likely we will be in the Baltic again in 2003 and the Mediterranean in 2004.

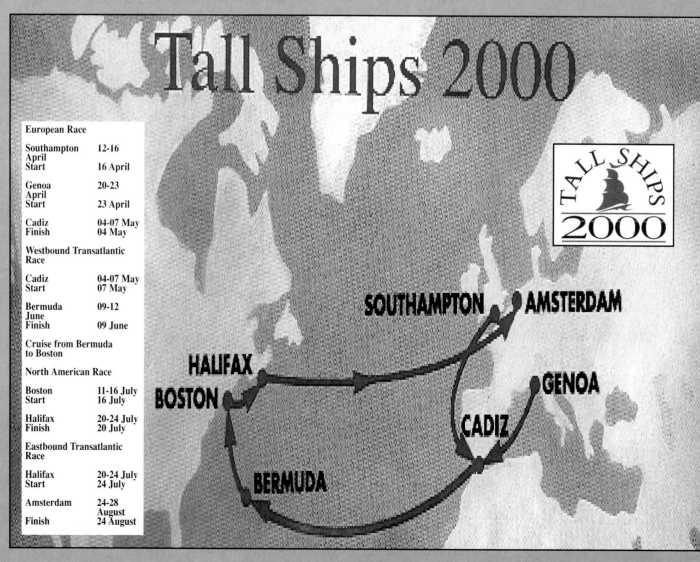

Tall Ships 2000

European Race	
Southampton April	12-16
Start	16 April
Genoa April	20-23
Start	23 April
Cadiz	04-07 May
Finish	04 May

Westbound Transatlantic Race	
Cadiz	04-07 May
Start	07 May
Bermuda June	09-12
Finish	09 June

Cruise from Bermuda to Boston

North American Race	
Boston	11-16 July
Start	16 July
Halifax	20-24 July
Finish	20 July

Eastbound Transatlantic Race	
Halifax	20-24 July
Start	24 July
Amsterdam	24-28 August
Finish	24 August

TALL SHIPS 2000

SOUTHAMPTON AMSTERDAM

HALIFAX
BOSTON

GENOA

CADIZ

BERMUDA

THE CUTTY SARK CONNECTION

John Rudd, Chairman of Berry Bros. and Rudd, presenting the Cutty Sark Trophy to the Captain and Crew of Shabab Oman, owned by the Sultanate of Oman, the winner in 1997.

The Cutty Sark Tall Ships' Races are named after their sponsor, Cutty Sark Scots Whisky. The whisky in turn is named after one of the most famous tall ships of them all, the 19th Century Scottish clipper which is now laid up at Greenwich, London.

Here is how it came about. One day in 1923, at lunchtime, the partners of London wine merchants Berry Bros. & Rudd were entertaining a well known Scottish artist, James McBey. The conversation turned to the new brand of pale whisky which the firm was planning to put on the market. McBey suggested that the whisky should be called "Cutty Sark", after the ship which was in the news at that moment. She had just been bought back from the Portuguese by Captain Wilfred Harry Dowman, a Cornish master mariner who had seen her outrace a steamship in 1894.

The partners, two Berrys and a Rudd accepted McBey's suggestion that the whisky should be called Cutty Sark, and they commissioned him to design a distinctive label. His design remains unchanged to this day, complete with the illustration of "Cutty Sark" and hand-drawn lettering on a yellow background.

Since its launch in 1923, Cutty Sark has grown to become one of the world's largest selling Scotch whisky brands, exported to 130 countries and winning the Queen's Award for Export Achievement.

In 1972, the attention of Berry Bros. & Rudd directors was drawn to the plight of the Tall Ships' Races which were in danger of lapsing due to shortage of funds. Once more the joint topics of Tall Ships and whisky were discussed at the firm's historic premises at No. 3, St. James's Street, London. The conversation revolved around the growth of the races, since the first one in 1956, their international character and their contribution to worldwide understanding and goodwill amongst young people.

The decision was taken. Cutty Sark Scots Whisky would sail to the rescue of the Tall Ships. Ever since, Cutty Sark has worked closely together with the International Sail Training Association, the organisers of the event, in the development of the Cutty Sark Tall Ships' Races worldwide. Through this long-term sponsorship, many thousands of people from all over the world have raced in friendly rivalry at sea and formed lasting friendships ashore.

The coveted Cutty Sark Trophy (above) is awarded each year to the ship and crew which, in the opinion of other participants, have contributed most towards promoting international understanding. For more information, contact Deborah Arnold, Peter Smales, at Public Relations, Cutty Sark Scots Whisky, 3 St. James's Street, London SW1A 1EG, England. Tel +44 207 3969666.Fax +44 207 3969641.

List 1 is the major part of our Guide, of ships you can get aboard, most sailing European waters

Alba Venturer

NATIONALITY	*Scottish*
HOME PORT	*Ardrossan*
SIZE OVERALL	*20.7 metres 68 feet*
STAFF	*5*
CREW	*12*

HISTORY
Established in 1960 the owners, Ocean Youth Trust (once the Ocean Youth Club), have the largest youth sailing fleet in Europe. They have seven yachts, of about 20 metres with crews of around 16. They are based in different ports around the British Isles.

ON BOARD
The aims of OYT are the enjoyment and adventure of life at sea, with crews of different sex, ability, backgrounds, and ethnic origin. OYT takes people aged 12 and up to 24, and for those 25 and over there is a 'Friends' Membership scheme. 'Friends' sail, with other adults, on special voyages. If you can fill all 12 berths, the OYT will waive the age bands. All OYT vessels are under the command of a skipper with an RYA/DTp Yachtmaster Offshore Certificate. The Mate is an experienced person holding a Mate's certificate issued by the OYT and an RYA/DTp Coastal Skipper certificate, or equivalent.
As an educational charity, OYT can offer grants for those between 12 and 24 years old, and assist in fundraising ideas. If you can't afford an OYT voyage, the club has a proud boast that no young person is unable to sail because of cost, with bursaries available, though all are encouraged to contribute. Over 60% of young crews have been subsidised.
Where any OYT vessel calls on any of her voyages depends on the weather, but in voyages over 3 days expect one port of call, and over 6 days, two.
OYT provides all safety equipment you'll require, and wet weather gear necessary for sailing. All food is included. On an OYT voyage you can gain OYT, Royal Yachting Association and Duke of Edinburgh Award Certificates.
School and youth groups studies into the environment can be catered for. All women voyages (staff and crew) can be arranged. For those with special needs, all OYT yachts are fitted with audio compasses, and some handicaps can be catered for. If you have a medical condition or disability, you must send a doctor's note, and bring adequate medicines, etc. One condition of sailing aboard, you have to be able to swim - 50 metres.

SAFETY CERTIFICATES AND INSURANCE
OYT Vessels are certified to the Department of Transport's Code of Practice for Sail Training Vessels. The OYT operates within the Statutory Code of Practice (DTp) which stipulates the qualifications of the sea staff and rigorous standards for vessels and their equipment. With so many ships in the club, it keeps its own 'once in 24 hour' reporting system from each of them. Insurance covers most eventualities, including loss of luggage, personal money, medical and other expenses when aboard due to illness or accident.

PROGRAMME
Alba Venturer is an Oyster 70, with two masts, and she has her sailing base at Ardrossan. She sails the west and east coasts of Scotland. Sample prices would show:

Voyage	Low season	Mid	High season
2 nights	£60	£98	£135
6 nights	£169	£304	£439

CONTACT   OYT Scotland
ADDRESS   24 Blythswood Square, Glasgow G2 4QS
PHONE   +44 141 300 5511   FAX   +44 141 300 5701
E-MAIL scotland@oyc.org.uk   WEB http://www.oyc.org.uk

Albatros

NATIONALITY	*German*
HOME PORT	*Bremerhaven, western Germany*
SIZE OVERALL	*35.7 metres 117 feet*
PERMANENT CREW	*6*
PAYING SAIL TRAINEES	*21*

HISTORY

This 3 masted schooner began life in Hobro, in Jutland, North Denmark, built as a fishing craft for the North Seas with her hold able to take 180 tons of fish. Her name changed from time to time to reflect new owners, and new rigs. Built as Dagmar Larsen in war time (1942), she was given plenty of sail area, as fuel was so scarce during the war. On her sale in 1951, she was re-christened Iris Thy. In 1953 her rig was reduced, and in 1957 she was again sold. In 1961 she again changed hands, and renamed Esther Lohse worked from Bornholm, an island in the Baltic. As a 'fisher of stones' she took on board granite for use elsewhere in quays and breakwaters.

She moved home again, in the early 1970s, out of the Baltic to Colchester, southeast England, where damage to her hull from carrying heavy loads required her to be extensively repaired. She was rebuilt almost to her original shape and with her original rig. By 1975 she was able to carry passengers. In 1978 and after her appearance in the Television series, the Onedin Line, she came to the attention of Clipper Deutsches Jugendwerk zur See e.V., who also owns and operates Johann Smidt, Seute Deern and Amphitrite. Renamed Albatros, she was extensively refitted and the object was to recreate exactly a typical Scandinavian schooner, above deck, with comfort and modern equipment

below. In order to achieve accuracy, the shipyard and the owner consulted historical records. To-day you see her reborn.

ON BOARD

There is comfortable accommodation aboard for 6 permanent crew in three two berth cabins, and 21 trainees in bigger cabins. All the sails are hoisted from the deck. The centre of life on board - besides the sailing activities on deck - is in a large saloon (combined with the galley) where there is space enough so that all the crew members and trainees can have their meals together and can have their 'social life'.

SAFETY CERTIFICATES AND INSURANCE

She conforms to the standards of Bureau Veritas classification, and GSHW.

PROGRAMME

Albatros' sailing programme is primarily centred on cruises from April to October in the Baltic, including the southern parts of Norway and eastern parts of Sweden as well as eastern Germany and Poland. She regularly takes part in sailing regattas. The cruises scheduled during spring time and autumn mainly last seven days and during summer time a fortnight, all usually beginning and ending on Saturday at about noon. Trainees from 15/16 years old pay £25 a day, as long as they are still in professional education (apprentices, students, etc). All others with a completed professional education (gainfully working) are charged £38 per day. These fees include food, coffee, tea and milk - that means, after coming on board, the trainees only need pocket money. The permanent crew consists of officers, an engineer and cook, who are sailing as voluntary helpers, spending their vacation time on board.

The ports visited for future years are a guide to her normal sailing pattern: Kiel, Hamburg, Århus, Flensburg, Köge, Travemünde, Stockholm, Karlskrona.

CONTACT	Clipper Deutsches Jugendwerk zur See e.V.,
ADDRESS	Hamburg Office, Jurgensallee 54, D-22609 Hamburg, Germany
PHONE	+49 40 822 78 103
FAX	+49 40 822 78 104
E-mail	ClipperDJzS-Knut-Frisch@t-online.de
Web	http://www.clipper-djs.org

Albanus

NATIONALITY	*Finnish*
HOME PORT	*Mariehamn, Åland Isles*
SIZE OVERALL	*21 metres 69 feet*
PROFESSIONAL CREW	*4*
PAYING SAIL TRAINEES	*20*

HISTORY

During the 19th and early 20th centuries several hundred ships with two masts, with the second mast substantial in size, traded in the Baltic with their cargo of firewood, fish and farm produce. Called in many countries galeasses - ketches to most of us - they laid the foundation for the great ship building tradition of the Åland Islands, off the west coast of Finland.

The original Albanus was one of these galeasse, built at the turn of the century. She is no more, but her name continues with a new ship, built using the traditional techniques of the past, preserved by and documented by a fading generation of craftsmen. For instance traditional flax sails were hand sewn for her by old Cape Horn sailors. She was built by the non profit organisation, Skeppsforeningen Albanus, to give young people of the archipelago the benefits and excitement of sailing a traditional ship. She was launched in 1988, during the Cutty Sark Tall Ships' Race visit to Mariehamn.

ON BOARD

The traditional rig of Albanus, with standing gaffs and big sails which furl into the masts, is easy to handle and ideal for young people. Most of the work with sails can be done from the deck, an advantage for those not keen on working aloft.

On board you are part of the crew and under a supervisor you participate in all the work. You handle sails, navigate, spend time at the helm, help in the galley. And you will have time off, as in any ship. No prior experience of sailing or ships is required.

Albanus sails throughout the night on occasion, but as with the original freight schooners she generally spends her nights at anchor or alongside in harbours, maybe off a small village of the outer archipelago, or at anchor in the beautiful bay of an uninhabited island, moored right up to smooth red granite cliffs. Sailing Albanus you get to know the vast and exciting archipelago of the northern Baltic, consisting of some 50,000 islands, few of which

are inhabited.

SAFETY CERTIFICATES AND INSURANCE

Albanus is inspected annually by the National Board of Navigation (Finland) and is fully equipped with rafts, etc, for traffic in the Baltic and adjacent waters to Skagen (Denmark) and Lindesnes (Norway).

PROGRAMME

She has cruised ten successful summers in the Baltic.

Two thirds of her time is spent on voyages for the young, and one third on charter work, which provides her with badly needed finance.

Usually she has one cruise for individuals, between 16 and 25 years old, while the rest is booked by groups or organisations. Her costs for boat, crew, and provisions, are from 600 Finnmarks a day for young people, and 700 FM per day for adults.

CONTACT	Freddie Olin
ADDRESS	Skeppsforeningen Albanus, Sjofartskverteret, FIN-22100 Mariehamn, Åland, Finland
PHONE	+358 18 17545 FAX +358 18 17595

NATIONALITY	Russian
HOME PORT	St. Petersburg, the Baltic
SIZE OVERALL	29.4 metres 96 feet
PROFESSIONAL CREW	4
SAIL TRAINEES	6/8

HISTORY

Designed by 'Grumant' at St. Petersburg, Alevtina & Tuy launched in November 1995 as a copy of a small mid 18th century merchant ship, with a typical topsail schooner rig. She is built of pitch pine and oak and equipped with modern navigation and safety equipment. She had a collision with a large cargo vessel in June 1996. Repaired over a two year period of 1996-7, she is back once again on the high seas, with confirmation of seaworthiness in her class. Her sister ship is Elena-Maria-Barbara.

ON BOARD

She has a main saloon for 12 people, a galley, two toilets with showers, and below she has 4 cabins, one four berth, one 2/4 berth, and two double berths. All the interior is of oak. She has a licence to carry 16 people overnight, including a captain, first mate, bosun, and cook. Special Russian food, and European food, are available.

SAFETY CERTIFICATES & INSURANCE

She is equipped according to SOLAS 74/78 standards, and is classified by the Russian Maritime Register of Shipping. Her insurers are Lampe & Shierenbeck of Bremen in Germany, and P & I Club in London. She is registered with the Russian Authorities for unlimited sailing areas.

PROGRAMME

She keeps mainly to the Baltic and North Sea, and on occasion sails further afield.

CONTACT	Boris Krishtal
ADDRESS	J/V "Erkon", 21 Linia 8a, St. Petersburg 199026, Russia
CONTACT	in Germany
ADDRESS	SCS Shipping Consulting and Services GmbH, Postfach 120429, D-27518 Bremerhaven, Germany
FAX	+49 471 9413857
PHONE ON BOARD	+7 812 9651120

Alexander von Humboldt

NATIONALITY	*German*
HOME PORT	*Bremerhaven, western Germany*
SIZE OVERALL	*62.6 metres 205 feet*
PROFESSIONAL CREW	*23*
OTHER SKILLED	*2*
PAYING SAIL TRAINEES	*35*

HISTORY

Launched in 1906 as Sonderburg, most of her early life was spent at anchor as a lightship on Germany's North Sea coast, guiding ships through difficult waters to the safety of a port. She had to be tough, and this attracted STAG (the Sail Training Association of Germany) who saw her potential as a sail training ship. She was bought in 1986 but disaster nearly struck in her last days as a lightship when at the Weser station north of Wangerooge, she was rammed by a 20,000 ton bulk carrier Ocean Wind. Her lookout managed to warn those below, and she suffered material damage only. Plating stove-in beneath the waterline in the aft area on the port side, and a mast cracked. She took in some water, but not sufficient to stop her being towed with a small list to Wilhelmshaven. After temporary repairs she transferred to a new port, Bremerhaven, under the provisional name Confidentia. Here she was converted. Out came the wheelhouse, radio cabin, and masts. The light tower was given to the Kiel Museum. The foremast now stands on a dyke in Wremen. The old windlass went to the Shipping Museum in Carolinensiel. The large centre hawsepipe (bringing the anchor onto the deck) came out and two side hawsepipes were installed instead. She was given a barque rig (square sails except on the last mast).

In 1988 she passed her sea tests in the Outer Weser, and later in that year, her first nucleus of crew, made up of experienced seafarers from the Pamir-Passat Association, and young enthusiasts, sailed her around Heligoland. In her first voyage under her new name Alexander von Humboldt she ran at 10.5 knots under an Easterly Force 7, on a bright sunny day - faster than she had ever run before under her engines.

SAFETY CERTIFICATES AND INSURANCE

Her safety assessment is under Germanischer Lloyd according to SOLAS, classified as 100 A4 Sailing Yacht +MC.

PROGRAMME

A regular at Cutty Sark Tall Ships' Races, she visits many regattas and ports in Germany and Scandinavia, visiting the Mediterranean and Canary Islands in the winter. Young people up to 25 years of age pay DEM80 a day, while adults pay DEM130 a day, all inclusive. She makes extensive cruises, including to Brest, Madeira, Lisbon, and Bremerhaven. In 1992 she made her first transatlantic crossing, and in 1998 sailed to South America to commemorate the voyages of the German natural scientist, Alexander von Humboldt. If you see her, you will recognise her from her green sails, the colour of the City of Bremen.

CONTACT	Martin Poetting
ADDRESS	Deutsche Stiftung Sail Training, Hafenhaus Columbusbahnhof D-27568, Bremerhaven, Germany
PHONE	+49 471 94588-0 FAX +49 471 94588-45

Amphitrite

NATIONALITY	German
HOME PORT	Bremen, western Germany
SIZE OVERALL	44.3 metres 145 feet
PERMANENT CREW	6
PAYING SAIL TRAINEES	23

HISTORY

Amphitrite has had many names, owners, and rigs. She was built in 1884 at Camper and Nicholsons at Gosport, south England, constructed of teak on oak as a two masted schooner, intending to cruise. However she took part in many races between 1900 and the early 1920s, and for instance raced against Kaiser Wilhelm's famous yacht Meteor. Her first name was Hinemoa, changing to Dolores in 1900. In 1915 an engine was added and she was re-named Joyfarer in 1922. During the second World War she became a barrage balloon carrier, moored in the centre of Plymouth Harbour, England, to protect the naval base against air attacks. For a while after the war she was laid-up and used as a houseboat. From 1957 she was mainly based in the Mediterranean and was changed into a three masted schooner. In the mid-1960s a Swedish millionaire renamed her Amphitrite of Stockholm, altered her rig to a barquentine and added luxurious cabins and saloons . Other owners followed and in the early 1970s she appeared on German TV in The Earl of Luckner and the Secret of the Marie Celeste. Since 1975 she has been operated by Clipper Deutsches Jugendwerk zur See e.V., and after a complete overhaul, her rig was changed once more, from barquentine to become a three masted schooner.

ON BOARD

There are comfortable wooden panelled two berth cabins aboard for the professional crew and larger cabins for trainees. The accommodation still echoes the days when she was a luxury yacht. The permanent crew - deck officers, engineer and cook - are all volunteers, spending their holidays aboard her.

PROGRAMME

From April to October she sails in the Baltic, Denmark, southern Norway, eastern Sweden, eastern Germany and Poland, usually on one or two week voyages.. Students and apprentices pay £25 a day Others pay £38 a day. These prices include food, tea and coffee. Ports visited in a year might include Århus, Travemünde, Flensburg, Köge, Kalmar, and Frederikshavn.

CONTACT	Clipper Deutsches Jugendwerk zur See e.V.
ADDRESS	Hamburg Office, Jürgensallee 54 , D-22609 Hamburg, Germany
PHONE	+49 40 822 78103 FAX +49 40 822 78104
e-maiL	ClipperDJzS_Knut-Frisch@-online.de
WEB	http://www/clipper-djs.org

Anna Kristina

NATIONALITY	*Norwegian*
HOME PORT	*Lysaker in Oslo*
SIZE OVERALL	*32 metres 105 feet*
PROFESSIONAL OFFICERS	*6*
CREW	*16*

HISTORY

Built 110 years ago, she is a restored Norwegian square rigged topsail ketch, built out of 600 selected trees from an area in Norway famous for its quality pine forests. She has famous sisterships. One is Gjøa, ship of the Norwegian explorer Roald Amundsen, who sailed in the Arctic and discovered the North West Passage in 1903-5. Another sister was Restauration, Norway's first emigrant ship to the Americas. A third sister was the first Norwegian passenger ship, Skjøldmoen, whose voyage in 1863 marked the start of the Norway-America line.

Anna Kristina started as Dyrofield, the name of a mountain at an island off Trondheim, half way up the Norwegian coast. For 88 years she traded cargo along the north Norwegian coast, and to north Russia.

First she used sails alone. Then an engine was added. In 1977 she was sold, and then sailed more sea-miles than any of the other thousands of jakts built in the last 300 years. In the last dozen years alone she has sailed well over 170,000 miles from the Arctic at 80 degrees North to the Roaring Forties down south.

Her yearly activity since 1984 has included Arctic Sailing; filming Norwegian TV's 'Hud', charter for two years to an American school for dyslexic students; the First Fleet Re-enactment from England to Australia to celebrate the 200th Anniversary of the first modern European landings in Australia, filming of an American documentary at Western Samoa; a whale research film 'Encounter with Whales' in Australia, to New Zealand and back to the Canaries, sail training with the Columbus 92 Grand Regatta Quincentenary, with a return to with a 'whales, sails and trails' programme in the Canaries since 1993. In her 110th year, 1999, she has been brought back to new Norwegian owners, after 22 years in Dutch hands.

SAFETY CERTIFICATES AND INSURANCE.

She is controlled by the Norwegian Maritime Directorate and yearly surveys are carried out on her by Det Norske Veritas.

PROGRAMME

She carries a passenger certificate for 40 persons, for day sailing. She accepts students for a whole year, but each summer she accepts applications from anyone who wishes to sail her.

CONTACT	'Anna Kristina', Sollerudstranda Skole
ADDRESS	Drammensveien 280, 0283 Oslo, Norway
PHONE +47 22 50 2090	FAX +47 22 50 3330
E-MAIL annakristina@c2i.net	GSM +47 959 36 869

Anny von Hamburg

NATIONALITY	German
HOME PORT	Hamburg, western Germany
SIZE OVERALL	38 metres 125 feet
PROFESSIONAL CREW	5
PAYING SAIL TRAINEES	10-14

HISTORY

The three masted schooner Anny was built in 1914 by C.Lühring of Hammelwarden on the Unterweser, as a cargo ship. The design was a commercial success and the yard built eight other steel-hulled schooners from the same plans. Anny's maiden voyage was to St. Petersburg. She arrived as the first World War broke out, and was seized by the Russians. In peacetime she was returned to Germany and in Hamburg she was given a reduced rig, and an engine was installed. Captain Walter Richter bought her in 1929 and her name became Hanna. In 1936 she was sold to Captain Max Both who renamed her Kurt Both and used her to carry cement between Bremen and Helgoland for the building of a naval base. Later she traded to Scandinavia. In 1940 the two forward wooden masts were removed as they had become rotten and were replaced by a single steel foremast. The mizzen mast was already steel and also acted as an exhaust for the engine.

After the war tonnage was scarce and in 1950 the ship was lengthened by 8 metres and had her bowsprit removed to complete her transformation from a beautiful old schooner into a motor vessel. In 1957 she was bought by a Swedish firm, renamed Ringo and then sold to Paul Gronquist of Finland. In 1980 this once proud vessel, now in bad condition and partially burned out, was bought by the Classic Schooner Club, a non-profit company with 44 co-owners. The new owners realised that never would they find another ship of comparable size so involved with Hamburg's history. They re-fitted and re-rigged her, giving her back her original sail plan.

ON BOARD

Accommodation is of a very high standard, with 5 guest cabins, each with a large berth, sofa, shower and toilet. The captain's cabin is aft while the 4 berths for the crew are forward. There is a large saloon/dining room and the entire accommodation is air conditioned.

The Classic Schooner Club aims to cultivate marine traditions and rediscover nautical skills. In addition to her commercial voyages she makes a point of taking part in Tall Ships' races with trainees between 16 and 25 years old.

SAFETY CERTIFICATES AND INSURANCE

She is classed by Germanischer Lloyd +100A5 Yacht with her last special survey passed in November 1996.

PROGRAMME

In the past her usual plan has been to charter during winter in the Caribbean and the Mediterranean, and at other times she has been an active part of the German sail training fleet based on Kiel.

For instance:

1 day cruises at Hamburg, or Kiel Week, or at Hanse Sail..

4 days, Hamburg-Heligoland-Hamburg.
6 days, Danish South Sea-Kiel Canal-Hamburg.
6 days, Brest-La Coruna-Porto-Lisbon.
14 days, Kiel-Bornholm-Kaliningrad-Riga-St. Petersburg.

In the Winter of 1997-8 she underwent a major refit at a German boatyard. She stayed in home waters for the spring and summer, then embarked once again on her more adventurous winter schedules - to the Canary Islands, en route to the Caribbean.

CONTACT	Classic Schooner Club e.V.,
ADDRESS	Platanenweg 10, D-21465 Reinbek, Germany
PHONE	+49 40 71097588 FAX +49 40 71097589

Antigua

NATIONALITY	*Dutch*
HOME PORT	*Franeker*
SIZE OVERALL	*48 metres 157 feet*
PROFESSIONAL CREW	*5*
PAYING PASSENGERS	*up to 32 for overnight voyages, and up to 80 for day trips*

HISTORY

Built in 1956 as an Atlantic fishing boat, Harry Smit carried out a re-build on her between 1993 and 1995, converting her to barquentine rig.

ON BOARD

Accommodation consists of 16 two berth cabins with shower and toilet en suite. Aft there is a large saloon located in a deckhouse under the bridge. Although her normal passenger complement is 32 for overnight voyages, she can carry up to 80 passengers on day trips.

SAFETY CERTIFICATES AND INSURANCE

She has all sailing permits issued by Register Holland and is insured worldwide. Trainees have to provide their own insurance.

PROGRAMME

Antigua's cruise pattern is mainly in the North Sea and the Baltic during the summer, and in the wintertime she leaves for the Caribbean. After crossing the Atlantic in October to December, Antigua is based on Antigua, and runs 7 and 14 day voyages, alternately north about or south about. A northern route takes her to Barbuda, Cocoa Bay, Basterre, St. Kitts to Monserrat; and on the southern route she sails to Nonsuch Bay, then Guadeloupe and Iles des Saintes. The price per person for 7 days is f990 and for 214 days f1,750. Prices are exclusive of a tourist tax of f16.50 per person per week, and flights, transfers, and excursions.

CONTACT	Hollands Glorie
ADDRESS	Industrieweg 135, 3044 AS Rotterdam, The Netherlands
PHONE	+31 10 415 6600 FAX +31 10 415 4545
E-MAIL	hgloire@whs.net
WEB	http:/www.hollandsgloire.nl

Arethusa

NATIONALITY	British
HOME PORT	Upnor, England
SIZE OVERALL	22 metres 72 feet
PROFESSIONAL CREW	2
OTHER SKILLED	3
PAYING SAIL TRAINEES	12

HISTORY
The Shaftesbury Homes and Arethusa Charity's first ship was the famous Cape Horn clipper, Peking, a 4 masted barque. Renamed Arethusa she was put into a mud berth on the Medway, and used as a training ship for boys from broken homes, or orphans, who were seeking a career in the British Royal or Merchant Navy. When she came to the end of her useful life in 1973 she was towed across the Atlantic, and under her old name Peking is in New York's South Street museum. She was replaced with the second and present Arethusa, built at Fox's Marina in Ipswich on the east coast of England, and she launched in 1982. She continues to run for the same charity to-day.

ON BOARD
Arethusa provides sail training for young people from the fourteen Shaftesbury Homes in south London. However she provides training for many other young people who can start at the age of 13.

SAFETY CERTIFICATES AND INSURANCE
A comprehensive policy covers all Shaftesbury Homes and Arethusa activities, so that payment for individual insurance is not necessary. She conforms to the MCA Code of Practice.

PROGRAMME
She has cruised extensively round Europe (and the Mediterranean) over the last 14 years. Her standard operating pattern is a 5 day cruise with young people, usually crossing the North Sea to a Dutch, French or Belgian port. Often at the weekend adult groups are embarked for a shorter cruise. This pattern is broken by sorties to the Cutty Sark Tall Ships' Races and appearances at other nautical events.

CONTACT Nicko Franks (Ketch Manager) or Angela Devlin (Secretary)
ADDRESS Arethusa Venture Centre, Lower Upnor, Rochester, Kent ME2 4XB, UK
PHONE +44 1634 711566   FAX +44 1634 295905

Asgard II

NATIONALITY	Irish
HOME PORT	Dublin
SIZE OVERALL	32 metres 106 feet
PROFESSIONAL CREW	5
PAYING SAIL TRAINEES	20

HISTORY

The first Asgard, a 34 foot gaff rig ketch, was built in Norway in 1905. In 1914 she ran a cargo of guns to Ireland from Germany, when owned by the author of 'Riddle of the Sands', Erskine Childers, with his wife and four others on board. He was discovered and executed. Later, after independence, his father became President of Ireland. Because of her history the Irish Government bought Asgard in 1961, and she was used between 1969 and 1974 for sail training, a role continued by the bermudian ketch, Creidne, whilst her successor, Asgard II, was planned and built.

In 1981 Creidne was transferred to the Naval Reserve, and the present Asgard II came into service. Designed by Jack Tyrell and built in Arklow, County Wexford, she carries as her figurehead a carving of Granuaile, the famous 16th Century Mayo pirate queen. She flies the Irish sail training flag, which has the variation of an old Nordic rune, the sun and moon symbols, representing freedom.

Asgard means 'Home of the Gods'. She has become so successful that by early in each year, her season is booked up and a waiting list is started. Asgard II is owned by the State, and the Minister of Defence is the registered owner. But she is not a naval service vessel. The ship is managed by Coiste an Asgard, the committee first formed in 1968 which is now a company limited by guarantee. The chairman is the Minister for Defence, and most directors are experienced yachtsmen with a keen interest in sail training.

ON BOARD

Asgard II's philosophy is that sail training schemes are best served by catering for individuals. But groups are also welcome, especially in early spring and late autumn, and preference is given to those who state clearly why they benefit more from sail training with a preformed unit rather than through an individual application.

There is also an Asgard Support Group who encourage young people to participate. They organise fund raising to help those who otherwise might not be able to afford a voyage. When Asgard II is in port, members assist with maintenance, shopping,

delivery of stores, etc, and team spirit and enthusiasm is their hallmark, as it is for those on board.

Asgard II sails all year round, (which includes winter in the Canaries) usually on one to three week voyages, and cruises involve visits to ports in Britain and France. During the summer, she spreads her wings in northern European waters and often she joins in the Cutty Sark Tall Ships' Races, or occasionally she sails to more distant shores - in 1985 she visited the USA, and in 1988 she participated in the Australian Bicentenary celebrations. Asgard II has a permanent crew of five, the master, mate, engineer, bosun and cook. She has a training crew of 20, and anyone over 16 years of age can apply. Knowledge of sailing is not necessary. There are four categories for which you can apply:
- Trainees are between 16 and 25 with or without previous experience.
- Watch leaders are young people with previous watch training experience aboard Asgard II.
- Navigator/coxwains are over 25 years old, experienced as offshore sailors and interested in youth training.
- Trainee adults are people over 25 with little or no experience in offshore sailing.

Keen trainees from each cruise are selected to take part in watch leader training programmes held at the start and end of each season.

PROGRAMME

A typical programme might be:

5 days, £IR 65; Dun Laoghaire-Howth (Watch Leader Training in Irish Sea).

6 days, £IR 65 Howth-Dublin (Watch Leader Training in Irish Sea).

7 days, £IR154; Dublin-Howth (via Irish Sea, Isle of Man).

7 days, £IR 196 Howth-Dun Laoghaire (via Irish Sea; Isle of Man).

Note prices are in Irish Punts, not pounds sterling.

Prices: where two prices are shown, the first is for trainees (16 to 25) and the second for adults (25+).

Fees are based on trainees paying £IR22 and adults £IR 28 in the low season, rising to £IR 25 and £IR 30 in high season.

CONTACT	G. Bradley
ADDRESS	Coiste an Asgard, Infirmary Road, Dublin 7, Ireland
PHONE	+353 1 679 2169 FAX +353 1 677 2328

Asgard II is usually fully booked.. so will the Republic of Ireland soon gain a second sail training ship? Maybe. The first Asgard could be refitted - some grants are already available - but her crew would be only ten or so. There are two replicas building of those 1840s ships which took emigrants to America during the Great Famine. They are Jeanie Johnson and Dunbrodie. Both are of similar size, 46 metres (150 feet). Dunbrodie's hull completed in 1999. Jeannie Johnson will return from the USA in 2001. The chances that one of them will be a sail training ship, look good.

Astrid

NATIONALITY	*Dutch*
HOME PORT	*Zutphen*
SIZE OVERALL	*43.3 metres 142 feet*
PROFESSIONAL CREW	*8*
PAYING SAIL TRAINEES	*27*

HISTORY

A checkered past, a rescue from obscurity by an enthusiast, a return to the problem of how to finance such a splendid old lady in need of constant and costly repairs, and then two changes of ownership in rapid sucession.

In 1918 she was built in The Netherlands as a working schooner. In 1937 she was sold to a Swedish farmer and she carried barley, wheat and rape seed along the Swedish coast. In World War 11 she traded timber and coal between Sweden and Poland.

She flew the Lebanese flag in 1976, and in 1977 she came under suspicion of drug trafficking by HM Customs. In mid channel, her crew set her on fire, leaving behind only her bare hull which was made of iron - and two bodies. Towed to Newhaven in southern England, she ended up neglected in the river Hamble near Southampton. Here Graham Neilson came upon her, liked what he saw, and paid out his naval retirement gratuity to buy her. The Astrid Trust was founded in 1985, and after four years of repair and renewal Astrid took to the seas again as a brig. Her new role was stated as 'Dedicated to the Service of Youth', as the Trust's brochure put it. Her first sail training voyage was in 1989. By early 1997 financial problems mounted and the Trust decided it should cease. Astrid was sold, and taken back to Holland. She now has a second new Dutch owner . Her accomodation has been improved, and she now sails in Dutch and German waters with trainees and day sailors on board. She also hopes to undertake voyages chosen with a variety of development programmes in mind.

CONTACT   TS Astrid
ADDRESS   Postbus 442, 7200 Zutphen, The Netherlands
PHONE 00 31 517 417 523
FAX 0031 517 417 114

Astrid Finne

NATIONALITY	Swedish
HOME PORT	Öckerö
SIZE OVERALL	24.7 metres 81 feet
PROFESSIONAL CREW	5
PAYING SAIL TRAINEES	12

HISTORY

A fine gaff rigged ketch, she was built in 1937 by Anker & Jensens in Oslo, Norway, for the Norwegian Safety And Rescue organisation. Her design was based on the classic lines of the Colin Archer type of rescue ships, although she is larger and has modifications to herengine. The hull is built of teak planking on iron frames, an unusual method of boatbuilding in those days, but developed by Johan Anker on his pleasure craft. Astrid Finne would show that this was a successful combination which produced a strong composite build that could easily withstand the roughest seas. Astrid Finne was amongst the first rescue ships to have an auxiliary engine fitted from her launching, and with such a piece of high technology at that time, she was stationed in the most difficult waters, off the north of Norway. Honningsvag near the Russian border was to be her station of service for many years, and she took part in many rescue missions in the area's cold, rough and unfriendly northern waters. She is known as an exceptionally seaworthy ship and one of her skippers once said "God can not make us such weather that Astrid Finne cannot put to sea". Closely involved in the Norwegian resistance movement during the Second World War, you can still see the marks in the teak deck from the bullets of the German airforce. She and her near sistership Hawila are owned by Mot Bättre Vetande, meaning 'towards better knowledge', a voluntary school sailing association, based at the port of Öckerö in Sweden. Gunilla is the school's third ship.

SAFETY EQUIPMENT AND INSURANCE

Astrid Finne is fully equipped with the latest navigation instruments; MARPA radar, Koden DGPS, Skanti SSB-radio, T&T Inmarsat C, etc. Other equipment includes crew suits, a watermaker and extensive medical equipment. She is fully surveyed by the Swedish maritime authorities and carries a passenger ship certificate. Personal insurance is included in the voyage fee.

PROGRAMME

In spring and autumn Astrid Finne cruises the archipelago of western Sweden, mainly carrying trainees from schools. She regularly participates in Cutty Sark Tall Ships' Races, and was the only Swedish ship to sail the whole 1997 race from Aberdeen to Trondheim, Stavanger to Göteborg. After the race, in September, she started on an 8 month voyage to the Caribbean, returning to Sweden in June 1998.

Her summer itinerary consists of an adventurous cruise up the Norwegian west coast with its scenic fjords and unspoilt nature. A years voyages could include: Florida USA to France, to Öckerö, Sweden, to Kristiansand, Norway, to Bergen, Norway, back to Kristiansand, and a return to Öckerö.

CONTACT	Erik Hermansson
ADDRESS	c/o MBV Skolskepp, Kabyssvägen 1, S-430 90 Öckerö, Sweden
PHONE	+46 31 962126
FAX	+46 31 962107
WEB	http://www.mbv.se

Atene

NATIONALITY	Swedish
HOME PORT	Skarhamn, west Sweden
SIZE OVERALL	24.15 metres 79.2 feet
CREW	25

HISTORY

Built in 1909 as the schooner Emanuel, she sailed for owners in Denmark, then Norway. Her present owners are Swedish, for in 1980 the port of Skarhamn on the island of Tjorn bought her, and established the organisation Foreningen M/S Atene in order to maintain old sailing ship traditions, on board her. The aim is to teach young people seamanship as practiced in years gone by.

ON BOARD

She sails between May and September with school classes aboard. The ship's complement, including crew, totals 25. These young people take sailing courses and participate in sailing races, including the Cutty Sark Tall Ships' Races. Out of season and at weekends Atene can be chartered by companies and private groups.

CONTACT	Mona Nestorson, Sailing Secretary
ADDRESS	Foreningen M/S Atene, Box 13, 471 21, Skärhamn, Sweden
PHONE	+46 304 67 0019 FAX +46 304 67 0019

Atlantic

NATIONALITY	German
HOME PORT	Bremen, western Germany
SIZE OVERALL	29 metres 95 feet
PROFESSIONAL CREW	3
PAYING SAIL TRAINEES	10-13

HISTORY

Atlantic is a gaff ketch of steel construction, built in 1871 by the firm of Norddeutsche Schiffbau A. G. at Kiel in northern Germany. She is thus one of the oldest steel hulled sailing vessels still afloat and in commission.

Later she spent some years as a general cargo vessel in the Baltic, and during the Second World War, she was used by an Army Officer as a private yacht under the name Forward. After 1952 she came down in the world, used as a sea-water-tanker. In 1982 she was purchased by Harald Hans, who brought her to Bremen and has carefully restored her as a sail training vessel. Since 1989, Atlantic has been used for sail training in the Bremen, Kiel and Baltic areas, and regularly takes part in the races organised by the International Sail Training Association

SAFETY CERTIFICATES AND INSURANCE

Her equipment complies with ISTA regulations for their races, and in September 1996 she was given the relevant sea-worthiness certificate by a recognised expert of the German Motor Yacht Association.

PROGRAMME

She has a regular programme of excursions in the Bremen, Kiel and Baltic areas, varying between four and eight days, between April and September each year.

The daily cost is some 110 DM, excluding on board expenses.

CONTACT	Harald Hans
ADDRESS	PO Box 750508, 28725 Bremen, Germany
PHONE/FAX	+49 421 653 221
SHIP'S PHONE	0171 520 8838

Atlantica

NATIONALITY	Swedish
HOME PORT	Göteborg, southern Sweden
SIZE OVERALL	26.2 metres 86 feet
PROFESSIONAL CREW	8
PAYING SAIL TRAINEES	24

HISTORY

SXK - Seglarskola, 'The Swedish Cruising Club's Sail Training Foundation', had excellent results with converted English sailing trawlers, such as their Gratitude. When they wanted a new ship, they kept to the same kind of design, and in 1981 built Atlantica, in Skagen, Denmark. Danish oak was used instead of British, accommodation below was to suit her sail training role, and a modern auxiliary engine was installed. Apart from these, she was built very much as a traditional English sailing trawler (though without, of course, the trawling gear). Rigging and fitting out was to a large extent done by the SXK Seglarskola's own people, as their knowledge gained from maintaining their other ships had created a wide range of craftsmen who had the necessary skills. In 1982 Atlantica took on board her first trainees and has sailed six months in each year, ever since.

ON BOARD

The objective is to teach young people sailing and seamanship.

This is done by letting the trainees perform almost all the duties on board, from steering and setting of sails to navigation and washing the dishes. All takes place under professional guidance and in a friendly atmosphere.

SAFETY CERTIFICATES AND INSURANCE

Atlantica is annually inspected and certified by the Swedish National Maritime Administration.

PROGRAMME

Traditionally SXK Seglarskola kept to home waters off Scandinavia. But Atlantica was, a new vessel with certificates enabling her to sail anywhere. It became possible to extend cruises all over Europe. Their Gratitude and Gratia were given major rebuilds, and then they too could make long journeys, including across the North Sea. So started a new era for SXK Seglarskola, and although its main activities are still at home, every year one of the ships now makes a substantial voyage. Atlantica, for instance, took part in Cutty Sark Tall Ships' Races and won the Trophy in 1986.

CONTACT	"Britt", SXK - Seglarskola
ADDRESS	Vita Gavein 38, Nya Varvet, 42171 Vastra Frolunda, Sweden
PHONE	+46 31 29 3505 FAX +46 31 69 3310°

Bel Espoir II

NATIONALITY	French
HOME PORT	Camaret
SIZE OVERALL	38.5 metres 126 feet
PROFESSIONAL CREW	5
PARTICIPATING SAIL TRAINEES	35

HISTORY

Designed and built by the Danish shipbuilder Ring Andersen, she launched in 1944 at Svendborg to work for Danish fishing enterprises between the Faeroe Islands, Greenland and Shetland Originally called Nett S, she was renamed Peder Most in 1946 and converted to transport up to 200 head of cattle on short routes such as Copenhagen to Hamburg.

In 1955 the British Outward Bound Trust acquired her. Re-registered in Glasgow, she became home to the Moray Sea School, one of Scotland's sail training organisations. Their old ship Prince Louis had reached the end of her useful life, and the new purchase was rechristened Prince Louis II.

In 1968 the Association Des Amis du Jeudi-Dimanche (the friends of Thursday-Sunday) came on the scene. Under the lead of Father Michel Jaouen this organisation helps young people who have severe problems dealing with modern life. A successor was required for their first ship, Bel Espoir. Prince Louis II was bought and once again her name changed, to Bel Espoir II.

By 1991 she was in bad need of repairs. Her long life carrying freight had taken its toll, and her hull had begun to sag. Her keel was deforming into an arc. It was time for her to be rescued or abandoned. Emptied and without masts, she was raised onto the quayside at Camaret, Brittany. The struggle began to find finance for her, and at first repairs were made thanks to donations from local collectives. Work was expensive, and Georges Pernoud, publisher of the magazine Thalassa, opened an appeal for funds in one of the magazine's issues, which was devoted entirely to the work of Father Jaouen and the rebuilding of the ship. Thousands of people contributed and with help from the City of

Paris, Finisterre's Consul General, the Region of Brittany, and many others, enough was raised for her complete restoration - thanks also to her being granted a new tax-saving classification as an 'historic monument'. During the three years of repair, Father Jaouen continued his work on board another three master, the Rara-Avis, and this ended in January 1995, when Bel Espoir II was relaunched and set off from Camaret for the Caribbean.

ON BOARD

Her main role remains to help the young who need to get back onto their feet again, and there are two main commandments on board - no alcohol, and no drugs. She has 40 couchettes in cabins of two or four.

SAFETY CERTIFICATES AND INSURANCE

Bel Espoir II has a certificate of Franc Bord certified by the Bureau Veritas. She complies with accepted navigation practices, and possesses all safety equipment required for 40 people, and abides by Category 1 of the maritime rules of France. The Association has a policy for civil insurance for the crew who embark on her.

PROGRAMME

Each year Bel Espoir II usually follows a similar pattern of voyages; to the Canaries in the winter, to the Caribbean in the spring, a return voyage via Canada, and a summer programme that includes visits to Tall Ships' events in Europe.

CONTACT	M.M.Gaouen, Association Des Amis du Jeudi-Dimanche
ADDRESS	4, rue de Colonel-Domine, 75013, Paris, France
PHONE	+33 4580 2233 FAX +33 9825 41 57

Or at the office in Brittany, Madame Loiselet

PHONE	+33 298 25 43 75 FAX +33 298 25 41 57

Belle Etoile

NATIONALITY	*French*
HOME PORT	*Camaret, Brittany*
SIZE OVERALL	*28.6metres 94 feet*
CREW	*12 couchettes or 27 for daytrips*

HISTORY

Harvesting sardines and then lobsters was the lifeblood of towns along the French coast of Brittany, such as Camaret. To service this trade a specific type of design evolved and Belle Etoile follows this tradition. She charters, and is also an ambassador for Camaret as a symbol of her famous past, reminding everyone that the town was once one of Europe's key fishing ports, and also a leading builder of wooden boats.

PROGRAMME

Daily rates are 6,000 FF to charter the whole boat or per person costs 230 FF, with half price for children under 14, and those with a student card.

CONTACT	Association Belle Etoile
ADDRESS	Mairie de Camaret, La Pointe 29570 Camaret sur Mer, France
PHONE	+33 2 98 27 8871 (8691)
FAX	+33 2 98 27 80 22

Belem

NATIONALITY	*French*
HOME PORT	*Nantes*
SIZE OVERALL	*58 metres 190 feet*
PROFESSIONAL CREW	*16*
PAYING SAIL TRAINEES	*48*

HISTORY

Built in Nantes as a merchant ship, in 1896, Belem is the last survivor of the great French square rigged fleet of the past. Not one of the largest, at 528 tons, she was nevertheless used for deep sea trade. At first she carried cocoa beans to France from Brazil's port of Belem. She was sold abroad, once, and then again, in 1913, for conversion into a luxury yacht. This included the addition of auxiliary engines, an exhaust put up the lower mizzen mast, and 'cosmetic' changes, for instance she was given turned teak poop rails instead of iron stanchions. Sold yet again in 1921, she made a circumnavigation in 1923-4. The war saw her laid up and fears grew that she would go to the scrapyard. It was then, in 1950, that she was bought by the Italian Fondazione Cini and made into a sail training vessel, based in Venice. In 1978 she had a second flirtation with the scrapyard. She was rescued and brought back under the French flag once more in 1979. In 1981 her masts came down, so she could pass under the bridges upriver to Paris, and there she was re-rigged, and remained moored alongside while attempts were made to raise funds. She was restored with the help of the Caisee d'Espargne (Savings Bank), and in 1985 she made her way back to the sea. Rerigged, she crossed the Atlantic in 1986 for the 100th Birthday of the Statue of Liberty, and a year later started a new life taking paying trainees on board, based on the port where she was built, Nantes.

ON BOARD

She takes anyone in good health above the age of 16, for courses between three and ten days, in the Channel, the Atlantic, or the Mediterranean.

Stopovers are made in places of nautical interest, but they cannot be specified in advance as prevailing winds dictate where she will go. Ports of departure and arrival are, however, firm.

Life on board is organised according to the rules, customs and traditions that developed under the dictates of experience with this type of ship, centuries ago. Trainees live with the permanent crew. They help with manoeuvres, are on watch day or night, and assist with everything from the humblest activity - care of brasswork and paintwork - to helming and climbing the masts. Trainees are initiated in all the disciplines. They helm, handle ropes and learn the care and handling of sails (gradually working up to climbing the masts and yards, if the instructors agree they are ready for it). They navigate day and night, make fixes within sight of land, navigate by the stars, and are taught safety at sea. Trainees sleep in comfortable marine type berths, 12 to a cabin. Separate showers and washbasins are provided for girls and boys. A modern electric galley run by chefs provides breakfast, two other meals a day, and hot and cold beverages.

PROGRAMME

The kind of voyages undertaken are:
3 days, Lorient, Belle-Ile, Lorient 2,430 FF.
4 days, Brest-Channel Islands-Cherbourg 3,200 FF.
5 days St. Malo-the English coast-Dunkerque 5,150 FF.
6 days, Canaries-Casablanca 4,100 FF.
7 days, St..Malo-Scilly Isles-Brest 5,150 FF.
9 days, Port-Vendres-Balearics or Algarve-Lisbon 5,950 FF.
Some reductions apply, and some insurance is included in the price.

CONTACT M. G. Le Fustec, Fondation Belem.
ADDRESS 23, rue de la Tombe-Issoire, 75014 Paris, France
PHONE   +33 1 40 78 46 46   FAX   +33 1 40 78 46 66
WEB   http://www.belem.tm.fr

Belle Amie

NATIONALITY	Swedish
HOME PORT	Stocksund
SIZE OVERALL	38 metres 124.7 feet
PROFESSIONAL CREW	6
PAYING SAIL TRAINEES	18

HISTORY

Belle Amie was built in Holland in 1915 to fish in the North Sea, all year round. She has a steel hull and a ketch rig. She has recently been completely re-built and is used for charter and sail training. Her owners are Segelfartygs Kompaniet.

PROGRAMME

She sails in the archipelago of Stockholm, and in the Baltic Sea. Prices are, from May to September, 25,500 Swedish Crowns (SEK) per day, for 2,700 SEK per hour.

CONTACT   Arne Welin
ADDRESS   Stocksund Hamn, 182 78, Stocksund, Sweden
PHONE   +46 8 247510   FAX   +46 8 8242090
SHIP'S PHONE   010214 0099

Birgitte

NATIONALITY	*German*
HOME PORT	*Lübeck*
Length	*25 metres 82 feet*
Crew	*9-10*

HISTORY

One of many 40 ton cutters built in Denmark for the North Sea, she fished off the Dogger Bank and even off Greenland. In 1981 she was bought by the present association of four owners, and was rebuilt at H.Behrens in Hamburg-Finkenwerder and H.Hattecke in Freiburg-Elbe, using historical plans for this type of ship. In 1983, rebuilt as a two master, she set off on trials, and since then has been based at Lübeck in the Baltic. She is a member of the Museum Harbour Lübeck e.V.. Since Sail Flensburg in 1984, she joined STA Germany, and took part in the Cutty Sark Tall Ships' Races in 1986, 1989, 1996 and 1998. She is an occasional sail training vessel for young people. Trainees learn about co-operation, teamwork, and leadership. In 1995 disabled people joined for 6 short cruises during their holidays.

CONTACT	Hans-Wilhelm Berns, Ruhrstr. 42, 40699 Erkrath
PHONE	+49 2104 46499 FAX +49 2104 46499

Boa Esperança

NATIONALITY	Portuguese
HOME PORT	Lisbon, Portugal
SIZE OVERALL	23.8 metres 78 feet
TOTAL CREW	22

HISTORY

Portugal led Europe's seafaring revolution, starting in the 15th century when Prince Henry the Navigator, brought astronomers, mathematicians, map makers and mariners from all over Europe, to his base at Sagres in the south west of Portugal. With new designs and ideas, he sent his ships into the 'Tenebrous Ocean Sea', as the Arabs called the Atlantic. Soon, the coast of Africa was known down to Cape NO (meaning that if you got there, you could return - or maybe not). First voyages were in small fishing caravels, seaworthy vessels descended from the Arab "qârib" (in portuguese cáravo) which used only the triangular lateen sail. New techniques then developed, for instance the control of the sail was moved from outside the shrouds (traditional to the Arabs) to within the shrouds, so enabling faster and safer manoeuvres, and allowing the ship to sail close to 40 degrees off the wind, far closer than any ship of its time.

Caravels developed in such a way that soon they carried a second mast, and during the time of John the Second, even a third mast was added. Crews could be between 25 to 100 men.

The Spanish ships of Columbus their famous voyage from Spain as caravels, with exclusively lateen rigs, but en route to the Caribbean Columbus changed, substituting with some square sails, at the Canaries. Technically, Columbus' three ships should be called naus and not caravels.

In Portugal the first modern caravel replica was named Bartolomeu Dias after the famous navigator who had been first to round the Cape of Good Hope in 1488. The replica was built in 1987 and recreated the original voyage, five hundred years later, in 1988. The impetus to build her came from South Africa and from Portugal. South Africa wished to celebrate the anniversary of this ship rounding the Cape of Good Hope, and Aporvela, dedicated to sail training in Portugal, wished to recreate a caravel. By 1984 her design was ready and by 1986 Bartolomeu Dias had completed her experimental voyages. She made her historic voyage from Portugal to the Cape of Good Hope, and ended up in South Africa's Dias museum at Mossel Bay.

By 1988 acclamation after the successful conclusion of the first project led to increased demand for another ship. Aporvela considered the problems of building a second caravel, learning from experience from the first. The decision of the Portuguese to engage in such an enterprise was made with the provision that the new ship should fit with Aporvela's sail training aims. She could not be a true replica even if that were possible, but she must be able to sail efficiently with trainees on board. A powerful auxiliary engine was included. The changes did not get in the way of the desire to study the behaviour and handling of such a ship at sea and to discover what the mariners of the past were up against.

ON BOARD

The interior design was changed to accommodate 22 crew instead of 17, with a separate accommodation to enable 4 young women to participate. Rigging was altered to make the hoisting of sails less arduous, and the handling of sails easier. In 1989 the building began. Named Boa Esperança (the name of the Cape of Good Hope at the turning point into the Indian Ocean) she launched in 1990 and she has successfully taken on her role as Aporvela's sail training ship, with the 'good hope' that she would inspire the young of Portugal and lead them through sail training at sea, to a better and more responsible future.

SAFETY CERTIFICATES AND INSURANCE

Boa Esperança is fully certified as an ocean going ship, according to Portuguese and International laws. Safety equipment complies with International regulations and personal insurance is included in the voyage fees.

PROGRAMME.

Boa Esperança appears at Cutty Sark Tall Ships' Ports, but is not ideal for racing. She entered the 1992 Columbus regatta and can be seen at many sailing events.

Vera Cruz

A third caravel is now building, named Vera Cruz - the first name given by Europeans to Brazil -and she too will be available for sail training. As is another ship newly under the charge of Aporvela, named Macau (see our separate entry for her)

CONTACT	Aporvela
ADDRESS	Doca do Terrieno do Trigo, P 1100 Lisboa, Portugal
PHONE	+351 1 8876854 FAX +351 1 8873885

Creoula

NATIONALITY	Portuguese
HOME PORT	Lisbon
SIZE OVERALL	67.4 metres 221 feet
PROFESSIONAL CREW	6 officers 6 petty officers
	27 ratings
TRAINEES	51 trainees, 1 teacher

HISTORY.

Creoula was built at the C.U.F. shipyards for the Parcelaria Geral de Pescarias, to fish off the Grand Banks of Newfoundland and Greenland. She was launched in 1937 after a record building time of 62 working days. As she was to sail the icy seas, her bottom was reinforced, especially in the bow area, and in particular her

stem. The central area was the fish hold, and she was divided fore and aft into three large sections by two watertight bulkheads. Water was stored in a double bottom. The fishermen's quarters, the provisions store and cold storage for the bait were forward, and aft were the officers' quarters, the engine room, fuel tanks, sail stowage, and fishing equipment. In 1973 her working life was presumed to be over and in 1979 she was thought to be fit only as a Fisheries Museum ship, tied up alongside.

But in drydock that year her hull was found to be in superb condition, and her future was reassessed. It was decided to keep her sailing as a sea training ship to train future fishermen and give other young people their first taste of the sea. Her mid-ship area, the former fish hold, was rebuilt and partitioned to create the trainees' deck and living quarters, petty officers quarters, crew and trainees mess, and WCs. Further alterations were made in 1992, including the adaptation of former trainees' quarters into a library and classroom. Creoula now has excellent on-board facilities for 51 young trainees, with quarters for 21 trainees in two areas, and a third for 9 trainees.

Although the permanent crew are from the Portuguese Navy, the trainees can be civilians.

CONTACT	Ministerio da Defensa Nacional,
ADDRESS	Av Ilbaa da Madeira,1400 Lisboa, Portugal
PHONE	+351 1 301 6259 FAX +351 1 301 5293

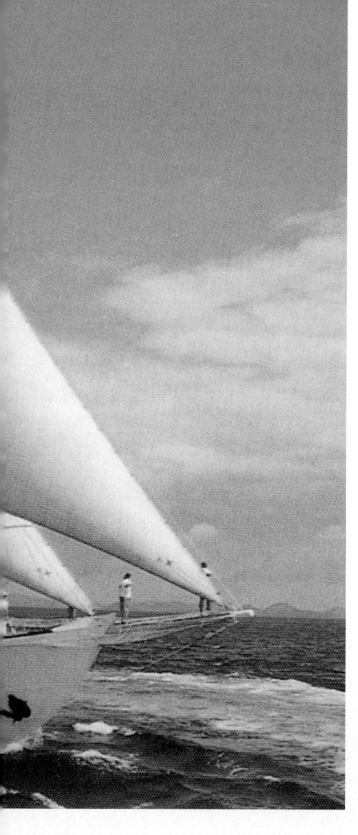

Carene Star

NATIONALITY	Danish
SIZE OVERALL	48.8 metres 160 feet
PROFESSIONAL CREW	7
PAYING SAIL TRAINEES	10

PROGAMME
Carene Star usually sails with disadvantaged youngsters aboard.

CONTACT	Paul Anders, Dora Svenson
ADDRESS	Thomash Brocklebank, Skorkaervej 8, 6990 Ulfborg, Denmark
PHONE	+45 75 343600 FAX +45 74 34 3800

Christian Radich

NATIONALITY	*Norwegian*
HOME PORT	*Oslo*
SIZE OVERALL	*72.1 metres 237 feet*
PROFESSIONAL CREW	*16*
PAYING TRAINEES	*up to 88*

HISTORY
Christian Radich was a merchant and sea captain who died in Oslo in 1884. He left in his will 90,000 Norwegian kroner for the building of a new schoolship. It took forty years, until 1936, for his dream to become reality. At that

55

time Statsraad Brichen had been Oslo's schoolship for 35 years, and a replacement was needed. Commodore and director of the navy's main yard in Horten, Christian Blom, designed the new ship. As many as eleven yards competed to gain the building contract and the best offer

came from Frameœs Mekaniski Veksted in Sandfjord. It had been 25 years since the yard had built a sailing vessel, and they took good care to get her right.

Since then, she has had many serious refits. One came after she had been seriously damaged in an air raid over Flensburg in Germany when she was dry docked. She had been used then as a submarine repair ship. Work on Christian Radich took place in 1945-47, and in 1949 she returned to sail training in Norwegian hands.

PROGRAMME
Since then Christian Radich has been used mainly to train navy and merchant navy personnel. She has also found other tasks. In 1956-7 she made an extended transatlantic voyage during which a wide-screen Cinerama film 'Windjammer' was shot. It was shown at the famous Chinese Theatre in Hollywood and in most cities of the world. She also starred in the British series 'The Onedin Line'. Recently she has started to take on board paying sail trainees, and she has taken to this actitivy with enthusiasm.

CONTACT Stiftelsen Skoleskipet Christian Radich
ADDRESS Skur 32, Akershusstranda, Postbox 666 Sentrum, 0106 Oslo
PHONE   +47 22 47 82 70
FAX   +47 22 47 82 71

Dar Mlodziezy

NATIONALITY	*Polish*
HOME PORT	*Gdynia, Poland*
SIZE OVERALL	*108 metres 358 feet*
PROFESSIONAL CREW	*33*
CADETS	*181*
PAYING SAIL TRAINEES	*20*

HISTORY

The Poles have a long history of sail training, and for years Dar Pomoza was their flagship, a beautiful ship, nicknamed affectionately 'The White Frigate'. When she became too expensive to maintain, she was moored alongside at Gdynia as a museum ship.

To replace her, designer Zygmunt Choren drew plans for the first of a new breed of three masted sail training ships. These were built in the 1980's at the Gdansk Shipyard. Dar Mlodziezy ('Gift of Youth') was the first and five others followed. All have modern interiors, engines and generators. Her five sisters are Khersones and Druzhba (Ukraine), Mir, Pallada and Nadezhda (Russia). Dar Mlodziezy is owned by the Merchant Marine Academy at Gdynia in Poland. Since her launch in 1982, she has sailed on numerous voyages including most of the Cutty Sark Tall Ships' Races. She represented Poland in the Australian bicentennial celebrations in

Sydney, when she passed under Sydney Harbour Bridge with all sails set and a metre between the top of her masts and the lowest part of the bridge. In addition to the 181 Merchant Navy cadets under training she welcomes about 20 fee paying "international trainees". She has also made her mark as an excellent vessel on which to hold hospitality parties.

Dar Mlodziezy's main role is the training of merchant naval officers and her voyages are mainly in the Baltic, European and American waters. She tries to take part in one sail training regatta in each year, and in 1997 she surpassed herself - completing two major sail training events on opposite sides of the world. She voyaged to Japan for Sail Osaka '97 and then sailed directly back to join in the second of the Cutty Sark Tall Ships' Races from

Norway to Sweden.

PROGRAMME

Her future programmes will be as varied as in the past, and will include Cutty Sark Races, Tall Ship events and a full programme of voyages especially around Europe, including the Mediterranean.

CONTACT P. Przeblowski, Gdynia Maritime Academy
ADDRESS Morska 83, 81-225 Gdynia, Poland
PHONE   +48 58 217047   FAX   +48 58 206 701

Den Store Bjorn

NATIONALITY	Danish
HOME PORT	Kolding Vamdrup, east Denmark
SIZE OVERALL	50 metres 164 feet
PROFESSIONAL CREW	8
SAIL TRAINEES	12

HISTORY

Several sail training ships started life as lightships. Anchored far outside harbours, or in estuaries, they hd to face all weathers and in open waters. Their hulls had to be extremely strong, and their shape had to deal with high and confused seas. One such was Den Store Bjorn, Denmark's former light-ship Number 18, built at the N.F.Hansens' shipyard in Odense, East Denmark, in 1902. Danish lightships came in three sizes. Den Store Bjorn was one of the largest, so she was often used in the most hazardous locations of the North Sea, also at Horns Rev near Esbjerg, and the Reef of Skagen in Skagerak. She had a Danish built B and W Alpha diesel engine added in 1959, so she could be used as a reserve ship in emergencies, able to motor to a new station under her own power rather than being towed there. Later, she was laid up, then bought by the shipping company D.s.i. Thomash Brocklebank in 1980 and rigged as you see her to-day, as a three masted topsail schooner suitable for sail trainingl.

Today she is used by young people in care, and is run by the Small School the Sailors-Denmark which is approved by the Vamdrup municipal council in the county of Vejle, and their pamphlet notes: "this small school may have a place for you if you have taken the first steps towards a criminal career, or a sombre future of drug abuse. In short, if you need a change in your life, if you have a zest for life, or if you would like to start afresh, then join the school". It has a campus ashore, with facilities for education, indoors and out of doors sports, a swimming pool, sauna, workshops, bodybuilding room and a small observatory with telescope. The school has a number of ships. Den Store Bjorn (which means the Big Bear) is one, and there are two other sailing ships Fortune and Gefion, inflatables, dinghies, and windsurfers.

The school accepts those between 14 and 20 years old, and has room for 30 students in all. Students may enroll at any time of the year.

PROGRAMME

For ten years she ventured far afield, even to the Caribbean, North America and the Mediterranean, but from the 1990's she has sailed mainly in Northern European and Scandinavian waters. Maybe in a year she will keep to southern Denmark and Germany in April, Norway in April/May, Denmark in June, to Scotland, the Faeroes and Norway in July/August, and back to Denmark for August, September and October.

CONTACT	Captain Klaus Bloch
ADDRESS	Smaskolen Fremtidens Danmark Sofolkene, Kaermindevej 8, 6580 Vamdrup, Denmark
PHONE	+45 75 58 32 97 FAX +45 75 58 37 49
E-MAIL	soefolkene@vip.cybercity.dk

Donald Searle

NATIONALITY	*British*
HOME PORT	*Hamble, southern England*
SIZE OVERALL	*22.8 metres 75 feet*
VOLUNTEER AFTERGUARD	*7*
PAYING SAIL TRAINEES	*13*

HISTORY

The owner, the London Sailing Project (LSP) was founded in 1960 by Lord Amory, then Chancellor of the Exchequer in the British government. He took parties of young sea cadets from London to sea in his own 40 foot sloop. Then he bought Rona, a 77 foot classic ketch, built in 1895, and he converted her to take a crew of 19. The project was then extended. After he died his Trust, which with the help of 'The Donald Searle Trust' and another, anonymous trust, now run three ketches, in length between 57 and 75 feet (17.4 metres to 22.8 metres).

In Lord Amory's words "Our aim is to provide opportunities for young men to acquire those attributes of seamen, namely a sense of responsibility, resourcefulness and team-work, which will help them throughout their lives". Trainees are between 14 and 25 years old and no previous sailing experience is necessary. Preference is given to those from the London area. The majority come from organisations such as Sea Cadets, Scouts, Boys Brigades, Boys Clubs and Childrens Homes. Only two are allowed from any one organisation in any one boat at a time. The result is a wide social mix. The remaining places can be booked by any young person. The LSP also organises a number of mixed 'special' voyages each year for the blind, the deaf, the mentally handicapped and pupils from schools with special needs. There are also opportunities for girls to go sailing.

ON BOARD

Each yacht normally carries an afterguard of 6 people, the skipper, a mate, two watch officers and two watch leaders. All have RYA (Royal Yachting Association) qualifications demanded by the Marine Coastguard Agency. At the end of each voyage a short report is written on each young man and a copy sent to any organisation or parent who asks for it. Trainees who give of their best can receive an 'Amory' award and an opportunity to sail in a Cutty Sark Tall Ships' Race. Those showing leadership can be recommended for watch leader selection. Indeed about 40 of the LSP skippers began as trainees.

Donald Searle is an 'Ocean 75' ketch, with a total crew of 20. She normally sails across the Channel to France and/or the Channel Islands, depending on the weather. The other two London Sailing Project yachts, Helen Mary R, and Rona II, are also ketch-rigged. Cruises begin and end at the LSP base at the Universal Shipyard, and last 6 days leaving on a Thursday and returning Wednesday, with special buses operating to London. The LSP publishes a voyage programme in November. Most of the berths are taken by the end of March but there are usually vacancies.

Trainees bring with them a sleeping bag, two sets of casual clothes, warm pullovers, trainers and a small amount of pocket money. The ship provides oilskins, lifejackets, safety harnesses, etc.

SAFETY CERTIFICATES AND INSURANCE

All yachts have complete cover including accident to crew members while on board, the exceptions are theft of personal belongings and personal accident when ashore.

PROGRAMME

The cost for a six day voyage is £50 a day for all, even the afterguard. Preference is given to anyone who cannot afford the full, economic fee of £300. The Trusts fund the difference. However the trainees are expected to contribute a part of their fee themselves and not rely on organisations, such as schools. Donald Searle normally sails across the Channel to France and/or the Channel Islands, depending on the weather, and a typical programme would last 9 days. There are voyages for special needs groups and individuals, schools and colleges, etc. Included in the itinerary are voyages as follows:
6 days, sail training voyages, 16-19 years olds.
6 days, voyages for special needs groups and individuals, schools and colleges, etc.
6 days, sail training voyages for 20-25 or 14-15 year olds.

CONTACT	Paul Bishop
ADDRESS	The London Sailing Project, Universal Shipyard, Crableck Lane, Sarisbury Green, Southampton SO31 7ZN
PHONE	+441489 885098 FAX +44 1489 579098
E-MAIL	office@lsp.org.uk
WEB	http://www.lsp.org.uk

Druzhba

NATIONALITY	*Ukraine*
HOME PORT	*Odessa*
SIZE OVERALL	*108 metres 358 feet*
PROFESSIONAL CREW	*45*
PAYING GUESTS	*80*

HISTORY

Druzhba was built at the Lenin Shipyard in Gdansk (Poland) in 1987 in a series of six ships, each very similar to the other. The first ship launched of this the "M108 class" (referring to the ship's length) was Dar Mlodziezy, which was ordered by the Polish government for the Gdynia Maritime Academy.

Five ships followed for Russia, as the Government of the USSR was considering the replacement of their two "Great Old Ladies" (Kruzenshtern and Sedov). The five were Mir meaning peace (with her home port of St. Petersburg), Pallada (Vladivostock), Khersones (Kerch), Druzhba meaning friendship (Odessa), and Nadzeshda meaning hope (Vladivostok). Khersones and Druzhba (and the Tovarisch, the former Gorch Fock of the German Navy), remained in the Ukraine when the Soviet Union broke up in 1990.

ON BOARD

Druzhba was originally built for sail training (as were her sisters) for 144 cadets, lodged in 12 cabins with 12 beds in each. More recently, she was converted into a cruising vessel. The 12 bed cabins were converted into 4 bed cabins with shower and toilet. A

bar was established on the main deck and the ships galley was converted into a cruising line kitchen.

Druzhba is now a training vessel re-equipped to a high standard. All 'sailing guests' are welcomed to participate in the crews duties: look out, sail handling, and keeping the helm of this huge windjammer.

SAFETY AND INSURANCE

Druzhba has the highest classification as a sail training ship (special purpose ship) under the Russian Register (similar to Lloyds). The ship complies with SOLAS (Safety of Life at Sea) standards. She carries a P&I insurance (required by all ships sailing in international trade).

PROGRAMME

Voyages are mainly in the Black Sea, Mediterranean, Red Sea, and across the Indian Ocean to the Maldives.

CONTACT	Inmaris Perestroika Sailing,
ADDRESS	Martin Luther Str 3, D-20459 Hamburg, Germany
PHONE	+49 40 37 2797
FAX	+49 40 37 1736
CONTACT	Primore Shipping,
ADDRESS	Odessa, Ukraine
PHONE	+38 04826 37332
FAX	+38 04826 367222

Duet

NATIONALITY	British
HOME PORT	Maldon, eastern England
SIZE OVERALL	19.2 metres 63 feet
PROFESSIONAL CREW	2
PAYING SAIL TRAINEES	7

HISTORY

The Cirdan Trust Sailing School now has three sailing ships based in east England, the 30.5 metre (100 foot) ketch Queen Galadriel, which is a converted Baltic Trader, Xylonite a 26.2 metre (86 foot) Thames Barge, and Duet is a recent addition.

ON BOARD

The Trust's aim is for youngsters to taste the adventure of sailing in larger ships, with youth organisation leaders deciding exactly what they want from a voyage. They can come aboard for a weekend, up to a fortnight, with mixed crews if necessary, and the lower limit is 10 years of age.

PROGRAMME

Duet sails the English east coast, in well protected waters, and she sometimes ventures to distant ports. The cost for individuals is £12 a day, with food extra. Group bookings can gain generous discounts. Royal Yachting Association courses are run, for instance Competent Crew and Day Skipper courses, for five day at £195, including food on board, harbour dues, and all tuition. Eighteen courses are held each year. Three courses are also held in preparation for Coastal Skipper/Yachtmaster Offshore certificates, in five day courses costing £250 - £275. The price does not include the RYA examination fee, which can take place after a course. Duet has taken part in many Cutty Sark Tall Ships' Races, and intends to continue with them.

CONTACT	The Cirdan Trust
ADDRESS	Fullbridge Wharf, Maldon, Essex CM9 7LE
PHONE	+44 1621 851433 FAX +44 1621 840045

Esprit

NATIONALITY	German
HOME PORT	Bremen, western Germany
SIZE OVERALL	20 metres 66 feet
PROFESSIONAL CREW	4
PAYING SAIL TRAINEES	12

HISTORY

In 1991 the shipyard Jugendkutterwerk Bremen e.v. (JKW) decided to built a modern schooner to enable young people to sail. This yard is unusual as it was not meant to operate at a profit, but as a place where boatbuilding skills could be encouraged. There, former long term unemployed and socially disadvantaged young people, and adults, found work in building boats, and became trained as qualified wooden boatbuilders. Finance was mainly covered by support programmes of the European Union, by several government institutions (thus the Ministry of Employment), and by some local Bremen authorities. In 1997 the yard changed its name to Bremen Bootsbau Vegesack. It built a reconstruction of an old flat bottom barge of the type used on the river Weser. And from 1999 BBV Sailing, the shipping office of the yard, has managed Esprit.

ON BOARD

Esprit is built of wood - cold moulded - to the standards of Germanischer Lloyd, using as little tropical timber as possible. She is planked with European larch and the frames and interior are of oregon pine and marine plywood. Under water she is protected by zincless antifouling. She is unusual in her main sails, one is bermudian, but the other has a gaff to increase her sail area. She has no bowsprit. She is designed for safe sailing with ease of handling by inexperienced crews, with good stability, and she makes little leeway. Below decks she has comfortable living conditions in a modern bright atmosphere. She is divided into three cabins with four berths forward and two cabins with two berths each, aft. Each cabin forward has its own toilet. The messdeck, galley and navigation area is amidships.

Launched in the autumn of 1995, her masts were rigged in 1996. She visited the Bristol Festival, and took part in Kiel Week before she made her first appearance with the Cutty Sark Tall Ships' Race, with a British crew from the James Myatt Memorial Trust.

SAFETY CERTIFICATES AND INSURANCE

Safety equipment complies with the German Sailing Association and the International Sail Training Association.

PROGRAMME

She usually cruises in the spring in the German Bight and North Sea waters. In autumn she sails in the Baltic. There are some special trips for instance one for women only. Esprit will enter future Cutty Sark Tall Ships' Races and in 1997 she won the Trophy, in a race entered by the Myatt Trust and JKW with a 50/50 British German crew. After Tall Ships 2000, her target is the Carribean.

CONTACT	Thomas Hinzen
ADDRESS	Bremer Bootsbau Vegesack GbmH, Schiffskontor Sailing, Teerhof 46, D-28199 Bremen, Germany
PHONE	+49 421 50 50 37
FAX	+49 421 59 14 00

Eendracht

NATIONALITY	Dutch
HOME PORT	Scheveningen
SIZE OVERALL	59.1 metres 194 feet
PROFESSIONAL CREW	13-14
PAYING SAIL TRAINEES	40-39

HISTORY

The Foundation 'Het Zeiland Zeeschip', and the National Society of the same name, were founded to promote the maritime traditions of The Netherlands as a seagoing nation throughout the world. And to offer active sail training experiences at sea to youngsters and adults at a reasonable cost.

In 1974, this was accomplished on board the first Eendracht (which means 'United We Stand'). She was a two masted schooner, easily recognised for many years by her blue sails. By 1986, she was too small for the growing numbers of enthusiasts for sail training in the country, and the decision was made to replace her. She was sold, and the go ahead was given for a larger, three masted schooner, intended to be one of the most comfortable and modern in the sail training fleet. For two years, designers and contractors, sailmakers and sparmakers were asked for ideas and quotations, and in 1988 her building contract was signed. The keel was laid that year and by August 1989 she was commissioned and blessed by H.M. Queen Beatrix. The Foundation is run by an all volunteer force with approximately 400 well qualified crewmembers. The 4000 members of the Society support the Foundation.

ON BOARD

Eendracht has been designed for safe handling during sail training, consequently prior sail experience is not required. The schooner has room for 39-40 trainees and of the 13-14 staff, 4 are paid crewmen, the boatswain, bosun's mate, engineer and cook. The other staff members such as skipper, mates, ship's surgeon, are all volunteers.

Trainee accommodation is in 8 two-bunk and 6 four-bunk cabins, with excellent provision of showers, toilets and drying space for clothing. The ship runs a four watch system, that is 8 to 12, 12 to 16, 16 to 18, 18 to 20, and 20 to 24, so you work in general for 4 hours and have 8 hours of rest. During the watch you perform all required ship's duties such as look out, helmsman, handling sail, and you make weather and pollution reports. The ship has to be kept tidy. Brass cleaning, washing, galley work and cleaning cabins are all part of the game. And there is a large saloon for relaxation, reading and music. A ship's stereo/CD installation in the saloon is provided, and trainees are encouraged to take along their own musical instruments. Eendracht operates throughout the year, from May to November in North European waters, and from December to April in South European waters, in the Mediterranean, around the Canaries and the Azores. During the summer and autumn holidays she is exclusively used by youngsters between 15 and 25, taking part in Cutty Sark Tall Ships' races, and in the rest of the year, she sails with anyone over the age of 15. The length of voyage is varied, between one and 20 days.

SAFETY CERTIFICATES AND INSURANCE

She has NSI classification as a 'special purpose ship', and is to Lloyd's sailing ship classification 100A1 for unrestricted worldwide sailing. She is also ISM code certified.

PROGRAMME

A typical year's programme could include:
1 day, 100G/130G; Scheveningen to Scheveningen.
2 days, 200G/280G; Scheveningen to Scheveningen.
4 days, 520G/640G; Scheveningen to Delfzijl.
7 days, 730G/930G/Transport 175G; Scheveningen to St. Malo.
16 days, 1150G/1515G/Transport 762G; Ponta Delgado to St. Malo.
18 days, 1690G/1690G/Transport 225G; Cutty Sark Tall Ships' Races.
Note: the two prices 100G/130G indicates the fees first for youngsters (aged 15 to 25) and second for adults. The third price shows the transport costs from Scheveningen by train or from there to and from harbours abroad. These transfers are arranged by the Foundation. Prices are 'all included'. Coffee and tea is free and no surprises are added on. It's just your own drinks you'll need pocket money for. The Foundation can arrange personal travel insurance if you wish.

CONTACT	P. Kroon, Stichting Het Zeilend Zeeschip
ADDRESS	P.O.Box 84108, 2508 AC The Hague, The Netherlands
VISITING ADDRESS	Schokkerweg 44, Scheveningen, The Netherlands
PHONE	+31 70 354 6261
FAX	+31 70 352 4183
WEB	http://www.eendracht.nl

Elena-Maria-Barbara

NATIONALITY	*Russian*
HOME PORT	*St. Petersburg*
SIZE OVERALL	*29.4 metres 96 feet*
PROFESSIONAL CREW	*4*
PAYING SAIL TRAINEES	*6-8*

HISTORY

This new sailing ship, like her sistership Alevtina & Tuy, is a copy of a small merchantman typical in Europe in the middle of the 18th century. As a Russian ship she has a special significance as she revives a Russian tradition of long sea voyages in such ships, a tradition almost forgotten. Her design was by 'Grumant' in St. Petersburg, and she launched in July 1995. Her hull is built of pitch pine and oak and her exterior is treated against rot and the growth of weed so that she shuld not need repair for at least 20 years. STS Elena-Maria-Barbara's rig is that of a two masted topsail schooner with an exceptionally long bowsprit.

ON BOARD

Aboard she is a comfortable modern vessel. There are two toilets with showers, a galley, and a comfortable main saloon for 12 people. Below are 3 double berth cabins for guests and one four berth cabin. Her 16 complement includes captain, first mate, bosun and cook. Special Russian food, and European food, are available.

SAFETY CERTIFICATES AND INSURANCE

She is equipped to SOLAS 74/78 standards and is registered in the Russian Maritime Register of Shipping. Her insurers are Lampe & Schierenbeck of Bremen in Germany and the P & I Club in London. She is licensed to carry up to 16 passengers overnight, and she has no-limit to where she can sail.

PROGRAMME

She has taken part in two Cutty Sark Tall Ships' Races, in 1995 and 1996, when she came second on the leg from Rostock to St. Petersburg. Her cruising area is 'unlimited'. She is a familiar sight in the ports of the Baltic, her usual stamping ground.

CONTACT	Boris Krishtal
ADDRESS	J/V "Erkon", 21 Linia 8a, St. Petersburg 199026, Russia
PHONE	+7 812 3251127
FAX	+7 812 325 1126 or +7 812 217 0682
CONTACT	in Germany
	SCS Shipping Consulting and Services GmbH, Postfach 120429, D-27518 Bremerhaven, Germany
FAX	+49 471 9413857
PHONE ON BOARD	+7 812 9651120

Etoile Maxi

NATIONALITY	French
HOME PORT	Saint-Malo, west France
SIZE OVERALL	25 metres 82 feet
CREW	25+

HISTORY

Famous as Kialoa IV under her previous owner, Jim Kilroy , she won of many ocean races throughout the world. Renamed Etoile Maxi she is the latest addition to the Etoile Marine fleet, which now has four very different types of ship at Saint-Malo.

ON BOARD

For day sailing, her capacity is 25 plus her crew, and for weekends and cruises the figure is 20 persons plus crew.

PROGRAMME

Such a fast yacht can undertake many commitments. Her plans includes her going to famous races (shadowing the last leg of the Whitbread Round the World Race), she can attend event race starts (such as the French singlehanded Route de Rhum), she makes 2 day cruises to the Channel Islands, and also takes youngsters to sea, maybe to participate in Cutty Sark Tall Ships' Races. In December she cruises to the Caribbean. A guideline price is 20,000 FF for a two day trip to the Channel Islands.

CONTACT	Bob Escoffier, Chantier Etoile Marine
ADDRESS	6, avenue Louis Martin, 35400 Saint-Malo, France
PHONE	+33 299 40 48 72 FAX +33 299 40 41 83

Etoile Molene

NATIONALITY	*French*
HOME PORT	*Saint-Malo, western France*
SIZE OVERALL	*35 metres 115 feet*
PROFESSIONAL CREW	*3*
PAYING SAIL TRAINEES	*20 and 28 for day trips*

HISTORY

Etoile Molene was built in 1954 by Auguste Tertu (nicknamed 'The Rostellec Carpenter'). She was one of the last ships built to be both a trawler and a tuna fishing ship. In 1990 she was due to be scrapped, but a few days before her intended destruction she was bought, and after 18 months of work she put to sea once again. She even took part in the singlehanded race, the Route de Rhum (from France to the Caribbean) in 1994. More usually, she charters.

If you are in Saint-Malo, her owners Chantier Etoile Molene also have a smaller sailing ship, the 15 metre long Popoff, a cruising catamaran, Etoile Filante, and they can be used together with their larger sister, Etoile Maxi, as a group.

ON BOARD

She sleeps ten in double couchettes, thirteen in single berths, and has one couchette for a child.

PROGRAMME

In April she sails for weekends in the Channel Islands, and in May up to 4 day voyages to the South Coast of England and the Channel Islands.

Usually, and from May to June, longer trips of seven days take her to the Islands off the French coast - including Belle Isle, Ile d'Yeu, Oléron, and to the Basque coast.

She has been made available for the Cutty Sark Tall Ships' Races, or for youth camps, or family cruises, depending on demand.

In the beginning of September she is in Brest, La Rochelle, and Saint-Malo. Then she is available for the last half of September and October, for weekends in the Channel Islands. Come January, February and March, she cruises in the Caribbean.

CONTACT	Bob Escoffier, Chantier Etoile Marine
ADDRESS	6, avenue Louis Martin, 35400 Saint-Malo, France
PHONE	+33 299 40 48 72 FAX +33 299 40 41 83

Europa

NATIONALITY	Dutch
HOME PORT	Amsterdam
SIZE OVERALL	45.5 metres 149 feet
PROFESSIONAL CREW	9
DUTCH NAVY VOLUNTEERS	2
PAYING SAIL TRAINEES	up to 50 overnight
	up to 100 by day

HISTORY

Europa launched in Hamburg, Germany, in 1911 as a lightship, Elbe 2. A role she fulfilled until the 1970s. Eventually, between 1987 to 1994, she was rebuilt into the three masted barque that you see to-day. She is now used for occasional sail training, and charters. In addition to a busy European sailing programme, Europa also undertakes worldwide voyages carrying up to 50 passengers.

ON BOARD

Guests have a choice of two, four, or six berth cabins with en suite showers and toilets. There are two saloons with a capacity of twenty and fifteen respectively plus a large deckhouse which seats thirty five.

SAFETY CERTIFICATES AND INSURANCE

The ship possesses the sailing permits issued by Register Holland, Bureau Veritas and Dutch Shipping and Inspection, the ISM Certificate, and international certificates. Trainees have to provide their own insurance.5

PROGRAMME

Over the weekend, 4-5 day voyages cost 150-780 Nfl a day, food included. Her ISTA Races, such as Tall Ships 2000, are usually 9-14 day voyages.

'Adventure Sailing' excursions are 14 days, and she visits seven countries, such as France, England, Holland, Norway, Denmark, Sweden, and Germany.

Her 7 days trips, to 'Discover the Baltic', are from Rostock to Sweden and back.

She carries out special sail training programmes as the official sail training ship of The Netherland's Nautical College at Enkhuizen.

CONTACT	Gert Tetteroo, Hollands Glorie		
ADDRESS	PO Box 11245, 3004 EE Rotterdam		
PHONE	+31 10 415 6600	FAX	+31 10 415 4545

Excelsior

NATIONALITY	*British*
HOME PORT	*Lowestoft, eastern England*
SIZE OVERALL	*33 metres 108 feet*
PROFESSIONAL CREW	*5*
PAYING TRAINEES	*12*

HISTORY

A hundred years ago over 2,000 sailing trawlers fished each winter in the North Sea, sailing from a number of English east coast ports. To-day only a few are left and Excelsior is one of them. She is a Lowestoft smack, a fine representative of this once famous and historic type. Incidentally a smack is usually a 'sloop' (one mast, while Excelsior has two), or a fishing ship with holds and equipment on board to keep fish alive (as had Excelsior). She was built to be fast and weatherly in all conditions, summer and winter, both for the quick delivery of her fishing catch into port, and for the safety of her crew. Built in Lowestoft in 1921, of oak on oak, she fished the North Sea for cod until 1935. Now she has been converted for sail training, especially offering a traditional sailing experience thus keeping alive the knowledge of how such craft were sailed and maintained. But don't despair if you think this 100 tonner has gear too heavy for you to handle. The trawlermen of the past did not expend energy needlessly, and she is fitted with every labour saving device of her day. And there is some modern equipment to help you sail her - though none of it affects her traditional feel. Her old steam capstan (to raise the anchor) is now operated by compressed air. And there's now an engine, a powerful Lister. Old time block and tackle and tiller steering still operate, not winches or a wheel. Down below she has been completely rebuilt and she was re-commissioned in 1989.

ON BOARD

You can sail her if you are over 14 (under 14s must be with an adult). There is no upper age limit. In addition to 12 trainees (no previous experience is necessary), she has a regular skipper, mate and bosun, with two watchleaders (the 'afterguard'). Excelsior usually operates a three watch system, 4 hours on watch and 8 hours off.

INSURANCE

She satisfies the requirements laid down by the Department of Transport in respect of sailing vessels.

PROGRAMME

Her usual voyage is for 7 days throughout the North Sea, including Scandinavia, the Faeroes, and Ireland. Ports visited recently include Lowestoft, Whitby, Inverness, Oban, Falmouth, Weymouth, Camaret, Vigo, Dublin, Newlyn and Rye.

CONTACT	The Excelsior Trust
ADDRESS	Riverside Road, Lowestoft, Suffolk NR33 0TU, UK
PHONE	+44 1502 585302 FAX +44 1502 585302
E-MAIL	excelsiortrust@excelsiortrust.freeserve.co.ltd
WEB	http://www.marina.fortunecity.com/reach/318/

Fryderyk Chopin

NATIONALITY	Polish
HOME PORT	Szczecin, Poland
SIZE OVERALL	55.5 metres 183 feet

HISTORY

Built in 1990, Fryderyk Chopin is named after the famous composer, and uses Polish spelling for after all, he was born near Warsaw, lived the first half of his life in Poland before moving west, and considered himself Polish.

She is the latest sail training ship designed by Zygmunt Choren, who was responsible for the Gdansk-built three masted ships of the 1980s including Dar Mlodziezy, Mir, Druzhba, Khersones, Pallada and Nadezhda, and the smaller Pogoria, Iskra, and Kaliakra.

Fryderyk Chopin appears more radical, with six foresails, and she carries six square sails on each mast. Her two masts are placed very well forward.

With this configuration, she is designed to have more speed than her relations, and in her debut in 1992 in the double transatlantic Columbus Regatta she came (on handicap time) fifth of 100 entries. She was the dream of singlehander Krzysztof Baranowski

and his International Class A Afloat Foundation, and her plan had been to sail train. Soon she faced stormy financial times and by 1996 the Polish Bank, Kredyt Bank, repossessed her. Interest to purchase came from Norway's City of Trondheim, and the Polish City of Szczecin. In 1998 the Polish Sail Training Association was asked to continue sail training her into 1999. Instead she cruised past Cape Horn into the Pacific, and back to Poland. The bank decided to keep her and has set up an operating company for her.

PROGRAMME

From Szczecin, she sails in the Baltic in summer, and into the Atlantic and beyond in winter, chartering, and also she is used by training groups.

CONTACT   Pawel Ryzewski
ADDRESS   Armatorski Dom Bankowy, ul Matejki 8, 71-615 Szczecin, Poland.
PHONE   +48 49 423 5902   FAX   +48 49 423 5902
E-MAIL chopin@cybersails.info.pl
WEB http://www.cybersails.info.pl.chopin

Eye Of The Wind

NATIONALITY	British
HOME PORT	Faversham, Southeast England
SIZE OVERALL	40.2 metres 132 feet
PROFESSIONAL CREW	9
VOYAGE CREW	20

HISTORY

Eye of the Wind's story is one of many in the fleet, of construction as a commercial ship, neglect, and careful rebirth in the hands of enthusiasts, in a form suited for sail training.

She was built by C. Luhring of Brake, Germany in 1923 to bring back animal hide from South America. She continued in Swedish hands for fifty years. Originally named Friedrich, and renamed Merry, she later carried general cargo in the Baltic and North Sea with summer spells drifting for herring off the coast of Iceland. Her first engine was installed in 1926, and her sailing rig was gradually reduced.

In 1969 fire in her engine room destroyed the wheel house and poop deck and her life seemed over.

Enter a group of square rig enthusiasts who bought her in 1973 as a hulk, and began the task of rescuing her. The Skandia air start engine and poop deck were rebuilt, and where the plating had buckled it was replaced with mild steel. She crossed the North Sea to Faversham in Kent, and here in 1975 her superstructure and rigging were painstakingly renewed. A master rigger came to live nearby. Local metal was used for her bowsprit, chain plates and a dolphin striker. Part of the breakwater of the nearby seaport and crossing timbers from a disused railway were fashioned into pinrails. A dance floor of teak became the deckhouse. Church pews became the seats. Panelling from a London bank embellished the new spacious lower saloon.

When ready, she was put to the test. First with a circumnavigation of the globe, averaging 100 miles a day to Sydney, Australia. Returning to Plymouth in 1978 she became the flagship of Operation Drake. This two year round the world scientific expedition involved over 400 young people from 27 nations, and ended in London in 1980. She took part in films such as 'Blue Lagoon', 'Savage Islands', 'Taipan'. and more recently 'White

Squall'. She is also the proud winner of the Cutty Sark Tall Ships 'Concourse D'Elegance Award' for the most beautifully maintained ship of the fleet. She was in Australia for the First Fleet Re-enactment and subsequent Bicentennial Celebrations. In early 1990 she sailed the southern Pacific Ocean to participate in the 200th anniversary of the settlement of Pitcairn Island by the descendants of the Bounty mutineers. In 1991 she sailed from Sydney round Cape Horn for Europe, joining in the Columbus Regatta celebrations in 1992, across the Atlantic and back. Today her voyages are just as adventurous.

ON BOARD

With Eye of the Wind you experience a traditional ship in comfort down below, but you don't have to know anything about sailing to join in. All cabins are two berth (except for one with four), each with wash basin, mirror, lights, fans, and storage, with toilets and hot fresh water showers adjacent.

The ship runs a three watch system, that is 8-12, 12-4, and 4-8 so you work for 4 hours and have a rest of 8 hours before the next watch. During the 4 hours you will do lookout, spend time on the helm, handle sails, and you can volunteer to work aloft, make safety checks, weather and pollution reports. Other duties

include washing the deck, brass polishing, cleaning bright work, etc. You will be on a galley roster and help with all aspects of meal preparation, washing up and cleaning, as allocated by the cook. Down below, you must help in cleaning to keep up a high standard.

Below, the saloon is for relaxation with a large library, and games. Personal stereos are permitted, but only during free time periods.

There's plenty of learning to do, helped by the permanent crew of 9, including fully qualified master, first officer, second officer, engineer and nurse. All are experienced with square rigged sailing ships.

SAFETY CERTIFICATES AND INSURANCE

She is fully surveyed by the Department of Trade (UK) as a Class XI sailing ship. Safety equipment complies with Department of Trade regulations for a sail training vessel. Personal insurance is included in the voyage fee.

CONTACT	Dianne Parsons
ADDRESS	Eye of the Wind, 102 High Street, Crediton, EX17 3LF, UK
PHONE	+44 1363 777990
FAX	+44 1363 773545

Fridtjof Nansen

NATIONALITY   German
HOME PORT   Wolgast, Baltic Germany
SIZE OVERALL 52 metres 170.6 feet
PROFESSIONAL CREW 12
PAYING TRAINEES 30

HISTORY

She has an unusual rig. If she had two or more masts of equal height with fore and aft sails on each mast, she would be a schooner. If she had a square sail only on her front (fore) mast, she would be a fore topsail schooner. These rigs are quite common in our guide. But Fridtjof Nansen has square rigged sails on her fore mast, and also on her middle (main) mast, hence her description as a main topsail schooner.

CONTACT	Traditionssegler Fridtjhof Nansen eV
ADDRESS	Hafenstr. 33, 22880 Wedel, Germany
PHONE	+49 4103 913161
FAX	+49 4103 913131

Fulton

NATIONALITY	*Danish*
HOME PORT	*Assens, Denmark*
SIZE OVERALL	*63 metres 206.6 feet*
PROFESSIONAL CREW	*3*
VOYAGE CREW	*Day sailing 72, overnight 42*

CONTACT	Fulton Stiftelsen
ADDRESS	Strandgade 7, DK-5610 Assens, Døgnvagt På, Denmark
PHONE	+45 64 71 16 14
FAX	+45 64 71 58 14

HISTORY

Built at Marstat in Denmark, in 1915, she was designed to sail a triangular trade route. Goods such as lead and stone were taken from Denmark to Newfoundland. From there she carried salted fish to Portugal. Wood and coal might be amongst the goods on board for the return journey to England, or to Denmark, or to Malmö in Sweden.

She was sold to Swedes in 1923, who owned her for a dozen years. During that time, an engine was added, in 1925. By 1960 she was in Aalborg, Denmark, and by 1970 she converted to the job she does to-day, taking out students between 13 and 18 years old, from Mondays to Fridays. Also on board are four youngsters at risk, taken from a house at Assens, Denmark, that cares for 25 at a time who might benefit from a controlled environment, and these may be asked if they wish to take a 15 day voyage on the ship. The State owns her, but financially, she has to pay her way.

Golden Vanity

NATIONALITY	British
HOME PORT	Brixham, South West England
SIZE OVERALL	12 metres 39 feet
PROFESSIONAL CREW	2
PAYING TRAINEES	6-7

HISTORY

Golden Vanity was built in 1908 in wood at Saunders Yard, Galmpton, on the River Dart, south west England for the marine artist, Arthur Briscoe. He insisted on a gaff cutter similar in design to working vessels of the time as he required a strong, seaworthy vessel to sail in any weather, and from her, he could sketch and paint the last of the commercial sailing ships trading in northern Europe.

In the 1970s she completed a number of transatlantic voyages, and then she was acquired by the Golden Vanity Trust in 1982. The Trust, a registered charity, was created to restore and operate her as a sail training vessel for local youngsters. After extensive work she was relaunched in 1988 and has been sailing ever since in her new role. In the winter of 1995 she underwent a major refit, including replacing several of the hull planks, and rebuilding the 33 year old engine. In 1999 she joined the Trinity Sailing Foundation, together with Provident and Leader (see entry 'Provident'), to provide three ships from the same port.

ON BOARD

Golden Vanity offers the advantage of a relaxed 'family' atmosphere where individuals' needs can be easily addressed and where everyone's effort is important.

Until 1997 she had a license to carry up to 8 people (usually a qualified skipper, an experienced mate, and 6 trainees). In the winter of 97/98 her accommodation was upgraded to 9. The Trust has gained considerable experience working with youngsters with learning difficulties. The present programme offers up to 20 days a year for local special needs schools, in which 5 pupils and 2 teachers sail with the skipper on 1 to 5 day cruises. These cruises are currently being sponsored by the BBC Children in Need Appeal.

PROGRAMME

Sailing from her home port of Brixham, Golden Vanity cruises extensively along the south coast of Devon and Cornwall, but she also ventures further afield. Every year since 1993 she has taken part in Cutty Sark Tall Ships' Races, in that year from Bergen in Norway to Oporto in Portugal. In 1995, she was proud to circumnavigate most of mainland Britain and to be overall winner of the Tall Ships Race series on corrected time.

In 1996 she went to the maritime festival at Bristol and she also took part in the Marine Conservation Society's national beach cleaning project. In both 1996,1997 and 1999 she took part in Cutty Sark Tall Ships' Races. She tries to provide as many opportunities as possible to disadvantaged and handicapped young people.

Golden Vanity takes between 250 and 300 people sailing each year. About 30% of the youngsters are those with special needs. Although the main aim is to provide sailing opportunities for the young of south Devon, she also takes people from further afield. Costs are based on £35 per person per day. However, there are possibilities of discounts for group bookings, for disadvantaged young people, and from those from the south Devon area.

CONTACT	Jean Border
ADDRESS	32 Courtland Road, Shiphay, Torquay PQ2 6JR
PHONE	+44 1803 613700 FAX +44 1803 856546

Götheborg III

NATIONALITY	*Swedish*
HOME PORT	*Göteborg, Sweden*
SIZE OVERALL	*58.5 metres 192 feet*
PROFESSIONAL CREW	*20*
SCHOOLSHIP CREW	*60*

HISTORY.

Many sail training ships are recreated from famous historical types. One type which has been largely ignored to date, is the East Indiamen. The route they plied was from Europe to the Far East in the 17th and 18th centuries. Portugal had the virtual monopoly of this trade in the 17th century. then came the British and Dutch. The city of Amsterdam has recreated two Dutch East Indiamen, Batavia and Amsterdam, but their main role is as museum ships, which can motor (but not sail) from event to event. This is about to be changed in Sweden, with the building of a fully fledged sailing East Indiaman, Götheborg III. Sweden came late to the trade, and their company started in 1731, following Denmark and Austria. The Swedish company was started by a Scottish nobleman, a German, and a Göteborg merchant, and their idea was to carry wood, tar, iron and copper to be sold en route at Cadiz for silver, which was then taken east and traded for tea, porcelain and silk.

A ship named Götheborg (the old spelling of the city) was one of Sweden's 38 East Indiamen. In 1745 she was on her way back from trading with China to her home port of Göteborg. In sight of the City, she sailed straight onto a well known rock, Hunnebåan, and slowly she sank. The reasons for her demise have been the subject of controversy ever since... excitement at seeing home again... insurance..the last of the wine on board. Nobody will know.

A decision was made in the 1980s to recreate a ship as a symbol of a proud sailing tradition at Göteborg through the centuries,and what better than an East Indianman. Why not build a replica of Götheborg? After all, her lines could be more easily recreated from knowledge provided by the wreck. The new ship, Götheborg III, will be launched in 2002, and her first voyage will be to China and back in 2004, with young people aboard. Then she will take up sail training nearer to home.

ON BOARD

The objective will be to teach young people sailing and seamanship by letting trainees perform all the duties on board, from steering and setting the sails to navigating and washing up. This all takes place under professional guidance and in a friendly atmosphere.

CONTACT ADDRESS	Svenska Ostindinaka Götheborg Companiet AB, Ostindiefararen Götheborg, Terra Nova Eriksberg, S-41764, Göteborg
PHONE	+46 31 7793450 FAX +46 31 7793455
E-Mail	flaskpost@rocketmail.com

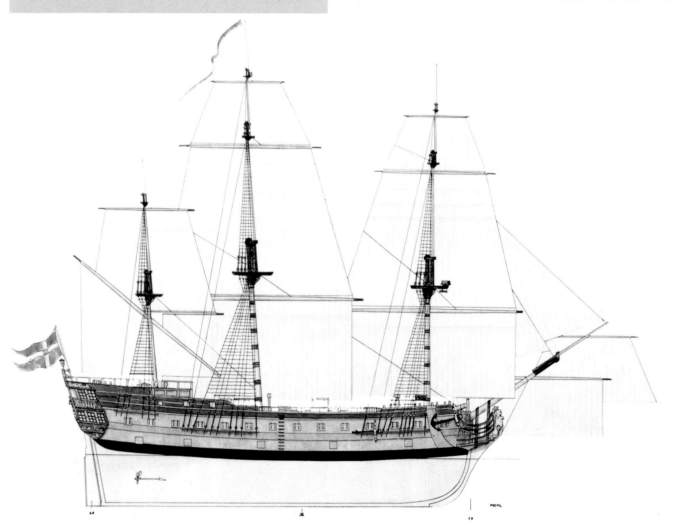

Gratitude

NATIONALITY	Swedish
HOME PORT	Vestra Frolunda
SIZE OVERALL	30.8 metres 101 feet
PROFESSIONAL CREW	7
PAYING SAIL TRAINEES	20

HISTORY.

Gratitude was built in 1903 in Porthleven, Wales, as a sailing trawler and she fished out of Lowestoft, East England, for almost thirty years. These sailing trawlers were well known for their exceptional seaworthiness and sailing capabilities. When steam trawlers took over, many of these sailing trawlers were sold to Scandinavia. Gratitude came to Sweden in the early 1930s. An engine was installed, the rig shrunk to a mere derrick, a steering house was fitted, and as a sailing ship she was degraded piece by piece.

The 1950s would have seen an end of her, if an fortunate purchase had not taken place. The SXK Seglarskøla 'The Swedish Cruising Club's Sail Training Foundation' had founders and active members many who were professional seamen with years of experience of large sailing vessels, and they believed that in an English sailing trawler would be ideal for sail training.

So, in 1957, Gratitude was bought by them and saved from the scrapper's jaws. With the help of many individuals and supporting companies, she was put back into good shape. The rig and deck layout were restored close to the original, and below decks accommodation was built for a larger crew. So she began her new career. The first trainees came on board in 1958, and she sparked the 'sail training boom' that now you see in Sweden. She has entered the Cutty Sark Tall Ships' Races four times, in 1978, 1980, 1992 and 1997.

ON BOARD

The plan is to teach young people sailing and seamanship. This is done by letting trainees perform all the duties on board, from steering and setting the sails to navigating and washing up. This all takes place under professional guidance and in a friendly atmosphere.

SAFETY CERTIFICATES AND INSURANCE

Gratitude is annually inspected and certified by the Swedish National Maritime Administration.

CONTACT	SKS-Segarskola
ADDRESS	Vita Gavien 38, Nya Varvet, 42671 Vestra Frolunda, Sweden
PHONE	+46 31 29 35 05 FAX +46 31 693 3310

Greater Manchester Challenge

NATIONALITY	British
HOME PORT	Liverpool, west England
SIZE OVERALL	23 metres 76 feet
STAFF	5
CREW	12

HISTORY

Established in 1960 the owners Ocean Youth Trust (formerly Ocean Youth Club), have the largest youth sailing fleet in Europe. They have seven yachts of about 20 metres with crews of around 16, and each is based in a different port around the British Isles.

ON BOARD

The aims of OYT are for the enjoyment and adventure of life at sea, with crews of different sex, ability, social backgrounds, and ethnic origin.

OYT takes people aged 12 and up to 24, and for those 25 and over there is a 'Friends' Membership scheme. 'Friends' sail, with other adults, on special voyages. If you can fill all 12 berths, the OYT will waive the age bands. All OYT vessels are under the command of a skipper with an RYA/DTp Yachtmaster Offshore Certificate. The Mate is an experienced person holding a Mate's certificate issued by the OYT and an RYA/DTp Coastal Skipper certificate, or equivalent.

As an educational charity, OYT can offer grants for those between 12 and 24 years old, and assist in fundraising ideas. If you can't afford an OYT voyage, the club has a proud boast that no young person is unable to sail with them because of cost, with local and national bursaries available, although everyone is encouraged to contribute so that they feel that they've given something. Of young crews, over 60% have been subsidised. Where any OYT vessel calls on any of her voyages depends on the weather, but in voyages over 3 days expect one port of call, and over 6 days, two.

OYT provides all safety equipment you'll require, and wet weather gear necessary for sailing. All food is included. On an OYT voyage you can gain OYT, Royal Yachting Association and Duke of Edinburgh Award Certificates.

School and youth groups studies into the environment can be catered for.

All women voyages (staff and crew) can be arranged.

For those with special needs, all OYT yachts are fitted with audio compasses, and some handicaps can be catered for. If you have a medical condition or disability, you must send a doctor's note, and bring adequate medicines, etc. Stowage space is small on these boats - jackets and dresses are left ashore.

Each yacht has a home base support group who help fundraise, and many who sail come back to see 'their' ship time and again. One condition of sailing aboard, you have to be able to swim - 50 metres.

SAFETY CERTIFICATES AND INSURANCE

OYT Vessels are certified to the Department of Transport's Code of Practice for Sail Training Vessels.

The OYT operates within the Statutory Code of Practice (DTp) which stipulates the qualifications of the sea staff and rigorous standards for vessels and their equipment.

With so many ships in the club, it keeps its own 'once in 24 hour' reporting system from each of them.

Insurance covers most eventualities, even including loss of luggage, personal money, medical and other expenses when aboard due to illness or accident.

PROGRAMME

Greater Manchester Challenge sails from Liverpool as her base, to ports around the Irish Sea, and included Saint- Malo to Greenock in the 1999 Cutty Sark Tall Ships' Races.

The exact ports she calls on during any of her voyages depends on the weather, but in voyages over 3 days expect one port of call, and over 6 days, two.

Example prices would show:

Voyage	Low season	Mid season	High season
2 nights	£60	98	£135
6 nights	£169	304	£439

CONTACT	Ocean Youth Trust NW Office
ADDRESS	Business Training Centre, Windmill Lane, Denby, M34 3QS, England
PHONE	+44 161 335 9032 FAX +44 161 320 0258
WEB	http://www.oyc.org.uk

Grossherzogin Elisabeth

NATIONALITY	German
HOME PORT	Elsfleth, Baltic Germany
SIZE OVERALL	66 metres 216 feet
PROFESSIONAL CREW	18
PAYING SAIL TRAINEES	36

HISTORY

This 3 masted gaff-rigged schooner was built in 1909 in Alblasserdam and launched with the name San Antonio. Designed to carry 600 tons of cargo in three holds she was the first sailing ship to be equipped with a diesel engine, which enabled her to berth without the aid of tugs. She traded in the North Sea and the Baltic and also ranged far afield to north and west Africa and made voyages to South America. By 1936 she had become a motor ship with a larger engine and auxiliary sails, trading on until 1972. Then she was converted at a German yard to allow her to carry passengers. She was fitted with 18 cabins built into the former cargo holds, each with shower and toilet and 2 or 3 berths. Her rig was also restored. A new large deckhouse was placed on the main deck for a galley and messroom and a wheelhouse was put on top of the existing superstructure. Renamed Ariadne she cruised mainly to the Mediterranean and the Caribbean.

In 1981 she was laid-up in Piraeus, Greece where she was found by the ship owner and captain, Horst Werner Janssen of Elsfleth who decided to take her home to make her a training ship, with accommodation for a new generation of young mariners who were being taught at the local nautical school. She arrived there after a stormy voyage, manned by a volunteer crew, in 1982. In March 1993 she had the misfortune to catch fire during a refit Today the Schulschiffverein Grossherzogin Elisabeth operates her

and the county of Landkreis Wesermarsch became her official owner, and it was the Schulschiffverein that rebuilt her within a year to the highest safety standards. Today she serves as a hostel for ships' mechanic apprentices during courses at the Trade School, and trains designated ship masters studying at the Nautical School. In the summer season guests are welcome for day and weekend cruises on the river Weser and the North Sea, or, during the school holidays, for more extensive trips into the North Sea or the Baltic. Grossherzogin Elisabeth has taken part in several Cutty Sark Tall Ships' Races.

ON BOARD

There are berths on board for up to 36 guests who live in 14 cabins each equipped with 2 or 3 beds, shower and toilet. The mess room can take up to 60 people. Trainees pay DM80 per day which includes accommodation and food.

SAFETY CERTIFICATES AND INSURANCE

The ship is classified at the top level of Bureau Veritas. She has all necessary modern nautical aids, and is constructed, equipped and manned according to German rules for sail training vessels. Guests are advised to cover their private risks for accidents, illness, etc, on their own.

CONTACT	Mrs Popken, Schulschiffverein Grossherzogin Elisabeth e.V
ADDRESS	Rathausplatz 7, D-26931 Elsfleth, Germany
PHONE	+49 4404 95000 FAX +49 4404 960224

Gunilla

NATIONALITY	Swedish
HOME PORT	Öckerö
SIZE OVERALL	49.6 metres 163 feet
PERMANENT CREW	10
CREW	38

HISTORY

Astrid Finne and Hawila were the first two ships owned and operated by the Swedish voluntary school sailing association, Mot Battre Vetande (MBV), meaning 'towards better knowledge'. After a search for a third ship, the association found Gunilla. Built in 1940 she only started to trade in 1945 as a three masted ship with bermudian sails on all of them. In 1954 she was lengthened and converted into a motor ship, carrying almost everything, from cars to lead and wheat. In 1997 she was sold to MBV, who formed Rederiaktiebolaget Gunilla to transform her into a modern sail training ship. She has regained her three masts, but now her rig is barque. She launched in the spring of 1999.

ON BOARD

Education on board will be to the Swedish version of pre-college education, called gymnasium, with a combined social and natural science programme. Students will spend a third of each school year on board, to learn about different countries and cultures, nature, and sailing. The students are all in cabins of four, and for their comfort she is fully air conditioned.

SAFETY CERTIFICATES AND INSURANCE

She is verified by Bureau Veritas. Her communications include a satellite link.

PROGRAMME

Gunilla will voyage from Sweden to ports in western Europe. She sails via the Canaries to Cape Verde, continuing to South America. Next she visits the Caribbean and the United States east coast. And so back to Sweden after calling at the British Isles. Students sail on a different leg of the voyage each year, so completing the whole tour, maybe, while at the gymnasium. Gunilla is also available for other events, and for instance entered the Cutty Sark Tall Ships' Race in 1999.

CONTACT	Mennart Martinson		
ADDRESS	MBV Skutoma, Kabbyssvagen 1, 430 90 Öckerö, Sweden		
PHONE	+46 31 962 670	FAX	+46 31 962 675
E-MAIL	gunilla@gunilla.nu		
WEB	http://www.gunilla.nu		

Hartlepool Renaissance

NATIONALITY	British
HOME PORT	Hartlepool, England
SIZE OVERALL	22 metres 72 feet
PROFESSIONAL CREW	4
PAYING SAIL TRAINEES	12

HISTORY

This 72 foot ketch, designed by Robert Clark, and originally built for the Ocean Youth Club (now Ocan Youth Trust) is one of three vessels now owned by The Faramir Trust. Other members of the fleet are Black Diamond of Durham, a 44 foot ocean racer, and the 34 foot Boromir. The Trust was established to introduce Adventure Sailing to people of all ages and abilities, and the aim is to help people to become fulfilled by learning about teamwork and personal development through sailing. Particular emphasis is placed on helping young people in deprived and disadvantaged circumstances, including the disabled and unemployed.

ON BOARD

Hartlepool Renaissance has been completely upgraded and refitted and offers 12 berths available for charter, as well as taking young trainees of both sexes to sea, usually for the first time.

SAFETY CERTIFICATES AND INSURANCE

Sail training and sea training vessels operate under the MCA Code of Practice governed by the Department of Transport. The Faramir Trust has Code of Practice Certification and upholds its strict safety standards. All their vessels are skippered by an officer holding a Professional Yachtmaster certificate, and crewed according to the RYA/DTp Code of Practice. Those on board are insured while on a Faramir Trust vessel or its accompanying support boat ('tender').

PROGRAMME

Based on the Durham coastline, the three ships' sailing ground centres on the north east of England. Throughout the year, they offer adventure sailing as an introduction to sailing and also provide the full range of RYA courses. They also go further afield. Hartlepool Renaissance embarked in 1998, for instance, on a Round Britain trip and the Cutty Sark Tall Ships' Races, taking her to Scotland, Ireland, Wales, and also The Netherlands, Belgium and France.

The basic cost is £42 a person a day. However bursaries are available to those in full time education and the long term unemployed, and a recent award from the National Lottery enables the Trust to offer a limited number of sailing days per year at only £9 per day when need is demonstrated.

CONTACT	Michelle Smith
ADDRESS	The Faramir Trust, The Boatyard, Middleton Road, Hartlepool, TS24 ORA, UK
PHONE	+44 1429 864794 FAX +44 1429 271583

Havden

NATIONALITY	Swedish
HOME PORT	Stenungsund
SIZE OVERALL	37 metres 121 feet
CREW	6
TRAINEES	28

HISTORY
Havden was built as a three masted trading schooner, but she has recently been rebuilt as a sail training ship.

ON BOARD
The crew are qualified with long experience of sailing ships, and include young people who are continually brought up to date on the latest techniques on seamanship. On board, there are 28 bunks in one open area, and 6 bunks separately for the crew in an after cabin.

SAFETY CERTIFICATES AND INSURANCE
The Swedish National Administration of Shipping and Navigation makes an annual inspection of the ship.

PROGRAMME
Havden runs 'Junior Sailings' for young people from 14 years old, 'Senior Sailings' for women and men past the junior age, and a 'Camp School' for school classes, who rent the ship and hold classes on board. Companies, societies and individuals can also make their own sail training plans, or just charter the ship with her professional crew.
Usually she stays in Swedish waters, but she has taken part in a Cutty Sark Tall Ship's Race.

ADDRESS Seglarföreningen Skutan, Box 247, S-444 23
         Stenungsund, Sweden
PHONE   +46 10 679 17 42   FAX   +46 303 866 95

Hawila

NATIONALITY	*Swedish*
HOME PORT	*Öckerö*
SIZE OVERALL	*25.5 metres 84 feet*
CREW	*30*

HISTORY

This sturdy gaff-rigged ketch was launched in 1935 from the same Norwegian Yard Lindstols which built the Norwegian square-rigged ship Sørlandet. Hawila is now owned and operated by the Swedish voluntary school sailing association, Mot Battre Vetande (MBV), meaning in English 'towards better knowledge'.

She was bought by MBV in 1978, and together with her 'sister' Astrid Finne they are ideal sail training ships concentrating on voyages in the Baltic and North Atlantic.

The school now has a third ship, Gunilla.

CONTACT	Erik Hermansson
ADDRESS	MBV - Skutoma, Kabbyssvagen 1, 430 90 Öckerö, Sweden
PHONE	+46 31 962126 FAX +46 31 34278

Helena

NATIONALITY	Finnish
HOME PORT	Uusikaupunki, south west Finland
SIZE OVERALL	38 metres 125 feet
PROFESSIONAL CREW	4
PAYING SAIL TRAINEES	20-24

HISTORY

Helena was Finnish built in 1992 to a design by Frenchman Guy Ribadeau Dumas. She is the flagship of the Sail Training Association Finland, whose aim is to give young people a chance to learn to live on board a sailing vessel, and to arouse their interest in navigation and seafaring. STA Finland has no ships of its own, but in the case of Helena it is a major shareholder. It looks after other ships for private owners, and uses them when mutually convenient. Two of the fleet, Helena, and Lokki, sail outside the Baltic.

ON BOARD

The lower age limit for trainees 16, with no upper limit. No previous experience is necessary. Different watch systems are used depending on experience. Four hours on watch and eight hours off is common.

STA Finland divides its activities into four groups.

First, for those who take part in basic sailing (14 to 25 year olds) who usually sail for 7 to 10 days.

Second, 'event' sailing, such as the Cutty Sark Tall Ships' Races.

Third, 'adventure sailing', for instance in the Caribbean, for spells of one week or more.

Fourth is 'Junior Sailing' for the young 12 to 13 year olds, for three days at a time.

SAFETY CERTIFICATES AND INSURANCE

Helena is fully surveyed by the Finnish Marine Administration and listed on the commercial vessel register as a Special Purpose Ship. Safety equipment complies with commercial vessels special purpose ship regulations and she is insured accordingly. Personal insurance is not included so you must take out your own policy which is compulsory.

PROGRAMME

A typical programme is for her to sail to the Canaries in winter, and to sail off Finland in the summer. She has also taken part in Cutty Sark Tall Ship' Races in 1992 and 1993, and in 1996 she took part in the Cutty Sark Tall Ships' Race from Rostock to St. Petersburg, and then to Turku.

A typical programme could be:

9 days Helsinki-Marienhamn-Rauma 1900 Finnmarks.

8 days Rauma-Mariehamn-Stockholm 1700 FM.

11 days Helsinki-Mariehamn-Stockholm 2850 FM.

7 days Stockholm-Tallinn-Kotka 1500 FM.

Note: The prices do not include flights to and from the ports, and personal insurance is up to each individual's choice.

CONTACT Pekka Toumisalo, The Sail Training Association Finland, Tarmonkuja 2, 00180 Helsinki Finland

PHONE   +358 9 685 26 16   FAX   +358 9 685 26 15

E-MAIL purjelaivasaatio@pp.kolumbus.fi

WEB http://www.koti.kolumbus.fi/^nuorpurj/

Helen Mary R

NATIONALITY	*British*
HOME PORT	*Hamble, southern England*
SIZE OVERALL	*17.4 metres 57 feet*
VOLUNTEER AFTERGUARD	*6*
PAYING SAIL TRAINEES	*10*

HISTORY

The owner, the London Sailing Project (LSP) was founded in 1960 by Lord Amory, then Chancellor of the Exchequer in the British government. He took parties of young sea cadets from London to sea in his own 40 foot sloop. Then he bought Rona, a 77 foot classic ketch, built in 1895, and he converted her to take a crew of 19. The project was then extended. After he died his Trust, which with the help of 'The Donald Searle Trust' and another, anonymous trust, now run three ketches, in length between 57 and 75 feet (17.4 metres to 22.8 metres).

In Lord Amory's words "Our aim is to provide opportunities for young men to acquire those attributes of seamen, namely a sense of responsibility, resourcefulness and team-work, which will help them throughout their lives". Trainees are between 14 and 25 years old and no previous sailing experience is necessary. Preference is given to those from the London area. The majority come from organisations such as Sea Cadets, Scouts, Boys Brigades, Boys Clubs and Childrens Homes. Only two are allowed from any one organisation in any one boat at a time. The result is a wide social mix. The remaining places can be booked by any young person. The LSP also organises a number of mixed 'special' voyages each year for the blind, the deaf, the mentally handicapped and pupils from schools with special needs. There are also opportunities for girls to go sailing.

ON BOARD

Each yacht normally carries an afterguard of 6 people, the skipper, a mate, two watch officers and two watch leaders. All have RYA (Royal Yachting Association) qualifications demanded by the Marine Safety Agency. At the end of each voyage a short report is written on each young man and a copy sent to any organisation or parent who asks for it. Trainees who give of their best can receive an 'Amory' Award and an opportunity to sail in a Cutty Sark Tall Ships' Race. Those showing leadership can be recommended for watch leader selection. Indeed about 40 of the LSP skippers began as trainees.

Helen Mary R is a 57 foot Bowman ketch, with a total crew of 16. The other two London Sailing Project yachts, Donald Searle and Rona II are 75 foot and 68 foot and are also ketch-rigged. Cruises begin and end at the LSP base at the Universal Shipyard, and last 6 days leaving on a Thursday and returning Wednesday, with special buses operating to London. The LSP publishes a voyage programme in November. Most of the berths are taken by the end of March but there are usually a few vacancies.

Trainees bring with them a sleeping bag, two sets of casual clothes, warm pullovers, trainers and a small amount of pocket money. The ship provides oilskins, lifejackets, safety harnesses, etc.

SAFETY CERTIFICATES AND INSURANCE

All yachts have complete cover including accident to crew members while on board - the exceptions are theft of personal belongings and personal accident when ashore.

PROGRAMME

Usually the younger trainees sail on her along the English south coast. The coast of France and Channel Islands may be included, weather permitting. A typical year could include:
6 day voyages for special needs groups and individuals, schools and colleges, etc.
6 day sail training voyages, 14 to 15 year olds.
6 day voyages for special needs groups and individuals, schools and colleges, etc.
6 day sail training voyages for 15 to 16.5 year olds.
The cost for the six days is £50 a day a head for all, even the afterguard. Preference is given to anyone who cannot afford the full, economic fee of £300. The Trusts fund the difference. However the trainees are expected to contribute a part of the fee themselves and not rely on organisations, such as schools.

CONTACT	Paul Bishop
ADDRESS	The London Sailing Project, Universal Shipyard, Crableck Lane, Sarisbury Green, Southampton SO31 7ZN, UK
PHONE	+44 1489 885098 FAX +44 1489 579098
E-MAIL	office@lsp.org.uk
WEB	http//www.lsp.org.uk

Hoshi

NATIONALITY	British
HOME PORT	Salcombe, Southwest England
SIZE OVERALL	26 metres 86 feet
PROFESSIONAL CREW	3
PAYING SAIL TRAINEES	9

HISTORY

This classic gaff-rigged schooner was built in 1909 by Camper and Nicholsons of Gosport, south England. Owned by the Salcombe based Island Cruising Club, Hoshi provides the ICC's members and visitors with sailing experience offshore. Our photograph shows her in her usual dark hull colour, though she's now changed to a light cream.

ON BOARD

Hoshi accommodates a total of 12, including skipper, mate and cook. Below the interior is fitted out to a high standard and includes 2 double-berth cabins, hot and cold water and a beautiful mahogany panelled saloon with all the elegance and style of the Edwardian era when she was built.

PROGRAMME

She is a frequent visitor from the English south coast to French ports in Brittany or to Scotland, and she takes part in the Cutty Sark Tall Ships' Races.

A typical year might include:

14 days, Salcombe-Eire-Oban £785
14 days, Oban-Western Isles-Oban £795
14 days, Oban-Orkney-Oban £795
14 days, Oban-Eire-Salcombe £785
7 days, Channel Cruise £395
7 days, Salcombe-Dartmouth £325
7days, Dartmouth-Salcombe £325
7 days, Channel Cruise £365.

CONTACT	Island Cruising Club
ADDRESS	Island Street, Salcombe, Devon TQ8 8DR, UK
PHONE	+44 1548 843481 FAX +44 1548 843929
E-MAIL	info@icc-Salcombe.co.uk

Hendrika-Bartelds

NATIONALITY	*Dutch*
HOME PORT	*Amsterdam, The Netherlands*
SIZE OVERALL	*49 metres 160 feet*
PROFESSIONAL OFFICERS	*2*
PROFESSIONAL CREW	*7*
PAYING TRAINEES	*36*

HISTORY

V&S Charters of Amsterdam have five schooners and barquentines which they charter. All are certified for sailing outside The Netherlands, and two of them have been on Cutty Sark Tall Ships' Races, Regina Maris and Jacob Meindert. These two are no longer with V&S. The ships they now have are Hendrika-Bartelds, the three masted schooner Bartele-Reinsink (46 metres), Willem, a brigantine looking rather like Royalist (29

metres), a sistership Wytske-Eelkje (29 metres) and Pedro Doncker (42 metres).

PROGRAMME

The ships usually sail from Kiel, northern Germany, with a favourite cruising ground in the Baltic, Scandinavia, and as far as the Baltic States and Russia, if you wish, with regular visits to Kieler fjord, the Danish island of Fyn, Gøteborg, Copenhagen, Oslo, Bornholm and Christiansø.

CONTACT   Janne Kopenaal
ADDRESS   V&S Charters Holland, Symon Meeszstraat 12,
              NL-2203 BM, Noordwijk, The Netherlands
PHONE   +31 7136 18265   FAX   +31 7136 15780

James Cook

NATIONALITY	British
HOME PORT	Hull, eastern England
SIZE OVERALL	21.3 metres 70 feet
STAFF	5
CREW	12

HISTORY

Established in 1960, the owners Ocean Youth Trust (formerly the Ocean Youth Club), have the largest youth sailing fleet in Europe. They have seven yachts of about 20 metres with crews of around 16 on each. They are based in different ports around the British Isles.

ON BOARD

The aims of OYT are for the enjoyment and adventure of life at sea, with crews of different sex, ability, social backgrounds, and ethnic origin.

The OYT takes people aged 12 and up to 24, and for those 25 and over there is a 'Friends' Membership scheme. 'Friends' sail, with other adults, on special voyages. If you can fill all 12 berths, the OYT will waive the age bands. All OYT vessels are under the command of a skipper with an RYA/DTp Yachtmaster Offshore Certificate. The Mate is an experienced person holding a Mate's certificate issued by OYT and an RYA/DTp Coastal Skipper certificate, or equivalent.

As an educational charity, OYT can offer grants for those between 12 and 24 years old, and assist in fundraising ideas. If you can't afford an OYT voyage, the club has a proud boast that no young person is unable to sail with them because of cost, with local and national bursaries available, although everyone is encouraged to contribute so that they feel that they've given something. Of young crews, over 60% have been subsidised. Where any OYT vessel calls on any of her voyages depends on the weather, but in voyages over 3 days expect one port of call, and over 6 days, two.

OYT provides all safety equipment you'll require, and wet weather gear necessary for sailing. All food is included. On an OYT voyage you can gain OYT, Royal Yachting Association and Duke of Edinburgh Award Certificates. School and youth groups studies into the environment can be catered for.

All women voyages (staff and crew) can be arranged.

For those with special needs, all OYT yachts are fitted with audio compasses, and some handicaps can be catered for. If you have a medical condition or disability, you must send a doctor's note, and bring adequate medicines, etc. Stowage space is small on these boats - jackets and dresses are left ashore.

Each yacht has a home base support group who help fundraise, and many who sail come back to see 'their' ship time and again. One condition of sailing aboard, you have to be able to swim - 50 metres.

SAFETY CERTIFICATES AND INSURANCE

OYT Vessels are certified to the Department of Transport's Code of Practice for Sail Training Vessels.

The OYT operates within the Statutory Code of Practice (DTp) which stipulates the qualifications of the sea staff and rigorous standards for vessels and their equipment.

With so many ships in the club, it keeps its own 'once in 24 hour' reporting system from each of them.

Insurance covers most eventualities, even including loss of luggage, personal money, medical and other expenses when aboard due to illness or accident.

PROGRAMME

James Cook was launched in the mid-1980s and her normal cruising grounds are the east coasts of England and Scotland, plus voyaging to Danish, Norwegian and Dutch waters. In 1997 she, and her sistership John Laing, returned from a round the world trip, calling in at 13 major ports en route, and sailing from Greenock to Alborg in Denmark on the 1999 Cutty Sark Tall Ships' Races.

Example prices would show:

Voyage	Low season	Mid season	High season
2 nights	£60	98	£135
6 nights	£169	304	£439

CONTACT	OYT North East
ADDRESS	13 Welbury Way, Southfield Lea, Cramlington, NE23 6PD, UK
PHONE	+44 1670 735736
WEB	http://www.oyc.org.uk

Jacob Meindert

NATIONALITY	Dutch
HOME PORT	Kiel
SIZE OVERALL	38 metres 124.6 feet
PROFESSIONAL CREW	2
PAYING SAIL TRAINEES	27 overnight, 35 daytrips

HISTORY
Under her owner Willem Sligting, an old tugboat, Oldeoog, had remarkable refit in 1989/90, to reappear as a topsailschooner, renamed Jacob Meindert. A small shipyard in Gdansk, Poland, took ten months to complete the metamorphosis. The form and lines of her masts and rig kept in mind the sleek and fast Baltimore Clippers of the eastern seaboard of the USA.

ON BOARD
Below decks there are 7 cabins which can take a maximum of 27 guests.

SAFETY CERTIFICATES AND INSURANCE
She is in the class Register Holland, Z.1.2.3.4.. Her seaworthiness certificate is from Nederland Scheepvaart Inspectie, her ship insurance with Kuiper verzkeringen (NL), her passenger insurance with Kuiper verzekeringen (NL), and P&I (Protection and Indemnity) with Luxemburg.

PROGRAMME
Since 1990 Jacob Meindert has sailed in the Baltic Sea from Kiel with charter crews and 'incentive' guests. She is fast and whenever possible her crew join in a race. She has once entered the Cutty Sark Tall Ships Race. Costs on her are DM4,000 for a weekend, DM5,400 for a schoolweek, and DM8,700 for a week.

CONTACT	Jacob Meindert
ADDRESS	Achterdijkje 8, NL 8754 EP Makkum
PHONE	+31 515 231712 FAX +31 515 232998
PHONE ON BOARD	+49 171 58 93 612
E-MAIL	andimanser@ad.com

Jean de la Lune

NATIONALITY	*British*
HOME PORT	*Leith, eastern Scotland*
SIZE OVERALL	*33.7metres 110 feet*
PROFESSIONAL CREW	*3 permanent 3 afterguard*
PAYING TRAINEES	*14*

HISTORY

Built in 1957 as a French MFV (Motor Fishing Vessel) designed to cope with harsh seas, she originally motored from Dounanarez in Brittany and fished off the Azores. She had fine traditional lines to her hull, and she was sturdily built. But she had no sails. Her second owner saw her potential as a sailing vessel, and an eight year conversion at Colchester, Essex, in the 1970s saw her stripped to her bare hull. Sails were added, making her a stays'l schooner. In 1983 she started work again taking scuba divers, particularly to St. Kilda in the Western Isles of Scotland. In the winter of 1985 she sailed for the Caribbean and the next year she had 3 months with Operation Raleigh.

There arrived on the scene an enthusiastic Scotsman, John Reid, a staunch advocate of traditional sailing, and his vision was to change her to square rig, and besides chartering he wished her also to follow the sail training path.

Each year more work is done to alter her for her new purpose. In 1992/3 her foremast was rerigged to accommodate the crossing of three yards and she changed from schooner to brigantine. Later rig alterations have seen a change from bermudian to gaff mainsail and a new bowsprit with 7 metre jibboom carrying three headsails.

During the winter of 97/98 JDL underwent a major refit to replace the ugly deckhouse and wheelhouse with something more akin to a traditional sailing ship but with improved safety and comfort. This has allowed the raising of the aft deck to form a poopdeck with pilot house and outside wheel and also the fitting of a fifth steel watertight bulkhead and improved crew accommodation. The ship has also been rewired, replumbed and refitted to a high standard. As a result of all this work, she is now a comfortable sailing ship.

ON BOARD.

Accommodation is in 2 and 4 berth cabins. There are 3 showers and 3 toilets. When sailing on longer voyages such as the Cutty Sark Tall Ships' Races a three watch (4 hours on 8 hours off) system operates, and trainees are expected to become involved in all aspects of day to day

activities. Traditional navigation methods are encouraged and there is the opportunity for tuition in celestial navigation. On shorter voyages, such as around the western islands of Scotland, she usually anchors at night in some secluded sea loch or ties up at one of the many island piers, where there is time to go ashore and explore.

SAFETY CERTIFICATES AND INSURANCE

Insurance is mandatory on all voyages and a guideline to the cost is £7.87 for an individual on a 7 day voyage and £9.75 for 11 days.

PROGRAMME

The kind of prices and voyages you'll expect are:
4 days, Round Oban £265. 7 days, Outer Isles £430.10 days, Outer Isles and St. Kilda £725. 10 days, Oban-Penzance via Ireland and Scillies £750
4 days, Dublin Oban £265
From October, she sails for the Canaries.
Prices are inclusive of port dues but do not include travel insurance.

CONTACT	John Reid or Fiona Brown
ADDRESS	JDL Marine Ltd, 14 Woodbine Terrace, Edinburgh EH6 8DA, Scotland
PHONE	+44 131 554 6551 FAX +44 131 554 6551

Jens Krogh

NATIONALITY	Danish
HOME PORT	Aalborg
HULL LENGTH	18.6 metres 61 feet
PAYING CREW	Skipper and 2 mates
SAIL TRAINEES	16

HISTORY

Built in 1899 at the H.V. Buhl shipyard AT Frederikshavn in the north of Denmark, Jens Krogh worked as a fishing vessel for 74 years. She was used for seine fishing in the Kattegat round the top of Denmark, and in the North Sea. Her gaff ketch rig was typical, and she had a large sail area. The middle of her hull was open to the sea so that fish remained alive from catch to harbour. She also had an innovation noted in the local newspaper which reported her launch - a motor. This was a 6hp kerosene engine which could propel her when there was no wind, and also lighten the work of the seine winch, used to drag the fish and nets aboard.

In 1912 her home port changed to Esbjerg on the west coast of Denmark and under a new name, Ida, she fished from there until 1957. She moved to Grenaa and then Saeby where she was re-named Ulla-Vita. In 1973, the year she stopped fishing, a newly formed FDF group of Alborg found her there. They purchased her and after an extensive refit lasting some years, she sailed again. The FDF is the national youth organisation in Denmark. It covers the whole country but the sailing division in Aalborg is unique. It offers exceptional opportunities to hundreds of youngsters to get to know the sea, with cruises of a weekend, a few days or a week. Since the first time the group saw the start of a Cutty Sark Tall Ships' Races, in 1978, there have been young sailors eager to take part. The first race they joined was in 1980 and since then they have hardly missed one. She joined in the Columbus Regatta across the Atlantic in 1992. At the end of the 1990 race series Jens Krogh received the prestigious award of the Cutty Sark Trophy at the prize giving in Zeebrugge. She is the only ship to have entered for the whole of Sail Osaka '97 from Hong Kong to Osaka in Japan, and also entered for the whole 1997 Cutty Sark Tall Ships' Race from Aberdeen to Göteborg. To enable her to fit all this into one year needed the support of the giant transport group Maersk, and she was shipped out on one of that company's container ships.

ON BOARD

Jens Krogh welcomes international trainees and although many of the youngsters on board are members of the FDF organisation, this is not an essential requirement. Those who are members can join FDF from the age of 10 and meet once a week as well as having the opportunity to sail on board. She sails every weekend in spring and in autumn and the long summer voyage which is divided up into legs of about 1 to 2 weeks lasts for two or three months.

CONTACT	Bo Rosbjerg
ADDRESS	FDF Aalborg Søkreds, Vestre Fjordvej 67, DK 9000 Aalborg, Denmark
PHONE	+45 98 154504 FAX +45 98 158129
ADDRESS	Stendalsvej 28, DK-9520, Skøping, Denmark
E-MAIL	br@ies.Lauc.dk

Johann Smidt

NATIONALITY	German
HOME PORT	Bremen, western Germany
SIZE OVERALL	36 metres 118 feet
PERMANENT CREW	7
PAYING TRAINEES	30

and apprentices who have not yet completed their education the cost is £25 per day. All other trainees are charged at £38 a day. The kind of ports visited in a year are Århus, Travemünde, Kalmar, Köge, Saint-Malo, Lisbon, Palma de Mallorca, Villamoura (Algarve), Las Palmas, and Hamburg.

HISTORY

Built in Amsterdam by the Cammenga shipyard in 1974 this schooner launched as Eendracht, the first sail training ship for Holland's Het Zeiland Zeeschip. She took part in many regattas including Cutty Sark Tall Ships' Races and she has crossed the Atlantic. From the outset she was designed with young people in mind to allow them to enjoy the adventure of tall ship sailing.

When it was decided to build a new and larger sail training ship, in 1989, Eendracht was sold to Clipper Deutsches Jugendwerk zur See, and she was renamed Johann Smidt after a Lord Mayor of Bremen in the 19th century. She is the only member of the Clipper DJS fleet to have a steel hull, typical of her original Dutch construction.

CONTACT	Clipper Deutsches Jugendwerk zur See e.V.
ADDRESS	Hamburg Office, Jürgensallee 54, D-22609, Hamburg, Germany
PHONE	+49 40 822 78 103 FAX +49 40 822 78 104
E-maiL	ClipperDJzS-Knut-Frisch@t-online.de
Web	http://www.clipper-djs.org

ON BOARD

Permanent crew and trainees are accommodated in two berthed cabins for the crew and four to twelve berth cabins for the trainees. The very large saloon can accommodate the entire ships' complement for meals or social functions. The permanent crew, deck officers, engineer and cook, spend their holidays working as volunteers aboard.

SAFETY CERTIFICATES AND INSURANCE

She conforms to Bureau Veritas Classification and to the rules of GSHW.

PROGRAMME

She usually sails from April to October in the Baltic, from the southern parts of Norway to eastern Sweden, north Germany and to Poland. Every second year cruises take her to Portugal and the Mediterranean, followed by a winter programme in the Canaries before she re-joins the Clipper DJS fleet again in northern waters in May. Fees include all meals, tea and coffee aboard. For students

John Laing

NATIONALITY	British
HOME PORT	Southampton, southern England
SIZE OVERALL	21.3 metres 70 feet
PROFESSIONAL CREW	5
PAYING SAIL TRAINEES	12

HISTORY

Established in 1960, the owners, Ocean Youth Trust, have the largest youth sailing fleet in Europe. They have seven yachts of about 20 metres with crews of around 16. They are based in different ports around the British Isles.

ON BOARD

The aims of OYT are for the enjoyment and adventure of life at sea, with crews of different sex, ability, social backgrounds, and ethnic origin.

OYT takes people aged 12 and up to 24, and for those 25 and over there is a 'Friends' Membership scheme. 'Friends' sail, with other adults, on special voyages. If you can fill all 12 berths, the OYT will waive the age bands. All OYT vessels are under the command of a skipper with an RYA/DTp Yachtmaster Offshore Certificate. The Mate is an experienced person holding a Mate's certificate issued by OYT and an RYA/DTp Coastal Skipper certificate, or equivalent.

As an educational charity, OYT can offer grants for those between 12 and 24 years old, and assist in fundraising ideas. If you can't afford an OYT voyage, the club has a proud boast that no young person is unable to sail with them because of cost, with local and national bursaries available, although everyone is encouraged to contribute so that they feel that they've given something. Of young crews, over 60% have been subsidised. Where any OYT vessel calls on any of her voyages depends on the weather, but in voyages over 3 days expect one port of call, and over 6 days, two.

OYT provides all safety equipment you'll require, and wet weather gear necessary for sailing. All food is included. On an OYT voyage you can gain OYT, Royal Yachting Association and Duke of Edinburgh Award Certificates.

School and youth groups studies into the environment can be catered for.

All women voyages (staff and crew) can be arranged.

For those with special needs, all OYT yachts are fitted with audio compasses, and some handicaps can be catered for. If you have a medical condition or disability, you must send a doctor's note, and bring adequate medicines, etc. Stowage space is small on these boats - jackets and dresses are left ashore.

Each yacht has a home base support group who help fundraise, and many who sail come back to see 'their' ship time and again. One condition of sailing aboard, you have to be able to swim - 50 metres.

SAFETY CERTIFICATES AND INSURANCE

OYT Vessels are certified to the Department of Transport's Code of Practice for Sail Training Vessels

The OYT operates within the Statutory Code of Practice (DTp) which stipulates the qualifications of the sea staff and rigorous standards for vessels and their equipment.

With so many ships in the club, the OYT keeps its own 'once in 24 hour' reporting system from each of them.

Insurance covers most eventualities, even including loss of luggage, personal money, medical and other expenses when aboard due to illness or accident.

PROGRAMME

John Laing is a Shipwright 70 ketch designed by Laurent Giles and launched in 1990. She proved her worth with a circumnavigation completed in the Spring of 1997, but her usual cruising ground is along the south west of England or voyaging across to ports in Brittany or the Channel Isles, sailing the Cutty Sark Tall Ships' Race from St. Malo to Greenock in 1999
Example prices would show:

Voyage	Low season	Mid season	High season
2 nights	£60	98	£135
6 nights	£169	304	£439

CONTACT	OYT South
ADDRESS	The Bus Station, South Street, Gosport Hants PO12 1EP, England
PHONE	+44 2392 501211 FAX +44 2392 522069
WEB	http://www.oyc.org.uk

Khersones

NATIONALITY	Ukraine
HOME PORT	Kerch, Black Sea
SIZE OVERALL	108 metres 358 feet
PROFESSIONAL CREW	40
TEACHERS	3
CADETS	maximum 154, of which
PAYING TRAINEES	up to 30

HISTORY

Khersones is sistership to Dar Mlodziezy, Mir, Druzhba, Nadezhda, and Pallada. Built in 1989, in Poland, her home port has been since then at Kerch in the Black Sea. On the break up of the USSR she came under Ukraine's flag, with the Kerch Marine Technological Institute as owners.

ON BOARD

Accommodation is in 12 berth cabins. Three meals a day are provided, with also bedding and linen for which a small additional charge is made.

On arrival, everyone is divided into watches, from 0000 to 0400, 0400 to 0800, and from 0800 to 1200. Duties include sail trimming, steering and lookout. Trainees work and live with the cadets under training, but separate instruction is given on practical seamanship and safety regulations.

PROGRAMME

She has an intense programme of voyages, particularly in the Mediterranean and north European waters. She has been a regular participant in the Cutty Sark Tall Ships' races.

A typical programme has been:

11 days, £750 Brest-Hamburg (via Cuxhaven)
7 days, £545 Hamburg-Cuxhaven (via Sheerness)
4 days, £273 Cuxhaven-Den Helder
10 days, £400 Den Helder-Cuxhaven
9 days, £680 Cuxhaven-Rostock (Langesund: Norway)
11 days, £750 Brest-Hamburg (via Cuxhaven)
6 days, £545 Hamburg-Cuxhaven (via Sheerness)
4 days, £273 Cuxhaven-Den Helder
9 days, £400 Den Helder-Cuxhaven
9 days, £680 Cuxhaven-Rostock (Langesund, Norway)
11 days, £750 Brest-Hamburg (via Cuxhaven)
7 days, £545 Hamburg-Cuxhaven (via Sheerness)
4 days, £273 Cuxhaven-Den Helder
10 days, £400 Den Helder-Cuxhaven
9 days, £680 Cuxhaven-Rostock (via Langesund, Norway)
11 days, £750 Brest-Hamburg (via Cuxhaven)
6 days, £545 Hamburg-Cuxhaven (via Sheerness)
4 days, £273 Cuxhaven-Den Helder
9 days, £400 Den Helder-Cuxhaven
9 days, £680 Cuxhaven-Rostock (Langesund, Norway)

Note: Experienced trainees pay £4.00 less than the above, for a day; and for voyages over 8 days, the reduction is 20%.

CONTACT	The Director
ADDRESS	Kerch Marine Technological Institute, Ordzhonikze 82, Kerch, Ukraine
PHONE	+380 6561 34584 FAX +380 6561 33080

Kruzenshtern

NATIONALITY	Russian
HOME PORT	Kaliningrad, Baltic Russia
SIZE OVERALL	113.4 metres 372 feet
CREW	76
CADETS	202

HISTORY

In the 1920's a famous line of clipper ships were built, most at Wesermunde, Germany, for the Hamburg-based 'Flying P' Line. They traded in the Atlantic, Indian Ocean, and Pacific, and passed Cape Horn many a time. Cargoes included wool from Australia and nitrates from Chile. All had four masts (one had five), and speedy hulls. Their original names included Padua, Peking, Passat, and Pamir, hence the 'Flying P'. Pamir sank with the tragic loss of 80 lives in a hurricane off the Azores. Peking ended up in a mudberth in Kent, England, as a static training ship until 1973, and then she crossed the Atlantic to become a museum in New York. Pommern is alongside in Mariehamn. Passat is now tied up alongside Travemunde, near the Kiel Canal, with masts but no sails on them, as a youth camp. Alone amongst them, still sailing, is Padua, launched in 1926. After the war, in 1946, she was awarded to Russia and renamed Kruzenshtern after their famous hydrographer and navigator. Her original task was to bring back nitrate for fertilizers, from South America, and then she too joined the grain trade from Australia. She had a history similar to so many clippers, of fast and dangerous voyages - she lost four crew in 1930 while rounding infamous Cape Horn. She made spectacular speed runs, including a reputed 351 nautical miles in 1933 over a 24 hour period. That is, over 14 knots. Today she displays black and white sides so popular in ships which traded with the East, where the colours and their design imitated gunports to scare away pirates. Now in the hands of the Fisheries Board of Russia, she trains their young for a life at sea, and has a crew of 232 people. She also takes a number of international paying trainees on each voyage, to help defray the formidable cost of keeping such an old a lady at sea.
The first Russian to enter the Cutty Sark Tall Ships' Races, in 1974, she is a regular participant. Of all the world's sailing vessels which still voyage, she is the second largest.

PROGRAMME

She travels worldwide, and enters many Cutty Sark Tall Ships' Races.

CONTACT	The Director
ADDRESS	Kaliningrad Marine Engineering Academy, 6 ul, Molodyozhaya, 236029 Kaliningrad, Russia
PHONE	+7 0112 499769

Klaus Störtebeker III

NATIONALITY	*Germany*
HOME PORT	*Wilhelmshaven*
SIZE OVERALL	*15.6 metres 51 feet*
PROFESSIONAL CREW	*3*
TRAINEES	*17*

HISTORY

She was built in 1921 as Bille III at the Schierhorn shipyard at Cranz, near Hamburg, Germany. Her hull and rig were based on a traditional design of shipbuilders at the turn of the century, and heavy and solid timbers were used in her construction. From 1934 to 1967 she flew the flag of the 'Segelkameradschaft (Sailing Friendship) Das Wappen von Bremen', and under that name she won the Burnham Race in 1936. In 1981 she was bought and completely re-built, re-rigged, and re-named Klaus Störtebeker III, by the 'Segelkameradschaft Klaus Störtebeker' at Wilhelmshaven, north west Germany. Her transom is covered with a wood carving of a lion on starboard carrying the Bremen arms, the town key, and of a lion on port with the Frisian arms. These wood ornaments are the unique mark of the yacht. Below deck she has 10 bunks for the total crew.

She is an excellent vessel for active vacations with traditional sailing, equally adapted for newcomers or 'seabears'..

CONTACT	Klaus Vogel
ADDRESS	Segelkameradschaft Klaus Störtebeker III, Kmiprodestraße 93, 26388 Wilhelmshaven, Germany
PHONE +49 4425 98 2565	FAX +4421 5 61 70

Kvartsita

NATIONALITY	Swedish
HOME PORT	Skaftö, Sweden
SIZE OVERALL	33 metres 108.3 feet
PROFESSIONAL CREW	6
PAYING SAIL TRAINEES	26

HISTORY

Kvartsita was built in 1945 at Holms Shipyard at Raa for the Höganäs Company. Constructed of oak she carried quartz to the company's factory at Höganäs. In 1953 she was sold to a Norwegian town, Farsund, who removed her sailing rig and re-named her Bono. She voyaged off southern Norway as a general freighter, carrying salt and timber, and other goods. In 1986 the newly formed society For Fulla Segel, meaning 'In Full Sails', bought her and gave her back her elegant schooner rig and original name.

ON BOARD

The Society, based at Skaftö, uses Kvartsita as a sail training ship and floating school to train both young and older boys and girls. Berths are available on board in particular for those people with a handicap. It is very much part of the Society's philosophy to encourage the younger generation to make use of the sailing 'know-how' of adults aboard and experience the excitement of big ship sailing.

SAFETY CERTIFICATES AND INSURANCE

She is fully surveyed and has safety equipment conforming with Department of Sail regulations for a sailing vessel.

PROGRAMME

Kvartsita takes part in Scandinavian regattas and is a regular entrant for the Cutty Sark Tall Ships' Races.

CONTACT	Thomas Falk
ADDRESS	Fur Fulla Segel, Kyrkekajen 10, S-450 34 Fiskebäckskil, Sweden
PHONE	+46 523 23188 FAX +46 523 23187

La Recouvrance

NATIONALITY	French
HOME PORT	Brest western France
SIZE OVERALL	22.8 metres 75 feet
PROFESSIONAL CREW	5
PAYING SAIL TRAINEES	12

HISTORY

In the wars between European nations in the 19th Century, involving constant contact with 'colonies' abroad, a breed of ship developed which were lightly armed, without the weight of cannon, with plenty of sail area, and a fast hull, to outsail ordinary men-of-war. They sailed fast with messages for far flung outposts, they spied on fleets as they gathered, and trailed them across oceans. Recently, a replica was built of an 1817 ship of this type, La Recouvrance. The inspiration came from a Breton publishing company , Le Chasse Maré, in 1990. The group had earlier been at the start of the Douarnenez '88 Sea Festival, and was planning 'Brest 92. An association from Brest formed, and proposed a 75 foot naval schooner. They researched the archives of the Service Historique de la Marine, and by 1991 in the spring, the preliminary studies were complete. The keel was laid in July in a purpose built shed on the Brest waterfront by shipwrights Chantier du Guip.

Her hull launched at the Brest '92 Sea Festival, and the following spring masts, rigging and sails were added. From 1993 to 1995 she sailed only for trial cruises as her interior was not complete. In 1996 the Association, having fulfiled its task of building the ship, decided to transfer her to a semi-public body, SOPAB, in which the City of Brest - from the outset the main sponsor - was the major partner. From the start, La Recouvrance has been a symbol of Brest. Her name recalls those women from the famous harbour district who used to pray to Our Lady of Recouvrance for the safe 'recouvrance' (or recovery) of their sea-faring sons and husbands. There were many from Brest and its region who contributed to the success of the project, by giving time, making a donation, or simply paying a visit to the building site which throughout had remained open to visitors. In 1998, fresh from a thorough maintenance and refit period, she embarked on a new ambitious programme, marked with her first entry in a Cutty Sark Tall Ships' Race.

ON BOARD

She has three main objectives. To be an ambassador for Brest and its region in French and foreign ports where important sea festivals or major economic and media events are organised. To be available, at least part of the year, for the people and enterprises of her home port. And to welcome passengers who might wish to discover what life was like on board a traditional sailing ship. All on board are introduced to and participate in the ship's manoeuvres, and may stand watch when the captain is satisfied they possess the necessary qualifications, or have acquired them on board with the help of the five professional crew members. Under the captain's orders, they are expected to follow the ship's regulations, share in routine maintenance and they are welcome to help with daily chores.

La Recouvrance can take 12 passengers offshore. Living accommodation is spacious with three independent WC/shower booths. The interior (passengers cabin, wardroom, crew and navigation quarters) are modelled on the actual officer quarters of an early 19th century French frigate. Passengers have to provide their own sleeping bag, toilet gear, and sea clothes.

CONTACT	Sylvie Avenel
ADDRESS	SOPAB/Recouvrance, BP 411 - 29275 Brest CEDEX, France
PHONE	+33 298 44 33 77 FAX +33 298 44 05 00
E-MAIL	seve2301@eurobretagne.fr

Le Don du Vent

NATIONALITY	French
HOME PORT	Marseille, Mediterranean France
SIZE OVERALL	32 metres 105 feet
CRUISING CREW 16	Day sailing 32
	Alongside a quay 80

HISTORY

In 1977 when he was 20 years old, Philippe Derain worked as an agent for France-Telecom, He saw Cala Virgili, a Spanish three master, anchored in the Old Port of Marseille. He joined ASCANFE (Association for the Safeguarding and the Conservation of Ships, both French and 'Etranger' (foreign)) which helped save the ship. And so began Philippe's love of wooden boats, and he sought to find a ship of his own to restore. First came failure. He saw a suitable ship at Les Sables-d'Olonnes, Gift of the Wind. Before he could buy her, she was sold.

Two years later he and his younger brother saw a ship at anchor within a stone's throw of his house. She was L'Ile Garo, built as a coast guard ship in 1943 by Burmeister at Bremen in Germany. She combined the tradition of old sailing ships with new concepts in safety materials. She has a composite hull of steel members and a hull of oak, aiming to give her a structure sufficient to resist the fierce weather which can spring up quickly in the North Sea. Three bulkheads divided her hull in the manner of contemporary ships.

She was one of a dozen built for coastal surveying, for military purposes. Some of her sisterships include Taino, owned by the marine painter Delfaut at Bordeaux, Fleur de Passion, at the Port de Balaguler at Seyne-sur-Mer, L'Occitan and Le Beer.

Her history between the end of the war and 1972 is obscure. Her name became La Danae under the Panamanian flag, and after chartering in the Mediterranean for several years, she was seized 'for administrative reasons'. Anchored without surveillance at St. Raphael, she was pillaged. She then became a floating home for five years. Philippe Derain saw her, bought her and renamed her Le Don du Vent. He took her back to Marseille where the extent of the damage to her became painfully clear. Thirteen years of work was needed before she was ready to sail again.

ON BOARD

Le Don du Vent has played numerous roles since her rebuild, as a ship for the 'redynamising and reinvigoration of the young in difficulty', for leisure cruises, for seminars, for events, for scientific research in the marine field, to be seen at sporting regattas and maritime gatherings, as a film set, and as a cultural base for music and the theatre. She has six double berths, and eight single couchettes.

INSURANCE AND SAFETY

Le Don du Vent is classified as a Sailing ship of the High Seas, Category 1. Her professional crew are from the Merchant Navy.

PROGRAMME

Her voyages are on an 'a la carte' basis, with Marseille and the Mediterranean as her base.

CONTACT   Philippe Derain
ADDRESS   38 Rue de Petit-Puits, 13002, Marseille, France
PHONE   +33 491 90 85 67 / +33 491 90 98 59
FAX +33 491 54 860 6
PORTABLE +33 06 09 98 52 67

Linden

NATIONALITY	Finnish
HOME PORT	Mariehamn, Åland Isles
SIZE OVERALL	48 metres 157 feet
PROFESSIONAL CREW	6 to 8
PAYING SAIL TRAINEES	29

HISTORY

In 1921 an Åland schooner, Linden, sailed her maiden voyage from Kotka in Finland to St. Helier, Jersey (in the Channel Islands), with a cargo of timber. She was one of the last timber ships built in Finland for such a trade, and until the 1950s her main routes were between Finland, Europe, and England.

The original Linden is no more, but today's Linden is built to look like her, and is rigged in similar fashion to her, as a three masted Baltic schooner of pine impregnated with Stockholm tar. Built in 1992 her masts and bowsprit are made of larch, from the famous Finnish mast forests of Kitee and Punkaharju, planted in 1880 by Tsar Nicholas with his eye to the creation of future fleets.

The new Linden is owned by over 2600 shareholders on Åland whose port is Mariehamn. This ship also has her own supporters club, 'The Society of Linden's Friends' who provide invaluable help with equipment and volunteer work.

ON BOARD

There are nine cabins, excluding the crew's accommodation. She has four 4 berth and one 3 berth cabins each has its own shower/WC and the remaining 4 berth and two 3 berth cabins share showers and toilets. On board facilities are of a high order and include a dining saloon and bar, a lounge, and a sauna. Linden's hull is divided into four watertight sections, each fitted with emergency exits.

SAFETY CERTIFICATES AND INSURANCE

She complies with De Norske Veritas rules for wooden ships. She has a Special Purpose Sailing Ship certificate, with a maximum number allowed aboard of 70 passengers. Trainees and crew are fully insured.

PROGRAMME

Her sailing season starts in April and ends in October. She is available for charter during the season, and you can choose whatever route you wish. She visits a number of ports around the entire Baltic Sea during a sailing season. She also has some scheduled cruises for individual travellers. Among the islands there are lots of fine natural harbours to anchor in for the night and enjoy a refreshing bathe. Her programme usually includes cruising in the northern Baltic and shorter voyages from Stockholm, Åland and southern Finland. She would like to do more sail training, when sponsors come forward, and she took part in the 1993 and 1996 Cutty Sark Tall Ships' Races.

CONTACT	Rederi AB Linden
ADDRESS	Box 197, FIN-22101 Mariehamn, Åland Islands, Finland.
PHONE	+358 18 12055 FAX +358 18 12145
TELEX	124491 Trade SF Cables
E-MAIL	linden@aland.net

Lokki

NATIONALITY	*Finnish*
HOME PORT	*Uusikaupunki, South West Finland*
SIZE OVERALL	*16.5 metres 54 feet*
PROFESSIONAL CREW	*2*
PAYING SAIL TRAINEES	*10*

HISTORY

The Sail Training Association of Finland is part owner of one ship Helena, and has a number of other privately owned ships on its books, to which it has access for part of the year. In return STAF helps to maintain and repair them. One of the private ships is Lokki, which like Helena is unusual in that for part of the year, she sails outside the Baltic. Lokki is a Sea Rover 51 type, a steel schooner built in 1980 in Finland. Since 1983 she has served as a sail training ship, and taken part in Cutty Sark Tall Ships' Races starting in 1988. In 1992 she was Finland's one representative in the transatlantic Columbus Regatta. With STAF her role is in teaching basic sailing to 14-19 year old youngsters without previous experience. Before the new flagship Helena came along, she made several cruises in waters south of the English Channel, bringing important experience to professional crews and providing trainees with many kinds of adventure. In October 1996 Lokki headed across the Atlantic for three months in the Caribbean.

ON BOARD

Foreigners, irrespective of sex and previous experience, can participate as paying crew. All the trainee yachtsmen and women have to take part in navigation, steering, sailing manoeuvres, preparing meals, cleaning ship, and seamanship manoeuvres. Different watch systems are used depending on the number and experience of the trainees and the areas to be sailed. Four hours on watch and eight hours off is common.

SAFETY CERTIFICATES AND INSURANCE

She is registered as a leisure boat and insured accordingly. She complies with the highest Finnish leisure boat safety regulations. Personal insurance is not included and taking adequate insurance is the trainee's compulsory responsibility.

PROGRAMME

When outside of Finland her voyages have been, for instance:
14 days, Guadeloupe-Grenadines-Martinique 4200 Finmarks;

7 days, Martinique-St. Lucia-Guadeloupe 2500FM;
24 days, Bermuda-Bermuda-Portsmouth 6150FM;
7days, Portsmouth-Neuwpoort-Göteborg 2500FM;
7 days, Göteborg-Visby-Uusikaupunki 2500FM;
11 days, Uusikaupunki-Visby-Hanko 2300FM;
12 days, Hanko-Kootka-Helsinki 250 FM;
14 days, Uusikaupunki-Copenhagen-Hanko 2900FM;
10 days, Hanko-Härnösand-Vaasa 2100FM;
12 days, Vaasa-Mariehamn-Helsinki 2500FM;
Note: flights to and from ports are not included, and insurance is up to each individual.
In the summer she sails, in principal, only with sail trainees aged 14-19 in the Baltic.
She made a suprise welcome at the final port of the Cutty Sark Tall Ships' race in 1999.

CONTACT	The Sail Training Association Finland
ADDRESS	Tarmonkuja 2, 00180 Helsinki, Finland
PHONE	+358 9 685 26 16 FAX +358 9 685 26 15
E-MAIL	purjelaivasaatio@pp.kolumbus.fi
WEB	http://www.kotii.kolumbus.fi/^nuorpurj/

Lord Nelson

NATIONALITY	*British*
HOME PORT	*Southampton, southern.England*
SIZE OVERALL	*55 metres 180 feet*
PROFESSIONAL CREW	*8*
OTHER SKILLED	**2*
PAYING SAIL TRAINEES	*40*

*Bosun's Mates - voluntary positions filled be people who have already sailed on the ship and have been recommended by the permanent crew.

HISTORY

Lord Nelson is unique in being the only tall ship purpose built to enable able bodied and physically disabled people to share the challenge of crewing a tall ship at sea. Since her maiden voyage in 1986, nearly 20,000 people of all physical abilities have taken part in this unique experience on 4 to 10 day voyages around the British Isles, Europe, and the Canary Islands.

The square rig design of the ship means that many people are required to work her which ensures participation by all members of the crew. Disabled crew members work side by side with able-bodied people (each disabled crew member is 'buddied' to an able bodied person). The special facilities on board include flat, wide decks for easy access to wheelchair users. Lifts between decks for those with limited mobility can be operated by the user. Vibrator pads fitted to the bunks alert those who are deaf or hard of hearing, in an emergency. An induction loop is fitted in the lower mess room to assist those with hearing impairment during the briefing sessions. She has a bright track radar screen. A speaking compass with digital readout screen enables blind people to steer the ship. Power assisted hydraulic steering makes it easy for people with little strength to steer her.

ON BOARD

Men and women between the ages of 16 to 70+ are eligible to sail her. No experience is necessary and all safety equipment is supplied.

She works a four watch system (six hours on watch and eighteen off). Each is led by a watch leader who like the bosun's mates has sailed on the Lord Nelson before and has been recognised by the permanent crew as a suitable candidate. Everyone is involved in every aspect of crewing, from going aloft to set/stow the sails, and helming the ship, to helping in the galley and cleaning the ship. Each voyage has four watchleaders and a doctor and these qualify for a 50% discount on the voyage price.

If you want to lead a team of 10 on a watch, you have to be skilled and a discount of 50% is offered. The same discount applies if you are a doctor, as Lord Nelson likes to have one on each cruise as well as the regular medical purser.

Below decks there are traditional bunks for most crew, and there's room for up to eight wheelchair users. Specially fitted WCs and showers are for those who need them. Epilepsy and diabetes are considered to be physical disabilities. Those with mental handicap and severe learning difficulties cannot be accommodated. For heavy weather, oilskins and harnesses are provided and below there is bedding and sleeping bags.

When without sails, she has two powerful engines (two 260 b.h.p. diesels). There are three generators for electricity, hot water, and heating.

SAFETY CERTIFICATES AND INSURANCE

Lord Nelson has all the requisite safety certificates, and prices for a voyage include insurance cover for personal accident, medical expenses, loss of baggage, and cancellation or curtailment of voyages for all crew.

PROGRAMME

Her typical programme is in and around the British Isles from April to October, and the Canary Islands from November to March. Voyage prices range from £295 (UK season) to £850 (Christmas voyage in the Canaries).

Due to the success of Lord Nelson, the Jubilee Sailing Trust is building a second ship in wood, in Woolston, Southampton. Building began in June 1996. Shorewatch shipbuilding holidays are run5ning throughout the project. The 'at sea' philosophy of integration has been brought ashore, and able bodied and physically disabled people are working alongside professional shipwrights in a working shipyard. The cost for 6 days at Jubilee Yard include food and accommodation is £100.

CONTACT	The Jubilee Sailing Trust Ltd
ADDRESS	Jubilee Yard, Merlin Quay, Hazel Road, Woolston, Southampton, SO19 7GB, UK
PHONE	+44 2380 449138 (voyage Bookings), +44 2380 449108 (Trust Office)
FAX	+44 2380 449145
E-MAIL	jst@jst.org.uk
WEB	http//www.jst.org.uk

"Lord Nelson II"

NATIONALITY	British
HOME PORT	Southampton, southern.England
SIZE OVERALL	63 metres 207 feet
PROFESSIONAL CREW	8
OTHER SKILLED	2
PAYING SAIL TRAINEES	20+20

HISTORY

The Jubilee Sailing Trust pioneered the building and operating of ships which enable able bodied and the physically disabled to sail. Their first ship to be purpose built was the 55 metre Lord Nelson (see previous pages). Such a success is she that a second ship was ordered. Her hull was completed at the end of 1998, with her first full season is 2001.

Many other countries follow the fortunes of disabled sailing with interest, and will be curious to know what lessons learnt from Lord Nelson were considered desirable in the second ship.

The designer is Tony Castro, whose first sail training ship this is. Fresh ideas were allowed from his side, with a strong input from the experience of the Jubilee Sailing Trust on the other.

A steel hull would have been easier than wood, from a design point of view, but wood was the choice, to give ordinary people including those handicapped, the chance of helping with their own ship. Gangs led by highly skilled shipwrights each looked after a small number of unskilled to shape the timbers.

Wood takes up more room than steel, so a careful adjustment of frames was required to interfere the least with the interior.

Construction just fits in under the upper limit of the existing wood rules of Lloyd's, with a blend of modern epoxy boat building with the best of traditional techniques. Steel is used wherever appropriate, for instance as a further fireproof barrier around the engine spaces.

Various hulls were put to performance and stability computer analysis, and two forms were then tested at Southampton University's Wolfson Unit Towing Tank and Wind Tunnel. The more traditional hull form was chosen, modified to give required seakeeping performance and stability. A deep forefoot was chosen to reduce the bow slamming into the sea. Tests in waves up to 5 metres high, and incidence of wetness were observed. She was given a long keel and her shape, not unlike a 19th century ship, gave her the best seakindly result. The keel would give her 'directional stability' - she would hold her course, for longer - although this would reduce manoeuvrability in restricted waters and in port - so she was given a pair of powerful 400HP engines and a bowthruster. Her rig was chosen as barque (as with her older sister). This was thought to be challenging to all crew, whilst being safe. The new ship has more sails, and more sail area for her size, than the first. To ensure those in wheelchairs or aloft would not lose control, the roll character of the ship was of special concern.

ON BOARD

Men and women between the ages of 16 to 70+ are eligible to sail her. No experience is necessary and all safety equipment is supplied. Her systems will be similar to those of Lord Nelson.

SAFETY CERTIFICATES AND INSURANCE

The new ship will have all the requisite safety certificates, and prices for a voyage will include insurance cover including personal accident, medical expenses, loss of baggage, and cancellation or curtailment of voyages for all crew.

PROGRAMME

Her typical programme could be in an around the British Isles from April to October, and the Canary Islands from November to March. Voyage prices range from £295 (UK season) to £850 (Christmas voyage in the Canaries).

CONTACT	The Jubilee Sailing Trust Ltd
ADDRESS	Jubilee Yard, Merlin Quay, Hazel Road, Woolston, Southampton, SO19 7GB, UK
PHONE	+44 2380 449138 (voyage Bookings), +44 2380 449108 (Trust Office)
FAX	+44 2380 449145
E-MAIL	jst@jst.org.uk
WEB	http//www.jst.org.uk

Lord Rank

NATIONALITY	British
HOME PORT	Carrickfergus, Northern Ireland
SIZE OVERALL	20.7 metres 68 feet
STAFF	5
CREW	12

HISTORY

Established in 1960, the owners Ocean Youth Trust (formerly Ocean Youth Club), have the largest youth sailing fleet in Europe. They have seven yachts of about 20 metres with crews of around 16. They are based in different ports around the British Isles.

ON BOARD

The aims of OYT are for the enjoyment and adventure of life at sea, with crews of different sex, ability, social backgrounds, and ethnic origin.

The OYT takes people aged 12 and up to 24, and for those 25 and over there is a 'Friends' Membership scheme. 'Friends' sail, with other adults, on special voyages. If you can fill all 12 berths, the OYT will waive the age bands. All OYT vessels are under the command of a skipper with an RYA/DTp Yachtmaster Offshore Certificate. The Mate is an experienced person holding a Mate's certificate issued by OYT and an RYA/DTp Coastal Skipper certificate, or equivalent.

As an educational charity, OYT can offer grants for those between 12 and 24 years old, and assist in fundraising ideas. If you can't afford an OYT voyage, the club has a proud boast that no young person is unable to sail with them because of cost, with local and national bursaries available, although everyone is encouraged to contribute so that they feel that they've given something. Of young crews, over 60% have been subsidised. Where any OYT vessel calls on any of her voyages depends on the weather, but in voyages over 3 days expect one port of call, and over 6 days, two.

OYT provides all safety equipment you'll require, and wet weather gear necessary for sailing. All food is included. On an OYT voyage you can gain OYT, Royal Yachting Association and Duke of Edinburgh Award Certificates.

School and youth groups studies into the environment can be catered for.

All women voyages (staff and crew) can be arranged.

For those with special needs, all OYT yachts are fitted with audio compasses, and some handicaps can be catered for. If you have a medical condition or disability, you must send a doctor's note, and bring adequate medicines, etc. Stowage space is small on these boats - jackets and dresses are left ashore.

Each yacht has a home base support group who help fundraise, and many who sail come back to see 'their' ship time and again. One condition of sailing, you have to be able to swim - 50 metres.

SAFETY CERTIFICATES AND INSURANCE

OYT Vessels are certified to the Department of Transport's Code of Practice for Sail Training Vessels.

The OYT operates within the Statutory Code of Practice (DTp) which stipulates the qualifications of the sea staff and rigorous standards for vessels and their equipment.

With so many ships in the club, it keeps its own 'once in 24 hour' reporting system from each of them.

Insurance covers most eventualities, even including loss of luggage, personal money, medical and other expenses when aboard due to illness or accident.

PROGRAMME

She has her sailing base at Carrickfergus in Northern Ireland and has the enjoyable choice of that beautiful coastline, including the famous Giant's Causeway; or, trips across the narrow 14 mile wide strait to SW Scotland or South to the Isle of Man. Further afield voyages include the Brittany coasts, sailing in the Cutty Sark Tall Ships' Race from St. Malo to Greenock in 1999. Example prices would show:

Voyage	Low season	Mid season	High season
2 nights	£60	£98	£135
6 nights	£169	£304	£439

CONTACT	OYC Northern Ireland
ADDRESS	Unit 18/217 Kilroot Business Park, Larne Road, Carrickfergus, Co Antrim, BT38 7PR, UK
PHONE	+44 1960 366776 FAX +44 1960 367670
WEB	http://www.oyc.org.uk

Malcolm Miller

NATIONALITY	British
HEADQUARTERS	Portsmouth, southern England
SIZE OVERALL	46 metres 150 feet
PROFESSIONAL CREW	16
PAYING SAIL TRAINEES	39

HISTORY

She's over 30 years old, one of the British Sail Training Association's famous twins, together with Sir Winston Churchill. Just how do you tell them apart? Sir Winston Churchill has TSK1 on her sails and has round tops to the doors amidships; Malcolm Miller's number is TSK2 and she's got flat tops to her midship doors.

In the 1950's a retired London solicitor, Bernard Morgan, dreamed of bringing together the world's great sailing ships. Earl Mountbatten was consulted, and Captain John Illingworth's committee organised the first ever Tall Ships Race. As a result the Sail Training Association was formed to run these races annually. Then came a question, why not build and sail ships under the same STA flag? In the 1960's the STA raised money and by 1966 the STA completed the first of the two, Sir Winston Churchill. Then came Malcolm Miller. They've both got three masts, and are schooners (all masts of similar size, or the back ones taller). In fact, they are 'topsail schooners', for on their first masts they have square sails above fore and aft sails.

Malcolm Miller was helped by significant donations from the Lord Provost of Edinburgh, Sir James Miller, who also became Lord Mayor of London. She was named after his son Malcolm Miller, who had recently died in an accident. Quite often the ship that carries his son's name carries all girl crews, or Scottish crews, determined to out-compete in their skills the crew aboard Sir Winston Churchill, who may be all boys, or from England. Friendly rivalry is a mark of these two sisterships.

ON BOARD

The 39 trainees are divided into three watches of 13 who do four hours on watch, and eight hours off. Each watch helps care for and maintain the ship and takes part in watch duties such as look-out, steering, sail trimming and assisting the cook in the galley. Most of the time is spent either on the bridge, perhaps taking the helm or keeping the ship's log - or working on deck or aloft. You don't have to go aloft, but most people do, for the experience of setting (letting loose) or handing (folding away) those two square sails on the foremast.

The permanent crew consists of master, chief officer, bosun, engineer and cook, with a voluntary afterguard comprising a qualified navigator, three watch officers, a purser, and a medical officer. The usual trainee age is between 16 to 24. This form of adventure training has proved highly successful in improving personal skills by providing a physical and mental challenge and an awareness of the value of leadership skills and team work. But it isn't only this age group who can benefit. There are also mixed sex voyages for those aged 16 -24.

CONTACT	The Sail Training Association
ADDRESS	2A The Hard, Portsmouth, Hants PO1 3PT, UK
PHONE	+44 2392 832055/6 FAX +44 2392 815769
E-MAIL	Tallships@sta.org.uk
WEB	http://www.sta.org.uk/sta/

If you can't afford the voyage, there are volunteer support groups nationwide who may be able to help, from their own resources or by helping you find a sponsor. All voyages qualify for the Residential Section of the Gold Award in the Duke of Edinburgh's Award scheme and the RYA Competent Crew Certificate may also be available. Voyages are in Northern European waters from March to November, and for the 'winter sun' voyages in the Canaries and the Azores from November to May.

SAFETY CERTIFICATES AND INSURANCE.

She is maintained to Lloyds Class AI and Department of Transport standards.

PROGRAMME

Usually voyages are in North European waters from March to November, and for 'winter sun' voyages in the Canaries and Azores from November to May.

An idea of a year's programme might be:

23 days, Weymouth-Lerwick Female 16/24 £1564

14 days, Lerwick-Aberdeen Male 16/24 £1008

12 days, Hartlepool-London Mixed 16/24 £682

14 days, Lerwick-Aberdeen Mixed age 16/24 £1008 (includes Cutty Sark Tall Ships' Race)

11 days, Greenock-Weymouth crew age16/24 £660

6 days, Weymouth-Shoreham Male 24/69 £360

5 days, Weymouth-Weymouth Mixed 24/69 £350

*Each Northern Europe youth voyage sails up to 1,000 miles and visits 2/3 foreign ports.

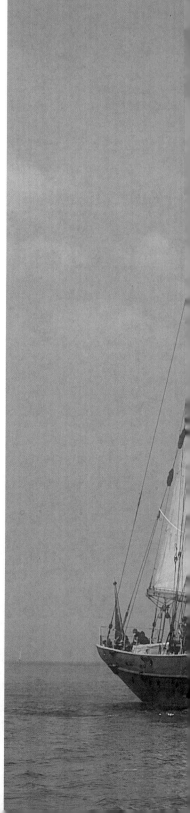

Macau

NATIONALITY	*Portuguese*
HOME PORT	*Lisbon, Portugal*
SIZE OVERALL	*34.1 metres 111.8 feet*
TOTAL CREW	*11*

HISTORY

Macau is a lorcha "a type of fast sailing craft built in China, with the hull after a European model, but rigged in Chinese fashion, usually carrying guns" according to the Oxford Dictionary. The origin of this remarkable type of sailing ship is still obscure, although there is no doubt that they were an adaption of the Portuguese caravel-type of hull, to the lighter, more efficient, Chinese traditional rigging of the junks. There is no definite proof of their place of birth or a reliable date for their first construction. There is, however, extensive evidence of their use by the Portuguese in the area of Macau, not only as 'traders', but mainly as warships, at least since the period of Fernão Mendes Pinto (1553) who mentions this type of ship in his "Peregrinação".

The first Portuguese adventurers in the Chinese Seas used such craft, that looked like Chinese junks but which were faster, more manœuvrable, and better armed. Worcester in "The junks and sampangs of the Yangtze" points out the possibilities of their earlier construction at Malacca, in the earlier period of Afonso de Albuquerque.

The Lorchas played an important role in the sea commerce of the China Seas, as they were employed either by Portuguese captains or even Chinese captains with honourary Portuguese captains on board, alone or in small 'flotillas' to trade, and convoy local trader junks, and they even contracted to local authorities. They were used to fight the local pirates, whose fleets exceeded 600 junks and about 1,000 small auxiliary craft, and with crews exceeding 60,000 people. They had surprising success.

By the end of the 18th century and during the whole of the 19th, namely until the generalised use of the engine on small traders, the lorchas were normally two masted and varied in size from 40 to 150 tons, the majority being between 50 and 100. The number of guns varied from 4 to 20 and from 1 to 24 pounds calibre and were normally manned by 30 men.

In 1976 the idea of building a replica of a lorcha started to gain acceptance, as it seemed appropriate to create a link between the Portuguese and the Orient. This idea gained the support of the Governor of Macau and the Portuguese Navy. The keel was laid in April 1987 and Macau was launched in November of the same year.

SAFETY CERTIFICATES AND INSURANCE

As with Boa Esperança, Macau will be fully certified as an ocean going ship, according to Portuguese and International laws. Safety equipment will comply with International regulations

PROGRAMME.

Since her building, Macau has been employed in sail training, and as an ambassador to explain Portuguese culture in the Far East, with two voyages from Macau to Japan and one to India. In 1998 she went to Portugal for Expo '98 and the Portuguese Navy decided to offer her to Aporvela, to continue her sail training activity.

As with Aporvela's Boa Esperança, Macau is not ideal for racing. She will play a full role in sail training around Portugal, she will appear at Maritime Festivals, and at Cutty Sark Tall Ships' Race ports. She will also teach the modern generation about sailing such a famous and unusual type of ship.

CONTACT	Aporvela
ADDRESS	Doca do Terrieno do Trigo, P 1100 Lisboa, Portugal
PHONE	+351 1 8876854 FAX +351 1 8873885

Marabu

NATIONALITY	British
HOME PORT	Brighton, southern England
SIZE OVERALL	17.7 metres 58 feet
PROFESSIONAL CREW	2
PAYING SAIL TRAINEES	8

HISTORY

Marabu was built by Germany's Abeking and Rasmussen in 1935 as a 100 square metre sloop (the 100 square metres refers to the sail area, and the sloop meant she then had one mast). She was one of a number of fine yachts built between 1935 and 1938 for the German armed forces, and some 200 of them were taken by the allies as 'Windfall' reparations after the war in 1945 when Marabu went to the British Armed Forces. By 1953 her one mast had became two, for ease of maintenance and handling. In 1978 she was sold to the Marabu Syndicate. Her main activity nowadays is cruising, although she still participates in some 'fun' races, such as the Cutty Sark Tall Ships' Races, and the Royal Escape Race. Designed for high sailing performance, rather than comfort, she has slim, overhanging lines, five times as long as her beam.

ON BOARD

The Marabu Sea School teaches sailing ashore and afloat to Britain's Royal Yachting Association (RYA) standards. Her smaller sistership Kestrel (50 sq metres) runs five day practical courses and shorebased evening classes. The RYA levels taught are for competent crew, day skipper, coastal skipper, yachtmaster offshore, and yachtmaster ocean. Members of the Club are graded as deckhand, coxwain, watchkeeper, mate and skipper, according to their RYA qualifications.

PROGRAMME

Marabu has an adventurous programme which aims to visit interesting ports and waters. The range to date has included Lisbon, St. Petersburg and the Faeroe Islands. The sailing season is from mid March to the end of December, with a refit in January and February. An example of her voyages was a programme, centred around the Cutty Sark Tall Ships' Races. Two prices were given, for adults (over 26) and cadets (unwaged under 26). They were £849/£466 for 21 days. There is an extra £5/£10 a day needed for food, fuel, mooring costs, etc..There are many opportunities for shorter and more local cruises including evening sails from Brighton and Portsmouth (£18/£9). Marabu is based in Brighton in spring and in the autumn she moves to Portsmouth.

SAFETY CERTIFICATES AND INSURANCE

Marabu is maintained to RYA/Dep of Transport Code of Practice standards.membership to the Club, a 'kitty' (joint collection) for food, drink, fuel and mooring charges, (paid to the skipper), and an instruction fee for the certificated courses or educational cruises (paid to the instructor).All bookings are taken on a first come, first served basis. Cruises last from between one evening and three weeks.

CONTACT	John Kapp
ADDRESS	Marabu Sailing Club, 55 Hove Park Road, Hove, BN3 6LL, UK
PHONE	+44 1273 501708 FAX +44 1273 291166
BOOKINGS	Hazel Parker, 5 Richmond Close, Fetcham, Surrey KT 22 9NX, UK
PHONE	+44 1372 451162

Mir

NATIONALITY	Russian
HOME PORT	St. Petersburg, Baltic Russia
LENGTH OVERALL	108 metres 358 feet
PROFESSIONAL CREW	49
CADETS	125
PAYING TRAINEES	25

HISTORY

Built in 1987 in Poland Mir, meaning 'Peace', now belongs to the Admiral Makarov State Maritime Academy. She is a three masted full rigged ship and her elegant lines were drawn by Zygmunt Choren. She is instantly recognisable by the recently added broad blue band along her hull which marks her out from her near sisters Dar Mlodzeizy, Khersones, Pallada, Druzhba and Nadezhda. Mir has covered more than 160,000 nautical miles in 9 years at sea and over 700 students have served their 5 months of sea training aboard. In 1992 she came first overall amongst the 35 Tall Ships in the Columbus 92 transatlantic regatta, which sailed from Cadiz to North America and back to Liverpool. She has been a regular participant in Cutty Sark Tall Ships' Races, and under Captain Victor Antonov has won many cups and trophies.

In 1996 she played host to the fleet when it visited her home port of St. Petersburg, and the view that she is the fastest of all the large Tall Ships was enhanced by her winning the leg from Rostock, Germany to St. Petersburg, and she was first Tall Ship to cross the finishing line, first in Class A and first overall. The second leg of the races was from Turku, Finland to Copenhagen, Denmark, and she was first overall in the second race as well, on corrected time. For speed amongst the large ships, she is still the one to beat in the new Millenium. She is regarded as very much a maritime symbol of the port and city of St. Petersburg, which celebrates the 300th anniversary of its founding in the year 2003.

PROGRAMME

Recent voyages costed in German Marks (DM):
7 days, Kiel-Cuxhaven (1)770 Students(2)660
7 days, Cuxhaven-Aberdeen (1)770 (2)660
11 days, Aberdeen-Trondheim (1)1200 (2)1000
11 days, Trondheim-Stavanger (1)1100 (2)850
9 days, Stavanger-Göteborg (1)1100 (2)850
3 days, Göteborg-Copenhagen (1)390 (2)300
6 days, Copenhagen-Kiel (1)720 (2)660
6 days, Kiel-Thorshavn (1)770 (2)660
7 days, Thorshavn-Bremen (1)770 (2)660
6 days, Bremen-Travemunde (1)770 (2)660
6 days, Travemunde-Copenhagen (1)770 (2)660
6 days, Copenhagen-Rostock (1)770 (2)660
8 days, Rostock-St. Petersburg (1)770 (2)660
(1) = Adults. (2) = Students.

CONTACT	The Director
ADDRESS	Admiral Makarov State Maritime Academy, Kosaya Linia 15a, St. Petersburg, 199026, Russia
PHONE	+7 812 356 6069
FAX	+7 812 217 0682
TELEX	121 137 SMA 5P

Najaden

NATIONALITY	Swedish
HOME PORT	Stocksund
SIZE OVERALL	47 metres 154 feet
PROFESSIONAL CREW	7
PAYING VISITORS	24 or 82 for day trips

PROGRAMME

The cost is 39,500 Swedish Crowns (SEK) per day or 3,700 SEK per hour with a minimum of 6 hours.

HISTORY

Najaden was built in Holland in 1918 as a commercial sailing vessel carrying a whole variety of cargoes, and over the years she changed ownership and flag several times. In 1988 she was totally rebuilt as a passenger sailing ship. She retains her original lines with clipper bow, deckhouse, and gaff rig, but below there are 12 air-conditioned double cabins, each with shower and WC. She is available in the Baltic Sea from April to October, and is moored 100 metres from the Royal Palace in central Stockholm. The other ship owned by Segelfartygs Kompaniet, Belle Amie, has entered a Cutty Sark Tall Ships' Race.

SAFETY CERTIFICATES AND INSURANCE

Najaden has a Swedish international passenger certificate and is classified by Bureau Veritas.

CONTACT   Arne Welin
ADDRESS   Stocksund Hamn, 182 78, Stocksund, Sweden
PHONE   +46 8 247510   FAX   +46 8 8242090
SHIP'S PHONE 010214 0099

Nobile

NATIONALITY	*German*
HOME PORT	*Wolgast, Baltic Germany*
SIZE OVERALL	*38.5 metres 126 feet*
PROFESSIONAL CREW	*6*
PAYING SAIL TRAINEES	*14*

crew of six, and fourteen trainees. Groups of adults and youth aged sixteen years and over sail on her. Adults and seminar groups are also catered for.

PROGRAMME

Nobile now sails on the North Sea and in the Baltic on 7 to 14 day voyages. Her sailing programme runs from late May to late October. Trainees (16-25 year olds) pay an average fee of 80 DM per day, adults 136 DM a day.

CONTACT	LebenLernen auf Segelschiffen e.V.
ADDRESS	Friedensallee 41, D-22765 Hamburg, Germany
PHONE	+49 40 390 8892 FAX +49 40 390 5551
WEB	http//www.segel.de/windjammer
E-MAIL	windjammer@segel.de

HISTORY

Nobile was built in Britain, worked in Norway, was rescued by Germany and named after an Italian hero. In 1919 she launched at Lowestoft, England, as a two masted sailing ship called Kathleen. Sold to Norway in 1947 she was used for many years as a fishing boat and named Jodnafjell. In the mid 1980s her rig was cut down and a new main engine installed, and it was in this state that she very nearly ended her days as an ex-dynamite freighter in a scrapyard in Trondheim, Norway. In 1992 she was sold to Detlev Löll and converted into a sail training ship, part of the LebenLernen fleet.

She was re-rigged as a racing cutter, with a tall mast 36 metres high, a long bowsprit, and a 22 metre main boom. The main part of the conversion was carried out by long term unemployed people through a German Government grant.

Nobile is the third ship in a row to be given a new life through the efforts of LebenLernen. The others are a coaster which is now the three masted top sail schooner Fridtjof Nansen, and a former small oil tanker transformed into the brig Roald Amundsen. The original grant ran out before Nobile could be completed so at least half the remaining work was done by volunteers. Now she is active in sail training, a distinctive sight in the fleet with her low freeboard, and massive single mast.

She is named after Umberto Nobile, an Italian polar explorer and aeronautical engineer.

On her first voyage after conversion, Nobile was manned by an all girl crew consisting of 15 apprentice boatbuilders between 16 and 20 years old.

ON BOARD

Nobile carries a professional

Noorderlicht

NATIONALITY	Dutch
HOME PORT	Enkguizen, The Netherlands
SIZE OVERALL	46 metres 150.9 feet
PROFESSIONAL CREW	3
VOYAGE CREW	20

HISTORY

'De Zeilwaart' from Enkguizen, The Netherlands, has over 120 yachts for charter, most of them in the more sheltered waters of Holland such as in the Zuider Zee. All of their ships are built in traditional style, and can take between 8 people and 34 people on board.

Of these 16 ships have the certificates needed to sail on the high seas, and are available for charter to sail training organisations, with 9 of them specialising in the Baltic Sea, while 6 go to Greece, Turkey, the Caribbean, and the Canaries. Maybe the most interesting boat for possible sail training use is Noorderlicht, the only one with the strength of hull to have permission to sail into the Arctic, with her on board heating and other arrangements able to deal with severe cold weather. She sails to Spitzbergen in summer and winter.

ON BOARD

She can take 20 people, in ten two berth cabins, and she has four showers and 5 toilets.

PROGRAMME

There is no set programme for the ship: you book her after discussing where you wish to go with the skipper.

The prices are (In Dutch guilders) 8340 for a week aboard, 4340 for a weekend, 2170 for a day, 1430 for an extra day, 6255 for Monday to Friday, and 4000 as a week's school tariff. Outside Holland, the rates are 9591 for the week, 4991 for the weekend, 2496 for the day, 1645 charge per extra day, 7193 mid weekly rate (Monday to Friday), and 4600 for a school excursion rate. The tariffs include payment for two permanent crew members, fuel for one hour's motoring per day, and extras such as windsurfing. Not included are oilskins, meals, and cleaning the boat. Insurance is all-risks, and the crew has third party with respect to the 'trainees'.

CONTACT	Sandra Canderplas
ADDRESS	Stationsplein 3, 1601 EN Enkhuizen, The Netherlands
PHONE	+31 228 312424 FAX +31 228 31 37 37
E-MAIL	zeilwaart@zeilwaart.co.nl

Notre Dame des Flots

NATIONALITY	*French*
HOME PORT	*La Rochelle*
SIZE OVERALL	*28.5 metres 94 feet*
PROFESSIONAL CREW	*3*
PAYING VOYAGERS	*16 a day and 8 for cruises*

History

Built in Gravelines in 1942, and based on a 1910 herring boat design, Notre Dame des Flots worked as a fishing trawler in the North Sea until 1974. Fishing techniques had changed by then, and as a ketch she was no longer suitable as an efficient working vessel. She was laid up and voluntarily sunk in Dunkerque's boat graveyard. In 1976 Jean Pierre, Pitchoune and Philippe refloated her and for the following seven years, they lovingly restored her and adapted her to give her a new life at sea. In 1983 she sailed on a round the world charter (through the Atlantic, Panama Canal, Pacific Ocean, Indonesia, Indian Ocean, Cape of Good Hope, Brazil, the West Indies and back to France). She has made fishing voyages to Iceland, taken part in Tall Ships' Races, sailed round the Pacific, and sailed on a humanitarian mission from Canada to Haiti.

ON BOARD

Each cabin is a double or a twin. All can be seated in the saloon, where Jean Pierre, Pitchoune and Fabien are available for information on sailing manoeuvres, coastal navigation, and astro-navigation.

SAFETY CERTIFICATES AND INSURANCE

All required sailing permits are gained from the French Marines Affaires and the merchant marine service, in the category of a ship used for 'collective utility'.

PROGRAMME

She sails along the coasts of France, England, Scandinavia and Portugal, and goes on transoceanic voyages. Costs for day trips are 300FF per person, and 450FF per day per person when on cruises.

CONTACT	Notre Dame des Flots,
ADDRESS	Musée Maritime, 1700 La Rochelle
PHONE	+33 610 100078 FAX +33 546 410787

Otama II

NATIONALITY	Australian
PRESENT BASE	Europe
SIZE OVERALL	16 metres 52 feet
PROFESSIONAL	2
PAYING SAIL TRAINEES	10

HISTORY

Otama II is an Australian registered sail training ship (TSKA 485) with bermudian cutter rig, of modern shape and sail area. Designed by Dutchman Van der Stadt, she is a 'Pacific II' type, launched in Friesland in The Netherlands in 1987. She was not completed to International Sail Training Standards until 1992, when she took part in her first Cutty Sark Tall Ships' Races in the Baltic. Since then, she has taken part in many Cutty Sark events.

ON BOARD

She is modified below to make it crowded and uncomfortable, as - says her owner - befits a sail training vessel. However, she has far more room below than her 52 feet would suggest and it always seems easier to fit another visitor around the saloon table than to see one leave.

Trainees are given far more responsibility than is usually possible on larger vessels and so have plenty of opportunity to learn the different aspects of sea-sailing.

SAFETY

Otama II is fully insured and has complied with the Cutty Sark Tall Ships' Races committee safety requirements.

PROGRAMME

Apart from participating in Cutty Sark Tall Ships' Races, she is in principle available for charter. The basic rate is $Au75 a day per trainee.

CONTACT	Frank Wolfe
ADDRESS	Otama II, PO Box 1015, 7550 BA, Hengelo, The Netherlands
PHONE	+31 652 931391 FAX +31 74 2500463
E-MAIL	106217.1630@compuserve.com

Oosterschelde

NATIONALITY	Dutch
HOME PORT	Rotterdam, The Netherlands
SIZE OVERALL	50 metres 164 feet
PROFESSIONAL	6
PAYING SAIL TRAINEES	36

HISTORY

Oosterschelde began life in 1918 as a schooner, and after many changes she has returned to this rig - although please note - in Dutch the term 'schooner' differs from that used by many European countries where such ships are identified by the aft mast being equal to or taller than any masts forward. A Dutch schooner indicates a type of ship with flared clipper bows and a rounded cabin with an overhanging bulwark at the stern.

Three and four masted Dutch schooners sailed all over the world and Oosterschelde was no exception, working the European and African coasts carrying 400 tons of cargo ranging from clay and bricks to salt herring and bananas.

In the 1930s she started to lose her identity as a sailing ship. Topmasts and bowsprit were removed and a heavier diesel engine fitted. Renamed Fuglen, she was sold to a Danish company who in 1954 passed her on to a Swedish firm, who totally rebuilt her as a motor coaster, and called her Sylvan. In 1988 Dick van Andel bought the ship with plans to restore her to her former glory as the last representative of the many three masted schooners which sailed under the Dutch flag at the beginning of this century. Restoration started in the spring of 1990 under the Rotterdam Sailing Ship Foundation, which was responsible for finding support for the rebuild through publicity and fundraising, for this project was going to be costly in spite of the good condition of the ship. Three maritime museums and many ship design offices provided expert knowledge to ensure absolute authenticity as well as sound construction and safety. In August 1992 Oosterschelde was relaunched by HRH Princess Margriet and she took to the water again as a sailing ship.

ON BOARD

Cruises are made to destinations outside The Netherlands and anyone can be a passenger. However Oosterschelde enjoys her voyages as a sail training ship just as much as the task of acting as a floating embassy representing the City of Rotterdam.

SAFETY CERTIFICATES AND INSURANCE

All required sailing permits are gained from Register Holland, and she undergoes Dutch shipping inspection.

PROGRAMME

The price to sail her is 140 to 180 Hfl a day. Typical programmes are
Boston to Halifax 5 days, Halifax to Amsterdam 32 days, 2 trips to the Antarctic of 26 days each, round Cape Horn 40 days, to the Galapagos 26 days, transatlantic from Rotterdam via Las Palmas, Recife, and Buenos Aires to Ushuaia, Oban to Rotterdam 14 days.

CONTACT   Gert Tetteroo
ADDRESS   Holland Gloire, PO Box 11245,
3004 EE Rotterdam, The Netherlands
PHONE   +31 10 4156600   FAX   +31 10 4154545

Pogoria

NATIONALITY	*Polish*
HOME PORT	*Gdynia, Poland*
SIZE OVERALL	*48 metres 157 feet*
PROFESSIONAL CREW	5
VOLUNTEER OFFICERS	5
PAYING SAIL TRAINEES	38

HISTORY

Porgoria was built in 1979-80 in Gdansk for the Iron Shackle Fraternity, a sail training organisation linked with Polish Television. She made her debut a few weeks after completion by taking part in the Cutty Sark Tall Ships' Race between Kiel and Amsterdam. Then began voyages of adventure. The first was in 1980/81. Chartered by the Polish Academy of Sciences she sailed to the Antarctic to relieve and re-supply the Polish Station on King George Island.

In 1982 she took part in her first Cutty Sark Tall Ships' Races from Falmouth, England to the finish at Southampton, calling at Lisbon, Portugal and Vigo, Spain. Then followed long distance voyages to circle Africa, plus a side trip to Bombay, to fulfil the 'Class Afloat' aim of introducing young Polish people to the sea and to new horizons.

In the late 1980s Pogoria was chartered full time by the Canadian Educational Alternative as a floating school. Since then, she has operated mainly in the Atlantic between Europe, the Caribbean and the USA. In 1993, financed by the City of Gdynia and the Sailing Foundation of that City, who became joint owners together with the Polish Yachting Association, she re-fitted for her new sail training role. And in 1995 the Sail Training Association of Poland became the ship's operator.

ON BOARD

Trainees are split into four watches, three are 4 hours on watch and eight hours off, the fourth is a daywork watch to help with keeping the ship clean and assisting in the galley. Most on-watch hours are at the helm, keeping the log up to date, on lookout and sail trimming. Going aloft is not compulsory but most trainees do so for the thrill and learning experience.

The permanent crew consists of chief officer, bosun, engineer, motorman, and cook; plus a voluntary master and four mates. Trainees are usually aged between 15 and 25.

PROGRAMME

A typical programme is:
April-Mid June, one to two weeks cruises in the Baltic.
Mid June to End of August, two to three weeks cruises to join the Cutty Sark Tall Ships' Races.
September and October, one and two week cruises in the Baltic.
November to March, occasionally she sails in the Atlantic for various sail training or class afloat programmes. If not, she stays in Gdynia for a refit.

CONTACT	Sail Training Association Poland
ADDRESS	Al. Zjednoczenia 3, PO BOX 113, 81-964 Gdynia 1, Poland
PHONE	+48 58 614770 FAX +48 58 206225

Pen Duick VI

NATIONALITY	French
HOME PORT	Saint-Malo
SIZE OVERALL	22.3 metres 73 feet
PROFESSIONAL CREW	2
PAYING CREW	12

HISTORY

Few combinations in ocean racing are as famous as the six yachts called Pen Duick, and Eric Tabarly, who died recently in the west of the Channel on board the first Pen Duick, the family's beloved hundred years old classic yacht. His other yachts brought key innovations to yachting, and included Pen Duick II, winner of the singlehanded transatlantic, Pen Duick IV, a giant trimaran, Pen Duick V, in which he won the singlehanded transpacific, and she experimented with water ballast tanks, an innvoative Paul Ricard, a transatlantic three hulled yacht with

'foils' to keep the outer floats out of the water, and Pen Duick VI, his giant two master, controversial when she used, until stopped, depleted uranium in her keel. In 2002, five Pen Duicks will be brought together at Lorient in a living 'museum' (all except Pen Duick IV which, renamed Manureva, sank). There, they will sail train and cruise. Pen Duick VI has for 12 years been run by Club Croisière Pen Duick out of Saint-Malo. Earlier she took part in Whitbread Round the World Races, in 1973, 1977 and 1981, and in her, Eric Tabarly won the OSTAR (singlehanded transatlantic race) of 1976. The Club owns a share of Pen Duick VI, and also runs for other owners Poil de Carotte (the lad with carroty hair) a 21.6 metre (71 feet) modern ketch with 7 double cabins, and 3 bathrooms, and Kriter V, a long thin monohull famous in singlehanded races.

ON BOARD

Ocean racing is taught, and, the club states "only a passion for the sea must be essential" for you to want to sail her.

PROGRAMME

Pen Duick VI is available from March to September out of Saint-Malo, for voyages to the Channel Islands, Brittany, and Chausey. Costs include March 2 days for 1,200FF, April 3 days for 1,550FF, May 9 days for 3,600 FF (to the Channel Islands), June 2 days for !,400FF, July 5 days for 2,500FF. For food, fuel and port dues, estimate about another 100FF per day. Costs for a leg in the Cutty Sark Race are (9 days) 3,600FF, (12 days) 4,800FF and (17 days) 6,800.
Pen Duick sails round the world (as in 2000 and 2001) with a typical price tag of 15,600FF for 39 days from New Zealand to Ushuaïa (by Cape Horn).Travel to and from the ship is extra.

CONTACT	Club Croisière Pen Duick
ADDRESS	7, Avenue Louis Martin, 35400 Saint-Malo, France
PHONE	+33 299 404111 FAX +33 299 568813

Provident and Leader

NATIONALITY	British
HOME PORT	Brixham, southern England
SIZE OVERALL Provident	27 metres 80 feet
SIZE OVERALL Leader	33.5 metres 110 feet
PROFESSIONAL CREW Provident	3
PROFSSIONAL CREW Leader	3-5
PAYING SAIL TRAINEES Provident	12
PAYING SAIL TRAINEES Leader	12-14

HISTORY

These are two of the last of the famous Brixham sailing trawlers of southern England, renowned for wide decks, sea keeping ability and comfortable motion. Provident was built in 1924. The Maritime Trust bought her in 1951, and she was operated by the Island Cruising Club on behalf of the Maritime Trust and the Island Trust until the end of 1998, when the Island Trust took her on. To-day, the recently established Trinity Sailing Foundation, based on Brixham, will operate three ships - Provident, Leader, and Golden Vanity. Provident was extensively re-fitted in the early 1990s.

Leader, one of the largest Brixham trawlers, is older, built in 1892. She fished the English Channel and North Sea for 20 years, and was sold to the Swedes who kept her for 20 years as a sail training vessel. 10 years followed on the West Cost of Scotland and she returned to home waters in 1996. In private hands, she became part of the Trinity Sailing Foundation at the start of 1999.

ON BOARD

Passengers have spacious berths, and the saloons are large enough for the entire crew. The cruising pattern

CONTACT	Struan Coupar,
ADDRESS	Wallis Cottage, Bowden, Dartmouth, Devon TQ6 OLH
PHONE/FAX	+44 1803 770486
E-MAIL	leader@eclipse.co.uk

includes short cruises to ports in south west England - Devon, Cornwall, Brittany, the Channel Isles and Isles of Scilly - but on longer trips they visit Scotland, Ireland, Northern Spain and the North Sea. The cruising season runs from April to October.

PROGRAMME

Typical prices are 3 days, July £195; 6 days, Dartmouth-Salcombe £320; 6 days, Channel Cruise Sept £365; 6 days, Channel Cruise Oct £290; 7 days, Salcombe-Southampton £385; 10 days, Normandy Cruise £650; 10 days, Isle of Scilly (June) £550 ;13 days, Salcombe-Bilbao £795 ;14 days, Bilbao-Salcombe £795; 14 days, Britanny (July) £795

The Island Trust

'Provident'

Roald Amundsen

NATIONALITY	German
HOME PORT	Wolgast, Baltic Germany
SIZE OVERALL	50.2 metres 164.6 feet
PROFESSIONAL CREW	14
PAYING SAIL TRAINEES	26

HISTORY

In 1952 in East Germany, the National People's Army built an oil tanker. After Reunification Detlev Löll and friends in LebenLernen auf Segelschiffen (The young Learning to sail on a Sailing Ship) saw her at anchor, and thought of a quite different future for her. As part of a re-deployment project (to assist the unemployed in East Germany) she was completely renovated and masts and sails were added. She was rigged as a brig (two masts with square sails on both masts). She is now transformed into a traditional sailing ship, and as such she believes in practicalities instead of much luxury, but her safety equipment is of the latest. Her first voyage as a youth sailing ship was in August 1993.

ON BOARD

First you join the association, the LebenLernen auf Segelschiffen. If you are with a group you should be over 16, and if you come alone the lowest age is 18. Youth groups predominate, but groups of adults and seminar groups are welcome. You don't have to be experienced, but "we hope you've the spirit to 'have a go', accept responsibility, even if occasionally you don't feel so good". The philosophy is 'orientation'. On a sailing ship almost everything is different. People on board have to reorganise themselves and their priorities to find a place in the new 'microcosmos'. Each person aboard is valued as one of a crew, where each individual effort counts, but is only effective in cooperation with others. The experience of self-victory and sailing on an exclusive traditional ship is part of the fun of being aboard. On board, it's safety first. As in the old days the motto is one hand for yourself, the second for the ship. For safety reasons, as part of the philosophy, the consumption of alcohol is not allowed for youth groups and smoking is only allowed on the upper deck. Personal musical sets are unwelcome, but bring musical instruments please.

Most trainees sleep four to a cabin, some in traditional hammocks.

PROGRAMME

Roald Amundsen often sails the Baltic in summer and the Canary islands in winter, and since 1993 she has participated in Cutty Sark Tall Ships' Races. In 1998/9 she joined Alexander von Humboldt for a commemoration voyage to South America, where the famous natural scientist A. von Humboldt carried out various expeditions.

During European cruises (ports visited recently include Hamburg, Heligoland, Travemünde, Kiel, Bremerhaven, Eckernförde), average costs per day are 85 DM for trainees of 16 to 25 years old, and 125 DM for adults. Prices include all shipbound costs such as food, fuel and harbour charges, but exclude transport to and from the ship.

CONTACT	LebenLernen auf Segelschiffen e.V.
ADDRESS	Friedensallee 41, 22765 Hamburg, Germany
PHONE	+49 40 390 8892 FAX +49 40 390 5551
WEB	http//www.segal de/windjammer
E-MAIL	windjammer@segel.de

Rona II

NATION	British
HOME PORT	Hamble, southern England
SIZE OVERALL	20.7 metres 68 feet
VOLUNTEER AFTERGUARD	7
PAYING SAIL TRAINEES	14

HISTORY

The owner, the London Sailing Project (LSP) was founded in 1960 by Lord Amory, then Chancellor of the Exchequer in the British government. He took parties of young sea cadets from London to sea in his own 40 foot sloop. Then he bought Rona, a 77 foot classic ketch, built in 1895, and he converted her to take a crew of 19. The project was then extended. After he died his Trust, which with the help of 'The Donald Searle Trust' and another, anonymous trust, now run three ketches, in length between 57 and 75 feet (17.4 metres to 22.8 metres).

In Lord Amory's words "Our aim is to provide opportunities for young men to acquire those attributes of seamen, namely a sense of responsibility, resourcefulness and team-work, which will help them throughout their lives". Trainees are between 14 and 25 years old and no previous sailing experience is necessary. Preference is given to those from the London area. The majority come from organisations such as Sea Cadets, Scouts, Boys Brigades, Boys Clubs and Childrens Homes. Only two are allowed from any one organisation in any one boat at a time. The result is a wide social mix. The remaining places can be booked by any young person. The LSP also organises a number of mixed 'special' voyages each year for the blind, the deaf, the mentally handicapped and pupils from schools with special needs. There are also opportunities for girls to go sailing.

ON BOARD

Each yacht normally carries an afterguard of 6 people, the skipper, a mate, two watch officers and two watch leaders; all having Royal Yachting Association (RYA) qualifications demanded by the Maritime Safety Agency. At the end of each voyage a short report is written on each young man and a copy sent to any organisation or parent who asks for it. Trainees who give of their best can receive a 'Amory' award and an opportunity to sail in a Cutty Sark Tall Ships' Race. Those showing leadership can be recommended for watch leader selection. Indeed about 40 of the LSP skippers began as trainees.

Rona II is an Oyster 68 ketch, with a total crew of 23. The London Sailing Project has two other yachts, Helen Mary R, a Bowman 57', and Donald Searle, an Ocean 75'. They are also ketch-rigged

(which indicates they have two masts, the aft one shorter, with the rudder post behind the second mast). Cruises begin and end at the LSP base at the Universal Shipyard, Hamble, and last 6 days leaving on a Thursday and returning Wednesday, with special buses operating to London. The LSP publishes its programme in November. Most of the berths are taken by the end of March but there are usually a few vacancies.

Trainees bring with them a sleeping bag, two sets of casual clothes, warm pullovers, trainers and a small amount of pocket money: the ship provides oilskins, lifejackets, safety harnesses, etc.

The cost for the six days is £50 a day, per head for all, even the afterguard. Preference is given to anyone who cannot afford the full, economic fee of £300. The Trusts fund the difference. However the trainees are expected to contribute a part of the fee themselves and not rely on organisations, such as schools.

SAFETY CERTIFICATES AND INSURANCE

All yachts have complete cover including accident to crew members while on board - the exceptions are theft of personal belongings and personal accident when ashore.

PROGRAMME

Rona II normally sails across the Channel to France and/or the Channel Islands, depending on the weather, but in July/ August she takes part in the Cutty Sark Tall Ships' Race. A normal programme might include:

9 days, voyages for special needs groups and individuals, schools and colleges, etc.

6 days, sail training voyages, for 20-25 years olds.

6 days, voyages for special needs groups and individuals, schools and colleges, etc.

6 days, sail training voyages for 20-25 year olds.

13 days, voyages for special needs groups and individuals, schools and colleges, etc.

6 days, sail training voyages for 16 to 19 year olds.

CONTACT	Paul Bishop
ADDRESS	The London Sailing Project, Universal Shipyard, Crableck Lane, Sarisbury Green, Southampton SO31 7ZN, UK
PHONE	+44 1489 885098 FAX +44 1489 579098
E-MAIL	office@lsp.org.uk
WEB	http:/www lsp.org.uk

Rupel

NATION   *Belgian*
HOME PORT *Ostend*
SIZE OVERALL
           17 metres 56 feet

HISTORY

A steenschuit is an old name of a small ship of centuries past, which carried bricks which were made in the Rupel region, to Antwerp. These bricks were put into schooners and they sailed abroad - thus to England. It was the foundation of a flourishing export trade.

And so, when Eddy Stuer started to lay the foundations of a shipyard in Boom, Belgium, which was near the river Rupel, he called his project 'De Steenschuit'. His idea was to build a 17 metre ship using unemployed people, unqualified when they started work on his project. This way, he hoped they would be brought back into a working lifestyle, and learn a useful number of skills. In June 1996 the boat was ready and more than 200 unemployed had by then worked on her construction. More than 150 of them found work afterwards.

The ship, named Rupel, now sails from Ostend, mainly in the North Sea. She took part in a Cutty Sark Tall Ships' Race for the first time in 1998.

CONTACT
De Steenschuit VZW
ADDRESS
Hoek 76 b32m B-2850
Boom, Belgium
PHONE
+32 844 46 48
FAX
+32 844 78 19

Sedov

NATIONALITY	Russian
Home Port	Murmansk, Arctic Russia
SIZE OVERALL	121.7 metres 399 feet
PROFESSIONAL OFFICERS	70
Russian fisheries Cadets	114
Instructors	6
PAYING TRAINEES	50

HISTORY

Two giant four masted ships were built at the Krupp-Germania boatyard at Kiel, North Germany. The Hussar launched in 1931 as a luxury yacht, and this is what she is to-day, taking paying passengers under the name Sea Cloud. The other was Magdalene Vinnen II, now called Sedov. Built in 1921 as a cargo ship, she carried nitrates, especially from Chile, back to Europe. Designed as a sails-only ship, she had a 500 HP engine fitted and so for a while could compete with steamships. By 1936 she had become unprofitable as a cargo ship. The shipping company Norddeutscher Lloyds in Bremen wanted a schoolship and bought her. She still did carry some cargo but she was altered so she could also act as a schoolship at the same time. Under her second name Kommodore Johnson, she transported grain from Argentina and Australia to Europe. Her fastest passage was 92 days from Sydney, Australia back to the Isle of Wight, southern England. During the war she continued in the Baltic as a schoolship, and after the war's end, she was handed over to the Russians who renamed her after their famous Arctic explorer, Georgy Y. Sedov (1877-1914). A new role was given her as an oceanographic research vessel under the ownership of the Russian Navy until 1966. She was out of service for some time until a refit brought her back under sail in 1981, training cadets for the Russian Ministry of Fisheries.

Today Sedov is the largest sailing ship that still goes to sea. She is one of the few remaining with four masts. Her home port is in the far north of Russia beyond the Arctic Circle, in Murmansk,and to-day her usual voyages between spring and autumn are to the Baltic, North Sea and Western approaches. Owned by the Russian Committee of Fisheries for the Murmansk State Technical University, she trains officers and cadets in seamanship, navigation, and every aspect of seagoing life. The costs of such a huge vessel are vast, so she also takes paying passengers who experience the exhilaration of sailing on a ship which is also a part of maritime history.

ON BOARD

The Russian Fisheries cadets work the ship, learn their lessons, and study for their examinations. Most of them are between 19 and 25.

Sedov also has on board up to 50 paying people, young and old, and they share an 8 berth cabin, a 20 berth cabin, and a 22 berth cabin. Bedding is supplied, and each person has a locker and drawer to stow away personal clothes and belongings. There is also a cosy common room for free time on board. Food is simple. On the open sea, trainees get four meals a day, and in harbour, three. The minimum age for trainees is 16 years old. Regular crew members supervise on day to day operations on board, and provide a chance for trainees to participate in sail manoeuvres such as taking a turn on the wheel or as a look out. A trainee can also request to work in the rigging.

When in port, Sedov also has a social role, and parties and conferences are held aboard her.

PROGRAMME

She regularly takes part in Cutty Sark Tall Ships' Races, and is a focal point for cameraderie between people of so many nations. The kind of voyages she undertakes and recent costs in German Marks were:

16 days, Sevastapol-Malta DM 1800
10 days, Malta-Mallorca DM 1500
11 days, Mallorca-Lisbon DM 1650
11 days, Lisbon-Brest DM 1650

4 days, Amsterdam-Hamburg DM 600
7 days, Hamburg-Edinburgh DM 1050
12 days, Edinburgh-Emden DM 1800
4 days, Emden-Cherbourg DM 750
10 days, Cherbourg-St. Petersburg DM 1500
11 days, St. Petersburg-Aberdeen DM 1650
10 days, Aberdeen-Trondheim DM 1650
10 days, Trondheim-Stavanger DM 1650
9 days, Stavanger-Göteborg DM 1485
6 days, Göteborg-Plymouth DM 1050
13 days, Plymouth-Barcelona DM 2100
6 days, Barcelona-Ajaccio, Corsica DM 1050
5 days, Ajaccio-Monaco DM 750

CONTACT   Murmansk State Technical University
ADDRESS   Sportivnaya Street 13, 183056 Murmansk,
               Russia
PHONE   +7 815 226 2051
FAX ASHORE   +7 47 789 10548
FAX/PHONE
ON BOARD: +871/2/3 1406 721
(INMARSAT-A)
TELEX   1406720
INMARSAT-C   427300043

Seute Deern

NATIONALITY	German
HOME PORT	Oldenburg, Schleswig Holstein
SIZE OVERALL	36 metres 118 feet
PERMANENT CREW	5/6
PAYING SAIL TRAINEES	24/25

HISTORY
She was built in Denmark in 1939 by the Ring Andersen yard in Svendborg and launched with the name Havet, meaning 'The Sea'. For her first five years she sailed in coastal waters but records are sketchy as this was during the second world war. In 1956 she was sold to a Danish shipping company, Lauritzen, which used her for carrying freight in coastal waters. Under new ownership and named Noona Dan she carried an exploration team to Greenland. Later she was to go on other ocean exploration voyages. In 1963 she was sold again, this time to the former Pamir-Passat Stiftung in Germany now known as the Stiftung für Ausbildungsschiffe. She was to be used as a training ship for young deck officers, and renamed Seute Deern. In 1973 she was given to the then newly founded association Clipper Deutsches Jugendwerk zur See and became their first ship. Now they have a fleet of four, the others being Albatros, Amphitrite and Johann Smidt. Shortly after the end of the war a similar hull was built in the same shipyard, later to become Bel Espoir II.

ON BOARD
There are 5 two-berth, 1 four and 2 eight berth cabins to accommodate permanent crew and trainees. The main saloon is large enough for the entire ship's complement to come together for their meals. The permanent crew, deck officers, engineer and cook are all volunteers, giving their spare time to this vessel.

SAFETY CERTIFICATES AND INSURANCE
She has the Germanischer Lloyd Classification and conforms to the rules of GSHW.

PROGRAMME
The sailing programme is primarily centred in the Baltic and this pattern also applies to the other ships of the DJS fleet. Voyages are either of 7 or 14 days duration, beginning on Saturdays. She regularly takes part in regattas. Trainees who are still in an educational programme (students, apprentices etc) pay £25 per day. All others pay a daily rate of £38. Ports visited in a year might include Århus, Kiel, Flensburg, Köge, Kiel, Kalmar, Stockholm, Karlskrona, Travemünde, and Bremen.

CONTACT	Clipper Deutsches Jugendwerk zur See e.V.
ADDRESS	Hamburg Office Jürgensallee 54, D-22609, Hamburg, Germany
PHONE	+49 40 822 78 103 FAX +49 40 822 78 104
E-mail	ClipperDJzS-Knut-Frisch@-online.de
Web	http:/www.clipper-djs.org

Sandefjord

NATIONALITY	Norwegian
HOME PORT	Oslo
SIZE	16 metres 52feet
PROFESSIONAL CREW	3
PAYING TRAINEES	5/6

HISTORY

Sandefjord was designed early this century by Colin Archer as a sailing lifeboat for the Norwegian Lifeboat Service. She was launched in 1913 at the Olsen Yard at Risor. Traditionally these boats served in the area where the finance to build them had been raised. In Sandefjord's case her benefector was the sister of Consul Kristiansen, and she saw service mainly in the southern part of Norway. Sandefjord is an example of the second and slightly larger revision of the basic Colin Archer design and is classed as a 'Solli' type, carrying the same rig and a working crew of 4. When the decision was taken some 20 years later to introduce only motor powered lifeboats she was sold to the adventurer and author, Erling Tambs. During his ownership she suffered a pitch-pole capsize while crossing the Atlantic in bad weather, losing a crewman and the mizzen mast had to be cut adrift. After repair in the USA she returned to Norway and was sold to a South African owner just before the outbreak of the Second World War. There she was based in Cape Town and, later, Durban. In 1964 two brothers Barry and Patrick Cullen partly restored her, leaving a year later on a round the world voyage with a crew of seven. A film, still available, was made of this journey. In 1971 she took part in the Cape to Rio race, after which she sailed North to Mystic Seaport in the USA and was sold there to Erling Brunborg who took her back to Oslo. Some years later she was taken over by Petter Omtvelt when she was completely restored. Between 1985 and 1993 more work was done to make her into a comfortable private yacht. In 1993 she was sold to her present owner, Gunn von Trepka, with the express intention of using her for sail training, and who fitted her with a new mast, gaff and movable bowsprit.

ON BOARD

The design concept was to produce a sailing ship capable of operating in very strong weather. The present aim is to enable sail trainees to start by learning to handle the various ropes and sails and learn how to use her tiller steering. The boat operates with two mates, each with a watch of 3 trainees on duty for a four hour cycle. One member of each watch is responsible for feeding the crew and keeping the boat clean. Below, Sandefjord is very comfortable. There is a 3 berth fore cabin, 2 berths and 2 settee berths in the main cabin and 3 berths in the owner's cabin. The galley has a fridge/freezer and gas cooker and there is hot and cold water, a shower and adequate heads (WCs) aboard. All normal safety equipment is provided including safety harnesses but trainees are expected to provide their own foul weather gear.

CERTIFICATES AND INSURANCE

Sandefjord is registered with the Norwegian Registry of Shipping. She falls below the minimum size for full certification. The boat is checked annually prior to the Cutty Sark Tall Ships' Races and complies easily with ISTA guidelines. She is fully insured for her area of normal operation but certain specific exceptions render it advisable to have personal effects insured by each individual.

PROGRAMME

Sandefjord is used only for sail training during Cutty Sark Tall Ships' Races and planning starts early in the year. With only 5 places available competition is fierce and while preference is given to locals, the owner likes to take at least one non Norwegian. Thus a recent programme started on 5 July with a cruise from Oslo to Trondheim, when berths cost £25.00 a day which also covered food, with travel not included.

In 1998 Sandefjord was committed to a modest refit, with the intention of starting her sail training activities once more from the following year's Cutty Sark Tall Ships' Races.

CONTACT	Gunn von Trepka
ADDRESS	Heimlibakken 20, 0198 Oslo, Norway
PHONE	+47 22856328 (Office) +47 22290694 (Home)
	+47 94387435 (Bo at)
FAX	+3 80 6561 33080
E-MAIL	gtrepka @ admin.uio.no

Shtandart

NATIONALITY	Russian
HOME PORT	St. Petersburg
SIZE OVERALL	30.5 metres 100 feet
PROFESSIONAL CREW	10
PAYING SAIL TRAINEES	30

HISTORY

The original designer was Tsar Peter the Great, and the ship was built in six months at the Olonets shipyard on the river Svir. She was built quickly to supply an urgent need for the defence of the new capital of Russia, St. Petersburg, and the ship did not last long. In 1728 Catherine the Great ordered a replica to be built, which would last for ever as a monument to the art of Russian ship building. However the order was never fulfilled.....until 1984 when sailing ship enthusiasts under naval architect Vladimir Martous laid the keel for a full size sea going replica.

The spirit of this enterprise is to help rebuild Russia and bring her again into the world of nations.

Peter the Great had intended to make Russia a maritime as well as a military power. His visit to the west in 1698 was for the purpose of studying all matters relating to the sea, and he returned to Russia to found the new Baltic fleet. Based in his new city of St. Petersburg, he ordered and helped to design Russia's first large warship, Shtandart, in 1703, and he was her first captain. She received her name in honour of the royal standard which Peter changed to black on gold, with a double headed eagle holding the four seas that Russia had access to, including now the Baltic, and through the years, Shtandart has become the symbol of the city of St. Petersburg.

So now a replica is being built. The Royal Standard of Peter the Great Maritime Education Trust is an international charity, which supports the rebuilding of Shtandart, and the building of further historical ships, and the establishment of an historic shipyard in St. Petersburg, with maritime education a priority.

ON BOARD

Shtandart's gun deck has an authentic 18th century appearance with traditional hemp ropes, sails, capstan, 28 cannon, sleeping hammocks, and the beautiful carved furniture of the Great Cabin. Below deck the modern crew quarters, up to date engines and equipment conform to international safety regulations. The original had 150 people on board, the replica will have only 40.

SAFETY CERTIFICATES AND INSURANCE

She is built to Russian Register of Shipping rules as an A2 sail training ship.

PROGRAMME

Shtandart will be based in St. Petersburg and London. Her maiden voyage lies along the route of the 1698 Great Embassy of Tsar Peter to Holland and Britain. As an ambassador for Russia in other countries, Shtandart will take part in maritime festivals and tall ship races as a sea going sail training ship for international youth. The year 2003 will see Shtandart as the centrepiece of an international maritime festival in St. Petersburg, celebrating the 300th anniversary of the founding of the city by Peter the Great.

CONTACT
Vladimir
Martous
ADDRESS
PO Box 100,
195112
St. Petersburg,
Russia
PHONE/FAX
+7 812 230
3736
ON BOARD
PHONE
+7 812 960
4159
E-MAIL
vmartous
@shtandart.
main.ru
WEB
http://www.
shtandart.
main.ru

Sir Winston Churchill

NATIONALITY	British
HEADQUARTERS	Portsmouth, southern England
SIZE OVERALL	46 metres 150 feet
PERMENANT CREW	5
AFTERGUARD	11
PAYING SAIL TRAINEES	39

HISTORY

She's over 30 years old, one of the British Sail Training Association's famous twins, together with Malcolm Miller. Just how do you tell them apart? Sir Winston Churchill has TSK1 on her sails and has round tops to the doors amidships; Malcolm Miller's number is TSK2 and she's got flat tops to her midship doors.

She was there at the start of sail training in Britain. In the 1950's a retired London solicitor, Bernard Morgan, dreamed of bringing together the world's great sailing ships. Earl Mountbatten was consulted, and Captain John Illingworth's committee organised the first ever Tall Ships Race. As a result the Sail Training Association (STA) was formed to run these races annually. So, why not also build and sail ships under the same STA flag? In the 1960s the STA raised the necessary funds and by 1966 the STA completed the first of the two, Sir Winston Churchill. Then came Malcolm Miller. They've both got three masts, and are schooners (all masts of similar size, or the back ones taller). In fact, they are 'topsail schooners', for on their first masts they have square sails.

ON BOARD

The 39 trainees are divided into three watches of 13 who do four hours on watch, and eight hours off. Each watch helps care for and maintain the ship and takes part in watch duties such as look-out, steering, sail trimming and assisting the cook in the galley. Most of the time is spent either on the bridge, perhaps taking the helm or keeping the ship's log, or working on deck or aloft. You don't have to go aloft, but most people do, for the experience of setting (letting loose) or handing (folding away) those two square sails on the foremast. The usual trainee age is between 16 to 24. But it isn't only this age group who can benefit. This form of adventure training has proved highly successful in improving personal skills by providing a physical and mental challenge and an awareness of the value of leadership skills and team work. There are also mixed sex voyages for those aged 24-69.

There's a continuous effort to raise money to maintain the ships, from donations and covenants to berth endowments. The result: about 25% of the true cost of each berth is subsidised. If you can't afford the voyage, there are volunteer support groups nationwide who may be able to help, from their own resources or by helping you find a sponsor.

Sir Winston Churchill has two powerful engines, and also generators for heating the sleeping and living accommodation, and providing hot water for the showers (available all the time).

All voyages qualify for the Residential Section of the Gold Award in the Duke of Edinburgh's Award scheme and the RYA Competent Crew Certificate may also be available.. Voyages are in Northern European waters from March to November, and for 'winter sun' voyages off the Canaries and the Azores from November to May.

SAFETY CERTIFICATES AND INSURANCE

She is maintained to Lloyds Class I and Department of Transport standards.

PROGRAMME

A fairly typical year's programme might be:
12 days, Greenock-Swansea Mixed Crew 16/24 years old £696
23 days, Weymouth-Lerwick Male 16/24 £1564
(includes Cutty Sark Tall Ships' Race)
13 days, Lerwick-Dundee female 16/24 £1008
(includes Cutty Sark Tall Ships' Race)
13 days, Shoreham-Ellesmere Port Mixed 16/24 £754
12 days, Dundee-Newcastle Mixed 16/24 £748
13 days, Hull-London Mixed 16/24 £682
11 days, Santa Cruz (Tenerife) Mixed 16/19 £594
14 days, Azores-Greenock Mixed 24/69 £650
*Each Northern Europe youth voyage sails up to 1000 miles and visits 2/3 foreign ports.

CONTACT	Sail Training Association
ADDRESS	2A The Hard, Portsmouth, Hants PO1 3PT, UK
PHONE	+44 2392 832055/6 FAX +44 2392 815769
E-MAIL	Tallships@sta.org.uk
WEB	http://www.sta.org.uk/sta/

Skibladner II

NATIONALITY	Danish
HOME PORT	Copenhagen
SIZE OVERALL	27.8 metres 91 feet
CREW	18

HISTORY

This Danish gaff-rigged ketch was launched over a century ago in 1897. She is now owned and operated as a sail training ship by FDF Københavns Søkreds, who took her over from FDF Sokorpset in 1987. She was built by the Danish firm of N.F. Hansen, who also constructed another regular competitor in the Cutty Sark Tall Ships' Races, Den Store Bjorn. Skibladner II traded in general cargo around the Baltic for many years and only had her first engine fitted in 1924.

ON BOARD

Usually 9 sail trainees are carried and their cruises take them on occasion as far north in the Baltic as Riga and, in 1996, for the first time to St. Petersburg whilst taking part in that year's Cutty Sark Tall Ships' Races.

CONTACT   FDF Københavns Søkreds
ADDRESS   Strandgade 36G, 1401 Kobenhavn K, Denmark

Sodade (ex Tradewind)

NATIONALITY	*Dutch*
HOME PORT	*Cabo Verde*
SIZE OVERALL	*35 metres 115 feet*
PROFESSIONAL CREW	*6*
PAYING CREW	*16 - 20*

HISTORY

Built in Holland in 1911 as a sailing ship with no engine, with the name Sophie Theresia she traded around the North Sea and the Baltic as a general cargo ship. A survivor of both World Wars, she then acquired an auxiliary engine, a deckhouse and a wheelhouse, but lost her masts and sails. She worked the Dutch and English coastal ports until 1972 when she was retired to the canals of Amsterdam as being too old and too small for further work. She was bought by a Dutch couple who decided to make her into a floating home, renaming her Aaltje en Willem. This did not work out and the old ship found her way to the scrapyard. She was rescued by a group of Dutchmen who discovered that her hull was in excellent condition, and set about restoring her. Rebuilding started in 1981 and was completed in 1986 by a new owner from New Zealand who completely re-rigged her as a traditional schooner of her era, fitting her out for charter and/or exploration work. Re-named Tradewind she sailed from London to Sydney as a part of the Australian First Fleet Re-enactment, when she proved the fastest ship in the fleet. She made a number of voyages to the Sub-Antarctic, visited the Falklands and sailed round Cape Horn to Fiji. Tradewind appeared in films such as Colombia Pictures' 'Return to the Blue Lagoon' and the French documentary 'Chronicles du Pacific Sud'. New Finnish owners in 1993 used her for day charter, sail training and discovery voyages around the Northern Baltic. In 1998 she was sold again and returned to the Dutch flag. She is now based on the Cape Verde Islands, available for charter and sail training events under her new name Sodade.

ON BOARD

Sodade is a fast and stable ship, demonstrated when she survived a 'knock down' undamaged while rounding Cape Horn. She can take up to 40 people on day cruises and has accommodation for 16 to 20 for longer cruises. Her permanent crew of six - the master, mate, cook and three deckhands.

PROGRAMME

She offer charters and sail training trips off the Cape Verde islands, from day sailing to week long cruises.

SAFETY CERTIFICATES AND INSURANCE

She used to be surveyed by the Finnish Ministry of Transport as a Special Purpose Vessel for non restricted traffic. Tradewind and her passengers are insured according to Finnish Maritime law. Under her new owners she came under Dutch rules for sailing passenger ships, intendeing to travel world-wide, under the rules of The Netherlands' Register Holland. This has required a new main-engine, a Caterpillar 440 HP and a second auxiliary engine. Accomodation has been stripped out and rebuilt according to Dutch rules for this kind of vessel.

CONTACT	Trop-Scan-Sailing-Charters Lda, Mindelo, Cabo Verde, and in Europe Kees Rol, Vechtdijk 360, NL - 3563 - ME, Utrecht, Holland
PHONE/FAX	+31 30 266 2121
PHONE ON BOARD	+49 17 525 460088

Søren Larsen

NATIONALITY	British
HOME PORT	Auckland, New Zealand
SIZE OVERALL	44 metres 145 feet
PROFESSIONAL CREW	12
PAYING voyage crew	22

HISTORY

Originally built by Søren Larsen and Sons in Denmark, she earned her living for many years as a coastal trading ship carrying general cargo around the Baltic and the north Atlantic ports of Scandinavia. In 1978 she was saved from destruction by her present owners, the Davies family in Colchester, England. There they lovingly restored the ship to the graceful late 19th century brigantine she is today. She is one of the most well known Tall Ships as the result of various roles on film and TV. She took part in the BBC/TV series 'The Onedin Line' and then appeared in 'The French Lieutenant's Woman' and the TV film about Shackleton, the Arctic explorer, which involved sailing north to the Arctic circle and into the pack-ice off Greenland.
Early in the 1980s Søren Larsen changed tack and pioneered sailing for the physically handicapped with the Jubilee Sailing Trust, introducing many hundreds of people for the first time in their lives to the joy and excitement of sailing. She then became the flagship for the Australian Bicentenary first Fleet Re-enactment Voyage, and she led a fleet of eight ships on a 22,000 mile voyage from England to Australia via Rio de Janeiro and Cape Town, to Sydney. She then sailed to New Zealand to represent Britain in the 1990 anniversary celebrations. She discovered the superb Kiwi coast and found a new home port at Auckland. With Eye of the Wind she returned to Europe in 1991/2 and they became the first British square riggers to round Cape Horn since 1936. She went on to win her class in the Grand Regatta Colombus whilst making her latest BBC TV documentary 'The Last Great Adventure'. Following an extensive refit and further restoration work in Britain she returned to New Zealand via the Caribbean, Panama, Tahiti and the South Pacific.

ON BOARD

Following her extensive refit Søren Larsen now 'trades' worldwide. Below she is fitted out in English oak and walnut, the companionway opening out into a large dining saloon that accommodates the entire crew. The very comfortable 2 and 4 berth cabins are situated amidships and adjoin the library where you can relax with a book and a drink from the bar. The Davies family specialise in adventure holidays and encourage guests to participate in all aspects of ship-board life, but nothing is compulsory and no previous sailing experience is required. The one important requirement is that all participants must be in good health. There are no minimum age limitations other than children under the age of 16 must be accompanied by an adult. Equally there is no maximum age, with the caveat that older people must be in good health and on longer voyages will be required to complete a medical questionnaire. From time to time Søren Larsen undertakes 'Special Interest' voyages for those keen, for example, in bird watching or natural history.

SAFETY CERTIFICATES AND INSURANCE

She is surveyed for worldwide voyaging by the UK's MSA, and by Bureau Veritas.

PROGRAMME

Each May to November she cruises the romantic and inaccessible islands of the South Pacific, giving adventurers of all ages a genuine 'experience of a lifetime'. From November to April she sails the New Zealand coast, following Captain Cook's tracks and allowing individuals the chance to enjoy a glimpse of traditional square rig sailing.
Here's the type of voyage she has undertaken:
5 days, Wellington to Christchurch $NZ997
3 days, Dunedin to Bluff $NZ598
7 days, Bluff to Nelson $NZ1196
17 days, Tonga-Fiji $NZ3680
13 days, Fiji-Vanuato $NZ3360
10 days, Vanuatu-New Caledonia $NZ2500
17 days, New Caledonia-Sydney 1$NZ2975
16 days, Sydney-Auckland $NZ2800
3 days, Auckland-Hauaki Gulf £235
5 days, Bay or Islands or South Island cruise £389
South Pacific islands cruises May to November
10 nights, Island Cruise Tonga or Fiji or Vanuatu or New Caledonia £975
13 or 16 nights, Blue Water Voyage NZ-Tonga £889 or Sydney-Auckland £1095
$NZ are New Zealand Dollars.
Squaresail Pacific can provide flight and hotel packages, and also required holiday insurance. Prices include all meals onboard, use of ships' equipment, snorkels, boats and safety gear.

CONTACT	Squaresail Pacific Ltd
ADDRESS	P O Box 310, Kumeu, Auckland, 1250 New Zealand
PHONE/FAX	+649 411 8484
E-MAIL	Sorenlarsen@voyage.co.nz
WEB	http://www.squaresail.Q.co.nz
	Friends of Soren Larsen UK, Patrick and Olga Grant, Leyburn, Daviot, Inverness, Scotland IV2 5XQ
PHONE/FAX	+44 1463 772031

Sørlandet

NATIONALITY	Norwegian
HOME PORT	Kristiansand
SIZE OVERALL	64.3 metres 211 feet
PROFESSIONAL CREW	16
PAYING SAIL TRAINEES	70

HISTORY

Sørlandet was built in Kristiansand in 1927. Except for a break during the war years, she operated as a merchant navy schoolship until 1973, when her owners decided that she no longer answered the needs of modern seamen. So the great grandson of the original financial backer gave her to the town of

Kristiansand, in 1977. Rather than use her as a static tourist attraction, the town decided to refit and recommission her as an adventure training ship for youngsters and adults, whether they be from Norway or from other nations. Sørlandet was the first big sailing ship to offer such a chance to all, to sail a square rigged ship, and she has been doing so since 1981 through a non-profitmaking trust Stifleisen Fullriggeren Sørlandet.

The ship began her new career in 1980 after a complete renovation which was careful to alter neither her character nor outside appearance. The old open-plan mess deck was retained but the hammocks were replaced by settee-cots, an innovation that has since been copied by other schoolships. Air conditioning was installed during another refit in 1988.

ON BOARD
Anyone over the age of 16 is eligible to sail aboard Sørlandet and no previous sailing experience is required. There is no upper age limit but those over 50 must provide a medical fitness certificate. The working language aboard is English, besides Norwegian. Instruction in basic seamanship and safety routines is given by the ship's officers and crew. Some cruises offer a specific topic or theme for which expert lecturers are carried.

Trainees are divided into three watches, each of 4 hours duration with 8 hours off. They take part in all the shipboard activities, steering, keeping lookout, maintenance, cleaning and painting ship, docking and other manoeuvres. Working aloft for handing or setting sail is not compulsory.

Each day some trainees are taken out of each watch on a rota basis to become daymen assigned to help the bosun, the cook or the steward. They have a full day's work but enjoy 'all night in' in their berths. At sea the rhythm of the watch system makes for ample time to relax and socialise and 'runs ashore' during port visits are much looked forward to. Sørlandet's adventure training formula has proved highly successful with over 90% wishing to return again.

SAFETY CERTIFICATES AND INSURANCE
Sørlandet is a Norwegian Merchant Navy ship in the Norske Veritas Class +1A 1EO and she has certificates for worldwide voyages.

Participants are covered by the ship's P&I insurance against accidents caused by fault or gross negligence of ship and crew. However all participants must have their own personal travel insurance.

PROGRAMME
Most years the ship operates 14 day public cruises during the summer holidays in the North Sea and the Baltic, although she sometimes sails further afield. Out of the summer season she undertakes private cruises, mostly under charter by the Norwegian Government for the training of naval recruits. In the winter of 1995/6 she took paying passengers to and from the West Indies.

CONTACT   Stiftelsen Fullriggeren 'Sørlandet'
ADDRESS   Gravene 2, N-4160 Kristiansand S, Norway
PHONE   +47 38 02 98 90
FAX   +47 38 02 93 34

Spirit of Boadicea

NATIONALITY	British
HOME PORT	Chatham, southern England
SIZE OVERALL	23.5 metres 77 feet
STAFF	5
CREW	12

HISTORY

Established in 1960, the owners, Ocean Youth Trust (formerly Ocean Youth Club), have the largest youth sailing fleet in Europe. They have seven yachts of about 20 metres with crews of around 16. They are based in different ports around the British Isles.

ON BOARD

The aims of OYT are for the enjoyment and adventure of life at sea, with crews of different sex, ability, social backgrounds, and ethnic origin.

The OYT takes people aged 12 and up to 24, and for those 25 and over there is a 'Friends' Membership scheme. 'Friends' sail, with other adults, on special voyages. If you can fill all 12 berths, the OYT will waive the age bands. All OYT vessels are under the command of a skipper with an RYA/DTp Yachtmaster Offshore Certificate. The Mate is an experienced person holding a Mate's certificate issued by OYT and an RYA/DTp Coastal Skipper certificate, or equivalent.

As an educational charity, OYT can offer grants for those between 12 and 24 years old, and assist in fundraising ideas. If you can't afford an OYT voyage, the club has a proud boast that no young person is unable to sail with them because of cost, with local and national bursaries available, although everyone is encouraged to contribute so that they feel that they've given something. Of young crews, over 60% have been subsidised. Where any OYT vessel calls on any of her voyages depends on the weather, but in voyages over 3 days expect one port of call, and over 6 days, two.

OYT provides all safety equipment you'll require, and wet weather gear necessary for sailing. All food is included. On an OYT voyage you can gain OYT, Royal Yachting Association and Duke of Edinburgh Award Certificates.

School and youth groups studies into the environment can be catered for.

All women voyages (staff and crew) can be arranged.

For those with special needs, all OYT yachts are fitted with audio compasses, and some handicaps can be catered for. If you have a medical condition or disability, you must send a doctor's note, and bring adequate medicines, etc. Stowage space is small on these boats - jackets and dresses are left ashore.

Each yacht has a home base support group who help fundraise, and many who sail come back to see 'their' ship time and again. One condition of sailing aboard, you have to be able to swim - 50 metres.

SAFETY CERTIFICATES AND INSURANCE

OYT Vessels are certified to the Department of Transport's Code of Practice for Sail Training Vessels.

The OYT operates within the Statutory Code of Practice (DTp) which stipulates the qualifications of the sea staff and rigorous standards for vessels and their equipment.

With so many ships in the club, it keeps its own 'once in 24 hour' reporting system from each of them.

Insurance covers most eventualities, even including loss of luggage, personal money, medical and other expenses when aboard due to illness or accident.

PROGRAMME

Spirit of Boadicea, built in 1974, was designed by Robert Clark, based on his Sir Thomas Lipton which won the 1968 Singlehanded Transatlantic Race. She was formerly Arethusa when used by Shaftesbury Homes. She covers the south east of England, including London.

Example prices would show:

Voyage	Low season	Mid season	High season
2 nights	£60	98	£135
6 nights	£169	304	£439

CONTACT	OYT London
ADDRESS	Ground Floor, 207 Waterloo Road, London SE1 8XD
PHONE	+44 171 928 1066
FAX	+44 171 928 1993

For those from Norfolk unable to afford the full cost, apply to "Norfolk Boat", Harrisons Farm House, East Tuddenham, Dereham, NR20 3NF.

TEL/FAXI	01603 881121
WEB	http://www.oyc.org.uk

Spirit of Scotland

NATIONALITY	Scottish
HOME PORT	Glasgow, western Scotland
SIZE OVERALL	28 metres 92 feet
PROFESSIONAL CREW	4
PAYING SAIL TRAINEES	12

HISTORY

In 1851 pilot cutters were a familiar sight in Liverpool Bay, west England, waiting at the mouth of the Mersey estuary for days on end, in all weathers, to guide into port large sailing merchant vessels, through narrow and shallow waters.

Spirit of Merseyside was built between 1980 and 1986, as an exact replica of one of these ships. Unemployed young people worked on her under the supervision of craftsmen who were also out of a job. By 1991, financial pressures made her horizons bleak, but she was taken over by the charity Fairbridge. Her name was changed to Spirit of Scotland.

Fairbridge is a British charity which operates in 11 inner city areas, working with young people who are deemed at risk from long-term unemployment, drug or alcohol abuse, sexual or physical abuse or involvement in crime.

Fairbridge takes referrals from many sources, including social services, education welfare officers and the probation services.

All Fairbridge's personal development programmes start with a residential course which uses challenging outdoor activities to provide opportunities to experience success and increase self esteem. Professional development training techniques help young people to realise that, despite their circumstances, they have the power to set their own goals and by working constructively with other people they can overcome the barriers to achieving them. Upon returning home, personal mentors encourage young people to build their own personal development programme which may, if applicable, include sailing on Spirit.

ON BOARD

Trainees are between 14 and 25, and for many of them it is the chance of a lifetime. For some it may only be the first or second time away from home and city life.

Each year over 240 people sail with her on various courses of different lengths.

She is based on the Clyde, but every second year she circumnavigates Britain, visiting each of the Fairbridge teams throughout the UK. Spirit has taken part in Cutty Sark Tall Ships' Races and may do more in the future. Funds come from the Government, statutory bodies, corporate sponsors, and charitable trusts.

PROGRAMME.

Spirit of Scotland is used for development courses for disadvantaged, young inner city people. Her programme mainly consists of 4-8 day sailing courses. A recent programme included: 11 days Oban to Bristol; 1 day Bristol to Cardiff; 7 days Liverpool Glasgo; 4 days Glasgow to Clyde; 4 days, Clyde to Oban; 14 days Oban to Aberdeen; 4 days Aberdeen to Torness; 1 day Torness to Leith; 4 days Leith-Hartlepool; 1 day Hartlepool to Newcastle; 8 day. Newcastle to Chatha; 1 day Chatham to London.

CONTACT Liz Anderson, Administrator
ADDRESS Spirit of Scotland, Norton Park, 57 Albion Road,Edinburgh EH7 5QY
PHONE   +44 131 475 2303   FAX   +44 131 475 2312

Stad Amsterdam

NATIONALITY	Dutch
HOME PORT	Amsterdam
SIZE OVERALL	78 metres 255.8 feet
PROFESSIONAL CREW	25
TRAINEES	68
Passengers on daytrips	125

HISTORY

In 1995, after the Cutty Sark Tall Ships' Race and Sail Amsterdam, the fleet of ships, both old and new, sailed away in a magnificent Parade of Sail. Many were acutely aware that there was no Dutch fully rigged ship to lead the fleet. The search began to put this right by the year 2000, when Amsterdam had plans for another Sail Amsterdam, and had been chosen as the final port of call for Tall Ships 2000. A partnership between the public and private sectors discussed the matter, with Amsterdam Council and the Randstad Groep leading the way. Within a year the design for a clipper was on the boards. She would be built to the style of a ship of the second half of the 19th century, from the great days of the Clipper Ships. Each of the two principals put up half the initial investment, and both will be able to use her for promotional events.

She is also to provide work experience, act as a tourist attraction in Amsterdam, and be used for sail training for youngsters. Her designer is Gerard Dijkstra, her builder is Damen Oranjewerf Amsterdam, and the fitting out is at the Maritime Museum in Amsterdam. At the Museum is another and older replica, called Amsterdam, representing the East Indiamen of the previous century. She has an engine but does not use her sails.

A new sistership to Stad Amsterdam is the Cisne Branco, to fly the Brazilian flag.

ON BOARD

Her one unusual feature is that she can have on her foremast and/or mainmast, studdingsails (see drawing). These are similar to those used by the old Clipper Ships, seen in so many paintings. The yards have extensions outwards, and when the wind is aft, sails are placed on them to speed the voyage.

SAFETY CERTIFICATES AND INSURANCE

She is a Lloyd's +100 A1 Sailing Passenger Ship +LMC, UMS. Register Holland.

PROGRAMME

After Sail 2000 Amsterdam, she will sail to ports and events as opportunity permits, with crews of young people and paying guests.

CONTACT
Rederij Clipper Stad Amsterdam
ADDRESS
s/a Kattenburgerplein 1,
1018 KK Amsterdam.
PHONE   +31 20 569 5839
FAX   +31 20 569 1720
E-MAIL
mail@stadamsterdam.nl
WEB
http:/www/.stadamsterdam.nl

"STA New Brigs"

NATIONALITY	*British*
HEADQUARTERS	*Portsmouth, southern England*
SIZE OVERALL	*59.4 metres metres 195 feet*
VOLUNTEER OFFICERS (AFTERGUARD)	*11*
PERMANENT CREW	*6*
PAYING SAIL TRAINEES.	*45*

HISTORY

The Sail Training Association (STA) was a pioneer in so many matters relating to Tall Ships, and over 30 years ago, they built two sister ships of schooner rig, Sir Winston Churchill and Malcolm Miller, of 45.72 metres (150 feet), with 5 professional crew, 11 volunteer officers and 39 trainees. These two have done first class work, but have become prohibitively expensive to maintain for such rigorous work. To continue to meet demand of the STA's mission, it was agreed to build two new ships to replace the schooners. At 195 feet, (59.4 metres), these new vessels are larger than the schooners, with better facilities and living quarters for the 45 trainees they will each carry on a voyage.

These brigs, square rigged on two masts, are being built by Appledore Shipbuilders in North Devon.

Sir Winston Churchill and Malcolm Miller were originally built to accomodate young men only, but now almost half the young people who sail with the STA are young women and mixed voyages of both sexes predominate. The new brigs are better suited to the needs of mixed crews and the more sophisticated demands of today's and tomorrow's young people. They also have modern systems for fresh water, air ventilation and waste disposal, that will make them more suitable for longer passages to more distant ports.

They are sail training ships for tomorrow's world. The build became possible with a grant of £3.5 million from the Lottery Sports Fund. Their rigs are a switch away from the schooner rig, as they will be brigs, with square sails on two masts, rather than square sails on only the first of three masts.

ON BOARD

On STA ships, the trainees are divided into three watches who do four hours on watch, and eight hours off. Each watch helps care for and maintain the ship and takes part in watch duties such as look-out, steering, sail trimming and assisting the cook in the galley. Most of the time is spent either on the bridge, perhaps taking the helm or keeping the ship's log, or working on deck or aloft. You don't have to go aloft, but most people do, for the experience of setting (letting loose) or handing (folding away) the square sails. The usual trainee age is between 16 to 24. But it isn't only this age group who can benefit. There are also mixed sex voyages for the age group 24-69. If you can't afford the voyage, there are volunteer support groups nationwide who may be able to help, from their own resources or by helping you find a sponsor. All voyages qualify for the Residential Section of the Gold Award in the Duke of Edinburgh's Award scheme and the RYA Competent Crew Certificate may also be available.

Usually voyages will be in North European waters from March to November, and for 'winter sun' voyages in the Canaries and the Azores from November to May..

SAFETY CERTIFICATES AND INSURANCE

The ships will be maintained to Lloyds Class A1 and Department of Transport standards.

PROGRAMME

The idea is to keep to the type of programme carried out by Sir Winston Churchill and Malcolm Miller, which you will find elsewhere in this book.

CONTACT	Esther Tibbs
ADDRESS	The Sail Training Association
	2A The Hard, Portsmouth, Hants PO1 3PT, UK
PHONE	+44 2392 832055/6 FAX +44 2392 815769
E-MAIL	tallships@sta.org.uk
WEB	http://www.sta.org.uk/sta/

Statsraad Lehmkuhl

NATIONALITY	Norwegian
HOME PORT	Bergen
SIZE OVERALL	97.8 metres 321 feet
PROFESSIONAL CREW	22
PAYING SAIL TRAINEES	150

HISTORY

Statsraad Lehmkuhl was built in 1914 as a three masted steel barque, at Geestermunde, near Bremerhaven, as a training ship for the German merchant navy with the name Grossherzog Friedrich August.

During World War I she was used as a stationary training ship and after 1918 she was taken as a war-prize to become Norway's largest and oldest sailing ship. But what should Norway do with her? A former Government Minister Kristoffer Lehmkuhl, who by then was the Director of the Bergen shipping line, took up her cause in 1923. She was bought by the Norwegian Shipowners Association as a sea school training ship. In gratitude for all his work, she was re-named 'Statsraad' (which means 'Minister') Lehmkuhl. Her maiden voyage was a five month school training cruise for some 200 boys and thereafter she continued with her sail training role, except for the Second World War, when she was confiscated by the Germans. By the early 1970s ever increasing operating costs forces her to be laid-up in Bergen. In 1978 her owner Hilmar Reksten donated her to the Statsraad Lehmkuhl Foundation which in 1986 put her back into a seaworthy condition.

ON BOARD
She offers the basics of sailing a traditional square-rigged ship, with instruction in boat handling, navigation, rules of the road and practical seamanship. The ship's galley provides all meals on board but does not cater for special diets or eating habits. Travel to join and leave the ship is not covered in the fee. Sleeping is in hammocks on the gun deck, and you must take a sleeping bag.

SAFETY CERTIFICATES AND INSURANCE
It is mandatory to take out medical insurance to cover accident, illness and hospitalisation.

PROGRAMME
Cruises open to all might include: 5 days Bergen-Kiel NOK2850; 9 days Eemshaven (Holland)-Stockholm NOK4975; 3 days Stockholm-Mariehamn (Åland Islands Finland) NOK1800; 6 days Mariehamn-Karlskrona (Sweden) NOK2950; 5 days Karlskrona-Rostock (Germany) NOK2450; 5 days Rostock-Bérgen (Norway) NOK2400. Prices include all meals.

CONTACT   Stiftelsen Seilskipet Statsraad Lehmkuhl
ADDRESS   Skur 7, Bradbenken, N-5003, Bergen, Norway
PHONE   +47 5532 25 86
FAX   +47 5532 08 79
ON BOARD PHONE
+47 55 31 33 06
E-MAIL   lehmkuhl@lehmkuhl.no
WEB   http://www.lehmkuhl.no

Swan

LOCATION	Shetland Islands
HOME PORT	Lerwick
SIZE OVERALL	20.7 metres 68 feet
CREW	4
DAY TRIPS	11

HISTORY

At the turn of the century, two types of sail fishing vessels dominated the hundreds which packed into Lerwick for the summer herring season, the Fifies, with vertical sterns and stern posts, and the Zulus with a raking stern. They were unique to the Scottish herring fleets. Swan, a Fifie, took to the water in 1900, but before long steam drifters were pushing sail out of business. In 1935 Swan was only one of five herring sailboats left in Shetland. She had an engine fitted which gave her a new lease of life. In the 1950s she was retired and moved south to Hartlepool to become a houseboat. Found there by Shetland enthusiasts, the Swan Trust was formed in 1990 to give her new life, to purchase, restore and operate her as a living museum and sail training vessel. She relaunched in 1994.

ON BOARD

One main objective was to encourage the young to sail her and keep alive the techniques of sailing and of working a traditional Fifie. Special efforts are made to ensure she is available to local schools, She is indeed available to any school, youth club, business or private individual.

SAFETY CERTIFICATES AND INSURANCE

Swan conforms to the requirements of the Department of Transport's Code of Practice for Small Commercial Sailing Vessels.

PROGRAMME

Swan sails mainly out of Lerwick from April to October, with many local trips and longer charters to ports in north west Europe. The very young are normally afloat for up to 2 hours, primary school children for 3 to 4 hours, and older primaries maybe a day. Secondary classes can sail for anything upwards to a week, perhaps to Norway and back.
Her three paying categories are

	Day sail	Half-day	Overnight
Child under 11	£13	£7.50	£26
Youth 11 to 18	£21	£11.50	£42
Adult 18+	£26	£13.50	£53

CONTACT	The Swan Trust
ADDRESS	119 North Road, Lerwick, Shetland Isles ZE1 OPR
PHONE	+44 1595 697 406
MOBILE	0441 182 430
WEB	http://www.shetland-news.co.uk/websites/swan

Swan fan Makkum

NATIONALITY	*Dutch*
HOME PORT	*Makkum*
SIZE OVERALL	*61 metres 200 feet*
PROFESSIONAL CREW	*14*
PAYING VISITORS	*36 (up to 120 for daytrips)*

HISTORY

Swan fan Makkum was built in 1993, as the world's largest brigantine (two masts, with square sails on the first mast) and was designed by van Meer. Her hull is steel, and so are her masts and yards. She has a partly wooden superstructure, Iroko decks, and her topmast, mainboom, bowsprit, gaff and jibboom are also of wood.

ON BOARD

She has an especially large saloon/dining room and a comfortable lounge in which to relax.

While all the modern comforts are below, above she looks very like the sailing ships which plied the ocean in the 19th Century. On 'Swan', you can lie back in a deck chair, and watch the bustle of setting sails and sailing a tall ship, or you can take part, if you wish. For though comfort is a key, she is also a fast ship which likes to join in with others in the sail training fleets.

SAFETY CERTIFICATES AND INSURANCE

She is registered in Holland as Z1234+ (z = seagoing, 1234 = trading areas and together 1234 means all areas, worldwide, + indicates newly built ships under the Holland register).

PROGRAMME

Her main task is as a charter ship, for companies going on summer day cruises in the Baltic, from her base in Kiel. Up to 120 passengers can be carried in some style. She cruises two weeks at a time in the Baltic, North Sea and Mediterranean in the summer time, and during the winter off she goes to the Caribbean, for weekly or two weekly cruises, from December to April. Here the numbers on board are rather more limited, with 36

visitors in 16 double cabins.

She has also proved a worthwhile ship to charter for the Cutty Sark Tall Ships' Races, and her main rival in speed has been the quite different four master Sedov, with whom she has had friendly encounters.

Her latest Tall Ships events in 1997, 1998 and 1999 were with Cutty Sark Scots Whisky sponsored trainees on board.

CONTACT	Monique Touw, Swan fan Makkum
ADDRESS	Achterdijkje 8, 8754 EP, Makkum, The Netherlands
PHONE	+31 515 231712
FAX	+31 515 232998
E-Mail	swanfan@wxs.nl

Taikoo

NATIONALITY	*British*
HOME PORT	*Southampton, southern England*
SIZE OVERALL	*22 metres 72 feet*
STAFF	*5*
CREW	*12*

HISTORY

Established in 1960, the owners,Ocean Youth Trust (formerly the Ocean Youth Club), have the largest youth sailing fleet in Europe. They have seven yachts of about 20 metres with crews of around 16. They are based in different ports around the British Isles.

ON BOARD

The aims of OYT are for the enjoyment and adventure of life at sea, with crews of different sex, ability, social backgrounds, and ethnic origin.

The OYT takes people aged 12 and up to 24, and for those 25 and over there is a 'Friends' Membership scheme. 'Friends' sail, with other adults, on special voyages. If you can fill all 12 berths, the OYT will waive the age bands. All OYT vessels are under the command of a skipper with an RYA/DTp Yachtmaster Offshore Certificate. The Mate is an experienced person holding a Mate's certificate issued by OYT and an RYA/DTp Coastal Skipper certificate, or equivalent.

As an educational charity, OYT can offer grants for those between 12 and 24 years old, and assist in fundraising ideas. If you can't afford an OYT voyage, the club has a proud boast that no young person is unable to sail with them because of cost, with local and national bursaries available, although everyone is encouraged to contribute so that they feel that they've given something. Of young crews, over 60% have been subsidised. Where any OYT vessel calls on any of her voyages depends on the weather, but in voyages over 3 days expect one port of call, and over 6 days, two.

OYT provides all safety equipment you'll require, and wet weather gear necessary for sailing. All food is included. On an OYT voyage you can gain OYT, Royal Yachting Association and Duke of Edinburgh Award Certificates. School and youth groups studies into the environment can be catered for.

All women voyages (staff and crew) can be arranged.

For those with special needs, all OYT yachts are fitted with audio compasses, and some handicaps can be catered for. If you have a medical condition or disability, you must send a doctor's note, and bring adequate medicines, etc. Stowage space is small on these boats - jackets and dresses are left ashore.

Each yacht has a home base

support group who help fundraise, and many who sail come back to see 'their' ship time and again.

One condition of sailing aboard, you have to be able to swim - 50 metres.

SAFETY CERTIFICATES AND INSURANCE

OYT Vessels are certified to the Department of Transport's Code of Practice for Sail Training Vessels.

The OYT operates within the Statutory Code of Practice (DTp) which stipulates the qualifications of the sea staff and rigorous standards for vessels and their equipment.

With so many ships in the club, it keeps its own 'once in 24 hour' reporting system from each of them.

Insurance covers most eventualities, even including loss of luggage, personal money, medical and other expenses when aboard due to illness or accident.

PROGRAMME

Taikoo was designed by Robert Clark in 1973, based on his Sir Thomas Lipton, winner of the 1968 Singlehndedd Transatlantic Race. Her south coast programme includes visits to the Channel Islands and France.

Example prices would show:

Voyage	Low season	Mid season	High season
2 nights	£60	£98	£135
6 nights	£169	£304	£439

CONTACT	OYT South
ADDRESS	The Bus Station, South Street, Gosport Hants PO12 1EP, England
PHONE	+44 2392 501211 FAX +44 2392 522069
WEB	http://www.oyc.org.uk

Tangaroa

NATIONALITY	British
HOME PORT	Southampton, southern England
SIZE OVERALL	25 metres 82 feet
PROFESSIONAL CREW	2/3
GUESTS	8/12 maximum

HISTORY

Built by Søren Larsen of Nykøbing Mors in 1925, Tangeroa began life as a Danish fishing vessel . One of the last sailing boats built there, she kept fishing until 1988. Found that year in Esbjerg west Denmark under the name Bikea, she had a thorough survey and was taken to Hayling Island on the south coast of England for restoration. After over 2 years of work she is now transformed , thanks to her owner Tony Athill, to her primary job as a sailing charter ship.
Tangaroa is a New Zealand Maori word meaning 'God of the Sea'.

ON BOARD

Although not primarily used for sail training purposes, Tangaroa is equipped for this role. The accommodation is designed to provide all modern comforts while retaining traditional appearance with original oak beams, panelled doors and a wood burning stove.

There are four guest cabins, each of which has a double over a single bunk. Above, the airy deckhouse provides an area in which to relax and it also houses the navigation area. There is a full time professional skipper and a cook/mate. Guests are encouraged to participate in all aspects of running the ship though this is not compulsory.

PROGRAMME

She usually visits Ireland, France, the Channel Isles and the south coast of the UK. She visits most maritime festivals and is available for corporate events at these and at Cowes Week, and she has achieved good results in Team Building and Management Development. Berths are available for selected cruises on a per head basis (8 max), or booked by whole groups of up to 12. Trips range from a weekend in the Solent to 2 weeks anywhere in northern Europe. The cost per head per day is from £45.

CONTACT	Tangaroa Yachting
ADDRESS	Harbour House, Town Quay, Southampton, SO14 2AQ, UK
PHONE	+44 2380 636878 FAX +44 2380 636879
E-MAIL.	AAthill@aol.com
WEB	httpp://members.aol.com/sailhol

Thor Heyerdahl

NATIONALITY	German
HOME PORT	Kiel, northern Germany
SIZE OVERALL	50 metres 164 feet
PROFESSIONAL CREW	12
PAYING SAIL TRAINEES	32

HISTORY

Built in Holland in 1930, her present owners bought the hull in 1979 at scrap value and restored her at HDW at Kiel with the help of many friends, until 1983 when she was ready to take to the oceans again. The rig of a topsail schooner (which has some square sails on her foremast) was chosen, as it is a classic rig for working up and down a coast. Thor Heyerdahl is a solid and weatherly ship, built of riveted steel with wooden masts and spars with steelwire for the standing rigging.

She is capable of undertaking long voyages, as far as the islands in the Caribbean and further south. Like many other large sail training ships she earns her keep after her sail training summer season through charter work and long distance cruises to a warmer climate away from the European winter.

ON BOARD

When sail training she aims to further the development of responsibility of the young trainees, to help them find their limits and widen their horizons. To accomplish this, a novel system is used at the end of any voyage. After passing the necessary tests, the trainees take over the ship for a day or more. They have to help each other with teamwork and co-operation. This is the foundation of the ship's programme, to learn and to work together, and still have some fun. On board, trainees experience a traditionally rigged schooner under the guidance of an instructor, but there is no need to know anything about sailing to join in. The 32 trainees live in ten cabins amidships and everyone participates in the three watch system, which means four hours on duty, and eight hours off.

SAFETY CERTIFICATES AND INSURANCE

Thor Heyerdahl's membership of the German section of the International Sail Training Association under the number TSG 342 means that she complies with the safety regulations of that international organisation. She is equipped to SBG standards (German authorities). Her technical equipment is classified by the Germanischer Lloyd. She is manned to GSHW specifications.

The ship has insurance against accidents and third party liability, but generally speaking insurance is up to individual trainees.

PROGRAMME

A typical year may include: 6 days in the Danish Isles; 1 day Kiel Fjord; 11 days Norway, Sweden, Poland; 8 days, school groups; 14 days Carribean, South and North America.

CONTACT	Friedrich Bæßmann
ADDRESS	Segelschiff "Thor Heyerdahl" e.V. Kaistraße 33, D-24103, Kiel, Germany
PHONE	+49 431 67 77 57 FAX +49 431 67 83 67
E-MAIL	info@thor-heyerdahl.ki.uunet.de
WEB	http://www.pweb.uunet.de/thor_heyerdahl.ki

Ubena von Bremen

NATIONALITY	German
HOME PORT	Bremerhaven, north west Germany
SIZE OVERALL	23.2 metres 76 feet
PROFESSIONAL CREW	4
PAYING SAIL TRAINEES	12

HISTORY

Between the 11th and 15th centuries a score of merchant cities flourished around the North Sea and the Baltic, from Bruges and Bremen to Danzig and Novgorod. They were known as the Hanseatic League and - apart from Denmark which opposed their activities - the League controlled and kept safe any trade by sea. A special type of ship developed, known as 'cog-ships'. Ubena von Bremen is an exact copy of one whose remains, dating from 1380, were discovered in 1962 in the mud of the River Weser during dredging. The previous cargo carriers, Viking ships of 400 years before, had a cargo capacity of only about 8 tons. These Cogs could carry 80 to 200 tons.

The Cog discovered in the Weser was comparatively complete and she has been re-assembled and reconstructed at Bremerhaven by the German National Maritime Museum and is now being preserved in a polyethyleneglycol bath, using techniques similar to the preservation of the Swedish warship Wasa and Britain's Mary Rose.

The new Ubena von Bremen's lines and dimensions have been taken from the re-discovered original and great efforts have been made to re-create her sail plan and rig, helped by illustrations found on coins, carvings and even carpets. The result of this detective work has been to produce as closely as possible a ship which in her time was revolutionary in the art of shipbuilding. A private non-profit club, The Hansekogge-Werft Bremerhaven was founded in 1987 to undertake the recreation of this ship and to learn how she should be sailed. Like the original her hull and deck is built entirely of oak. The single mast is 21 metres tall, (68 feet) and the single square-sail is 200 sq metres (2150 sq ft). She was launched in 1990 and on her maiden voyage she visited ports in Northern Germany, and along the Baltic coast.

ON BOARD

Below she has accommodation for 16 people with up to date navigational equipment, plus an engine. The crew and trainees are all volunteers who have the opportunity to experience and learn how to sail the ship, and in particular discover how to tack against the wind. The crew have found that the loaded ship has a speed of about 6 knots in a force 5 wind. Experiments with the sail plan show that two rows of 'bonnets' may have been fastened along the foot of the mainsail and a loose footed jib may have been used to enhance performance to windward.

SAFETY CERTIFICATES AND INSURANCE

She is certified by Germanischer Lloyd and carries insurance for trainees and crew.

PROGRAMME

Her destinations vary but she likes to be at sailing events, including some Cutty Sark ports, and visits which included in 1997 the City of Gdansk in Poland for the 1000th anniversary of that port's foundation, and in 1998 to the Baltic (Kiel, and to Travemünde, Rostock, Wismar, Stralsund, Sassnitz-Rügen), and in the North Sea.

CONTACT	Hanse-Koggewerft e.V.
ADDRESS	Alter Fährweg 8, D-27568 Bremerhaven, Germany
PHONE	+49 471 946090
FAX	+49 471 946 0999

Vegewind

NATIONALITY	*German*
HOME PORT	*Bremen, western Germany*
SIZE OVERALL	*19.9 metres 65 feet*
CREW	*14*

CONTACT	Capt Klaus Tietze-Scheer
ADDRESS	Navigator sail training e.V. Alte Hafenstr. 26, 28757 Bremen
PHONE	+49 421 65 63 19
FAX	+49 421 65 64 78
E-MAIL	navigator.bremen@t-online.de
WEB	http://www.hansekogge.de/page/toerns

HISTORY

Vegewind is from the fleet of the European foundation, EUROCO, based in Bremen and founded in 1986 to encourage educational youth exchanges and sail training. Vegewind, launched in 1992, was designed and built by AUCOOP Bootswerkstatt which also organises sailing programmes in the Bremen area and abroad, for young people. As well as local Baltic and North Sea cruises, Vegewind makes voyages to the Mediterranean.

ON BOARD

Designed as a fast passage-making yacht Vegewind's 14 guests live mainly in 2 berth cabins. Other berths are in 'open-plan' areas. Facilities include a large open saloon, workshop, galley and navigation area. The saloon also doubles as a classroom. Her schooner rig sets 1940 sq ft of sail to windward. This sail area, her flat racing hull and her fin keel make her fast enough to fit more voyages into her annual cruise pattern. As well as carrying students and sail trainees the yacht also offers courses for skipper training and navigational trips.

PROGRAMME

From March she undertakes youth programmes in the North Sea area, including the Cutty Sark Tall Ships' Races. In November she leaves for the Mediterranean and sails in the Balearic Isles.

Vida

NATIONALITY	Swedish
HOME PORT	Stockholm
SIZE OVERALL	41.1 metres 135 feet
PROFESSIONAL CREW	10
PAYING SAIL TRAINEES	18

HISTORY
Vida was built at Vlaardingen, The Netherlands, in 1916. For several years she fished the North Sea under the Dutch flag, but in 1931 she was sold to Karlshamn's Dockyard in the south of Sweden. Her sail area was cut back, her engines increased in size and power, to make her a motor driven freighter. In 1942 an extra 6.4 metres of midsection was added, and she was re-rigged as a three masted schooner. Her switch between power and sail continued, and later, the rigging was completely removed and she traded solely under motor in Lake Malaren and the Baltic.
In the 1970s the search for commercial cargos for such small vessels became more and more difficult to find, so a group of enthusiasts bought her, to convert her back to sailing for charter. At first, lack of resources made this impossible, so in 1980 most of the old owners were bought out and new ones joined, providing fresh capital, work-force and enthusiasm. To-day, after 70,000 hours of hard work, Vida is a fine, comfortable ocean going sailing vessel.
To start her new career, she hosted business conferences in the Stockholm Archipelago. From 1987 to 1992 she sailed around the world with a paying crew on board. In 1993, she once more sailed as a charter ship in the Archipelago and Baltic, and she also took part in that year's Cutty Sark Tall Ships' Race in the

North Sea. In the winter of 1994/5 she shifted base and chartered in the Canary Islands. In the winter of 1996-7 she chartered in the Caribbean, and in the winter of 1997-8 she remained in Stockholm.

ON BOARD
Her voyages in the Caribbean, allow crews to experience the best of warm water sailing. She is available for normal or for sail training charters.

SAFETY CERTIFICATES AND INSURANCE
Vida is approved and certified for ocean cruises by the Royal Swedish Board of Navigation. Personal insurance for paying crew is not included in the Programme fee.

PROGRAMME
She is only an occasional sail training ship. Her main programme is charter in the Caribbean from December to the middle of March, with tours starting from Antigua along the chain of the Windward Islands and back. Her voyage home to Stockholm begins in March. Ordinary charter in the Stockholm Archipelago is from the end of May to the middle of September. Sailing to the Caribbean starts at the end of September from Stockholm.

CONTACT	Ake Fridell, Managing Director
ADDRESS	s/v VIDA, PO BOX 3233, S-103 64 Stockholm, Sweden
PHONE	+46 8611 0050 FAX +46 8678 8726

Williwaw

NATIONALITY	*Belgian*
SIZE OVERALL	*14.5 metres 47.6 feet*

HISTORY

The Sail Training Association of Belgium had for years no ship of its own. Members chartered, for races such as the 1998 Cutty Sark Tall Ships' Races when they sailed Lord of the Dance, a twenty year old white sloop of 11.7 metres. By late 1998 came the good news: at last STABelgium was offered a ship of its own, and a famous one at that. Williwaw was built in Thuin, Belgium, in 1970, to the plans of Omoo, a yacht that made a round the world voyage in 1954. Her designer was L. van de Wiele. Williwaw also made a round the world trip in 1970. In 1977 she was reinforced for polar navigation and made the North West passage from Greenland through the Bering Straight. Stopping at Vancouver, she sailed south and reached Antarctica in 1979. When she returned to Belgium, she became the first vessel in the world to have circumnavigated the American continent, anti-clockwise. In 1996 the Association 'Friends of the National Maritime Museum' bought her from her owner Willy de Roos and made a gift of her to the City of Antwerp, owner of the National Maritime Museum, with the aim of conserving this historic vessel, They in turn have

entrusted her for five years to STABelgium. Restored in 1998-99 by Danny Ghys, assisted by up to 18 enthusiastic youngsters, she will become a living museum ship and whenever possible she will compete in Cutty Sark Tall Ships' Races. Proof of Belgium's increased interest in sail training is another project, to build a successor to Belgium's former large sail training ship Mercator, now a museum ship at Ostend, but she has emerged under sail, recently.

CONTACT	STA Belgium,
ADDRESS	Grote Singel 6, B-2900 Schoten, Belgium.
Phone AND FAX	+32 3 658 0006.
e mail	gvdd.advo@glo.be
WEB	rttp://promin.net/mercator

Yuniy Baltiets

NATIONALITY	*Russian*
HOME PORT	*St. Petersburg*
SIZE OVERALL	*46.4 metres 152 feet*
PROFESSIONAL CREW	*15*
TRAINEES	*36*

HISTORY

Designed and built at the Baltic Shipyard at St. Petersburg in 1989, she is the first and only large sail training ship built in Russia since 1913, as the other Russian tall ships were all built in foreign yards. Her design was influenced by former ships' boys, who insisted on a high degree of seaworthiness.
Owner is the St. Petersburg Palace of Youth Creation (formerly the Leningrad School of Pioneers) and she is a sailing school for those 14 to 17 years old studying in the Maritime Club 'Yunga'. Students would like to be professional sailors, or to learn as a hobby.
She attends many functions at ports, including Kieler Woche, and Hansa Sail, and she can take up to 12 people as paying trainees.

CONTACT	Evgeny Okulich
ADDRESS	39 Nevsky av, St. Petersburg 191011, Russia
PHONE +7 812 2740731/3105421	FAX +7 812 3108577/2170682

Xylonite and Queen Galadriel

NATIONALITY	British
HOME PORT	Maldon, eastern England
XYLONITE	26.2 metres 86 feet
XYLONITE PROFESSIONAL CREW	2
XYLONITE PAYING SAIL TRAINEES	12
QUEEN GALADRIEL	30.5 metres 100 feet
QUEEN GALADRIEL PROFESSIONAL CREW	3
QUEEN GALADRIEL TRAINEES	17

HISTORY

The Cirdan Trust Sailing School now has three sailing ships based in east England, a converted Baltic Trader named Queen Galadriel, Xylonite a Thames Barge, and Duet of 19.2 metres (63 feet) has recently joined, and has a seprate listing in our Guide.

ON BOARD

The School's aim is for youngsters to taste the adventure of sailing in larger ships, with youth organisation leaders deciding exactly what they want of a voyage. You can come aboard for a weekend, up to a fortnight, with mixed crews if necessary, and the lower limit is 10 years of age.

PROGRAMME

Xylonite (below) and Queen Galadriel (above) sail along the east coast of England, with its well protected waters, and sometimes to distant shores. The cost for individuals is £12 a day, with food extra. Group bookings can gain generous discounts. Royal Yachting Association courses are run, for instance Competent Crew and Day Skipper, on five day courses costing £195, including food on board, harbour dues, and all tuition. Eighteen courses are held each year. Three courses are also held in preparation for Coastal Skipper/Yachtmaster Offshore certificates, in five day courses costing £250 - £275. The price does not include the RYA examination fee, which can take place after the course.

CONTACT
The Cirdan Trust
ADDRESS
Fullbridge Wharf, Maldon, Essex CM9 7LE,UK
PHONE
+44 1621 851433
FAX
+44 1621 840045

LIST II. Ships where you can get berths on board, but which are seldom seen in our chosen area (North Atlantic; North Sea, Baltic). They usually stay further afield, but could be of interest to the more adventurous.

Akogare

NATIONALITY	*Japanese*
HOME PORT	*City of Osaka, south Japan*
SIZE OVERALL	*52.2 metres 171.2 feet*
PROFESSIONAL CREW	*12*
PAYING SAIL TRAINEES	*40*

HISTORY

Akogare (meaning 'yearning') was built by Sumitomo Heavy Industries and completed in 1993 for the City of Osaka, as its first ship designed to carry out a sail training programme.

ON BOARD

A number of courses are offered, from one day cruises, to an introductory course which includes up to three nights on board, and a cruise course which includes up to more than four nights on board.

An authorised overseas course with international exchange is also included.

On her sail is a logo expressing her philosophy, of a sun emerging over the horizon, expressing the bowed beauty and strength of sail, with the curve arching upwards signifying human striving towards its goal. As the ship document states "A profound spiritual strength and the feeling of compassion towards others are nurtured through life together on board such a small world as a ship".

The introductory programme is for one day, for one night and two days, or for up to three nights and four days on board, with those eligible from ten years or older 'as of the day the ship sets sail'. One day courses start with ropework and instruction on the very first steps in sail handling, with experience of working the mast, during a four hour course. If you take part overnight, you get the same, plus the experience of 'riding the wind', and learning the skills necessary to navigate, such as learning how to calculate the ship's direction using navigation equipment, experiencing astronomical observation, polishing the deck and dishing out meals.

On the cruise programmes, you also work the masts as soon as you set sail, and operate the anchor. You can also learn to navigate.

PROGRAMME

For those living, working or studying in Osaka, the rate for the one day course is 3,000 yen for under 19s, and 4,000 yen for over 19 year olds, with 11,000 per night for the overnight course for the under 19s, and 16,000 yen for the over 19s.

For those outside of Osaka, the rates are 3,500 and 4,500 for one day courses, and 12,000 and 17,000 yen per night, for overnight courses.

From the seventh night on board, the basic fares are 25% less, and from the 13th night, 50% less. There are discounts of 20% for groups of 30 to 40; and for overnight courses, if the group is 20 to 25 people. For those who have already participated, there is a 20% discount.

Akogare sails out of Osaka, but on occasion undertakes longer voyages - thus during the Hong Kong to Osaka event of 1997.

CONTACT	Goro Taniguchi
ADDRESS	O's 636 ATC Building, 2-1-10 Nanko-kita, Suminoe-ku, Osaka 559 Japan
PHONE	+81 6 615 5381 FAX +81 6 615 5384

Alma Doepel

NATIONALITY	*Australian*
HOME PORT	*Melbourne, Victoria*
SIZE OVERALL	*45.5 metres 149 feet*
PROFESSIONAL CREW	*16*
PAYING SAIL TRAINEES	*36*

HISTORY

Alma Doepel was launched in 1903, built from local timber at Bellingen in Northern New South Wales for the trader and shipping entrepreneur Frederick Doepel, who named her after his daughter. This 3 masted topsail schooner proved a fast ship and in her first year plying the Tasman sea she set a record for the fastest voyage there by a sailing ship, and she became a familiar sight during the next 12 years in ports all along Australia's east coast. She changed owners in 1917 and traded between Hobart (Tasmania) and the mainland. As part of the 'Mosquito Fleet' she established a record sailing from Hobart to Melbourne Heads in 58 hours 30 mins. She was the only trading ship in the Bass Strait to carry square sails. In the Second World War Alma Doepel was requisitioned by the Australian Army and de-rigged to serve in the New Guinea area carrying supplies and troops. Post war she was re-rigged as a 3 mast 'bald-head' schooner and resumed trading across the Bass Strait. Later she became a limestone carrier in Tasmania. After lying idle for a year she was bought in 1976 for the scrap value of her engines and restored as a sail training ship. Initial restoration was slow. She was taken to Williamstown and spent 17 months there while supporters cleaned the hull below decks. In May 1978 the Port of Melbourne allowed the use of a berth and store facilities at 12 North Wharf and restoration moved forward at a greater pace. By early 1984 Alma Doepel was not wholly renovated, yet she appeared for the first time since 1937 with her square sails. Now complete, this historic vessel is fitted out with good accommodation and has modern safety and navigation equipment.

ON BOARD

She can take up to 100 passengers on day cruises and has accommodation for 36 excluding permanent crew. She runs six 9 day voyages each year which are confined to Port Philip Bay and timed to coincide with local school holidays. These voyages take mixed sex groups between 16-19 years old. Also she is available to schools for 3 hour excursions in the local Melbourne area to introduce students to life at sea.

SAFETY CERTIFICATES AND INSURANCE

She is surveyed by the Marine Board of Victoria, and is fully equipped with safety devices. Personal insurance is included in the voyage fees.

CONTACT	Sonia Russell
ADDRESS	P O Box 157, Port Melbourne, Victoria 3207, Australia
PHONE	+61 3 9646 5211
FAX	+61 3 9646 5604
SHIP'S PHONE	+61 018 364 307

Bill of Rights

NATIONALITY	USA
HOME PORT	Philadelphia
SIZE OVERALL	39.3 metres 129 feet
PERMANENT CREW	5-8
INSTRUCTORS	5
TRAINEES/APPRENTICES	52 day 39 overnight

HISTORY
Bill of Rights is a replica of an 1856 schooner which, from her launch in 1970, sailed for charter and was bought for charter by VisionQuest in 1987.

SAFETY CERTIFICATES AND INSURANCE
She is a registered as a Passenger Vessel (Subchapter T), indicating she is a small passenger vessel under 100 gross tons carrying passengers for hire, and required to pass regular US Coastguard inspections of the ship and her onboard equipment.

PROGRAMME
VisionQuest has two vessels, and Bill of Rights is one. Their trainees are usually young people referred to them, either privately or by court referral, giving an alternative to prison, to those who might benefit from eight months at sea under skilled supervision. A crew includes 19 youths, 10 treatment staff and 3 seamen. The trainees spend five days a week at sea. Bill of Rights sails in Maine in summer, and Florida in winter.

CONTACT	VisionQuest National Ltd.
ADDRESS	PO Box 447, Exton, Philadelphia PA 19341
PHONE	+1 602 881 3950

Brilliant

NATIONALITY	USA
HOME PORT	*Mystic Seaport*
SIZE OVERALL	*18.6 metres 61 feet*
CREW	*3 day 4 overnight*
TRAINEES	*10 day 6 overnight*

HISTORY
Designed by the brothers Rod and Olin Stephens of the US's Sparkman and Stephens design team in 1932, she raced frequently, including several times in one of the world's classics, the Newport-Bermuda Race. In 1953, she was donated to Mystic Seaport, which has run her ever since.

SAFETY CERTIFICATES AND INSURANCE
She complies with the Coast Guard's Subchapter R (as a sailing school vessel) and Subchapter T (as a passenger vessel).

PROGRAMME
In spring and autumn she runs adult voyages, while in the summer it is the turn of teenagers. Varied programmes include Friday to Monday 4 day cruises, 6 day cruises from Sunday through to Friday, and 14 day voyages. Along the coast, you don't have to have previous experience, but for the longer passages, you do. All must be able to swim. Individuals are welcome, as are groups - with the typical group (such as a scout group) of an adult and nine teenagers.

Her sailing ground is mainly in New England, Nova Scotia, and Chesapeake Bay.

The cost per day is $125 a person, or $110 per person a day, for groups.

CONTACT	George H.Moffett
ADDRESS	Museum Education Department, Mystic Seaport, Box 6000, Mystic, Connecticut CT 06355 0990
PHONE	+1 860 572 0711
FAX	+1 860 572 5328
Web	http:/www.mysticseaport.org

Challenge of Outward Bound

NATIONALITY	Australian
HOME PORT	Sydney
SIZE OVERALL	27 metres 89 feet
PROFESSIONAL CREW	4
PAYING SAIL TRAINEES	20

HISTORY

Outward Bound Australia is an independent non-profit educational organisation which operates sail training courses for a very wide range of people, children, school students, adults, management trainees and other special interest groups.

The first Outward Bound school was established by Lawrence Holt and the German born educator Dr. Kurt Hahn, who between them developed a sea training course which was all about young men developing an inner strength, a tenacity of spirit, and a compassion for others. From this beginning Outward Bound schools have now spread to over 40 countries

The Australian Outward Bound movement began in 1941 thanks to the efforts of Lawrence Holt of the Liverpool based Blue Funnel shipping line. It was wartime and Holt regretted the passing of the square-riggers which had fostered and developed in seamen a sense of wind and weather and self-reliance. It was the lack of these qualities that seemed to Holt to be responsible for the tragic loss of so many young seafarers' lives through enemy action during the Battle of the Atlantic.

In 1991 Outward Bound bought their first ship, Challenge of Outward Bound. She had been built in Thailand from rainforest timber 25 years earlier and, then called Shah Nijima, she was a trading vessel who then sailed to Darwin with over 100 refugees aboard. There she was converted to a 3 masted schooner and registered as a sail training vessel.

ON BOARD

The ship runs Australian Yachting Federation (AYF) endorsed sail training programmes and she serves as a place for basic sail training, expedition preparation, plus all the thrills of large ship sailing. She is also used as a base for other fun expeditions including rock climbing, abseiling, and overnight camping. Aboard, accommodation is informal and communal and the original trading boat style has been preserved with bunks lining each side of the main hold. Toilets are fitted in the fo'c'sle and in 1997 shower facilities were added. Trainees on Classic Challenge, Adult and Womens' programmes are able to complete their AYF Competent Crew Certificate.

SAFETY CERTIFICATES AND INSURANCE

Challenge of Outward Bound has an Australian commercial survey class 2D. And she is registered as a sail training vessel by the AYF enabling her to operate with trainees aboard in partially enclosed waters. This means the sheltered waters of Broken Bay, Hawkesbury River Estuary, Pittwater, Brisbane Waters and Sydney Harbour. She is fully covered for public liability. Personal insurance, if desired, can be applied for on enrolment.

SAILING PROGRAMMES

Public and Corporate cruises are offered, ranging from a one day 'Come'n Sea' experience up to the 22 day Classic Challenge on Broken Bay and the surrounding Hawkesbury River region. Programmes run throughout the year for schools, corporations, disabled and disadvantaged groups. The peak season is from September through to April inclusive

CONTACT	Rupert Good - Senior Manager - Marine Operations
ADDRESS	8 George Street, Brooklyn, NSW 2083, Australia
PHONE	+61 2 9985 7078 FAX +61 2 9985 7079
E-MAIL	rupertg@outwardbound.com.au
WEB	http://www.outwardbound.com.au

Concordia

NATIONALITY	Canadian
HOME PORT	Nassau, Bahamas
SIZE OVERALL	57 metres 188 feet
PROFESSIONAL CREW	8
TRAINEES	8
CO-EDS	48

HISTORY

Built in 1992, she was designed by West Island College International as a floating campus. She was built to rigorous standards for safety and to be as comfortable as possible for the five and ten month voyages which would take her crew worldwide. She was given a barquentine rig as the best compromise between the tradition of a square rig and the efficiency of fore and aft sails. As the vessel is on a tight schedule, this rig allows sailing closer to the wind and motor sailing when required to get her to her destinations.

She is owned by Class Afloat, a nonprofit educational programme affiliated with high schools across the United States and Canada. The mission is to broaden students' understanding of international issues while preparing them for responsible global citizenship in the 21st Century. The concept is to "take the classroom to the world", intended to encourage self-sufficiency, cooperation, and a clear awareness of other cultures. Each semester, 48 students work as crew and study aboard her.

A fully certified faculty instructs students in a curriculum that includes social studies and global issues, anthropology, marine biology, and physical education. Courses are also offered in seamanship, celestial navigation, and the history and traditions of the sea.

ON BOARD

Between decks she accommodates 48 students in twelve 4-berth cabins, each with heads (WCs), shower and air conditioning. Since students are at sea for at least 5 months, generally in tropical latitudes, little consideration was given to 'traditional' hardships which are generally a part of 'tall ship' sailing. The 16 working crew are in 2 berth cabins.

SAFETY CERTIFICATES AND INSURANCE

She is certified for sailing worldwide without restriction.

SAILING PROGRAMMES

Over 500 international students have joined Class Afloat and sailed the world for an entire academic year. Students are 11th and 12th grade co-eds, but applicants who are seeking a unique and challenging 'year out' programme can be accepted. Crews are selected on the basis of strong academic profiles, demonstrated strength of character and social suitability, health, fitness, and on their degree of dedication. A season onboard her coincides with the Academic Year. Summer programmes are also offered for students and adults.

The cost is US$14,500 per student per semester, and US $25,800 per student per year.

CONTACT	Sherri Holcman, Director of Admissions and Operations
ADDRESS	Class Afloat, 851 Tecumseh, Dollard des Ormeaux, Montreal, Quebec, H9B 2L2
PHONE	+1 514 683 9052 FAX +1 514 683 1702
WEB	http://www.classafloat.com

WEST ISLAND COLLEGE · CLASS AFLOAT

YOUR PASSPORT TO EDUCATION
Since 1984

*You cannot discover new oceans
unless you have the courage
to lose sight of the shore.*

Ernestina

NATIONALITY	*USA*
HOME PORT	*New Bedford, Massachusetts*
SIZE OVERALL	*47.5 metres 156 feet*
PERMANENT CREW	*11*
PAYING SAIL TRAINEES	*75 (day) 24 (overnight)*

HISTORY

Originally launched as Effie M. Morrissey in 1894, this Essex-built schooner fished the Grand Banks and served as a coastal packet for 31 years along the coasts of New England, Nova Scotia and Newfoundland. In 1925 the famous ice pilot and explorer Capt. Bob Bartlett purchased her as an Arctic expedition vessel, and for the next 20 years he made an annual trip north, collecting Arctic flora and fauna for museums and zoological societies in North America. The last two years of this period found the schooner engaged in hydrographic and supply work for the US Army and Navy during World War II in Baffin Bay and Frobisher Bay. After Capt. Bartlett's death in 1946, Morrissey was purchased by Capt. Henrique Mendes and renamed Ernestina and as such she was the last Atlantic sailing packet to regularly bring immigrants to the US under sail, making 24 crossings from the Cape Verde Islands to southeastern New England. In 1982 the schooner was returned to the US as a gift from the Republic of Cape Verde and now serves as a cultural and educational resource all along the New England coast.

ON BOARD

Crew members are chosen from a nation-wide pool of experienced educator-mariners who bring their collective skills together to create an exceptional environment aboard a historic ship. Offerings in marine and environmental science, geography, and maritime history are often designed in collaboration with accredited schools and universities, scouts, ElderHostel and other partners.

SAFETY CERTIFICATES AND INSURANCE

She is inspected by the US Coast Guard and carries Sailing School Vessel (Subchapter R) and Passenger Vessel (Subchapter T) certifications.

PROGRAMME

She operates from March to November from her home port of New Bedford and from various ports of call along the eastern seaboard of the US. Most often she is offering dockside and underway educational programmes for groups of all ages. Programme participants not only take part in the operation of the vessel, but are engaged in multi-disciplinary learning activities developed by the ship's educational staff in collaboration with local and regional educators of the Commonwealth of Massachusetts and beyond.

Individual citizens and visitors to America can sail her, through her Membership Programme.

CONTACT	Massachusetts Schooner Ernestina Commission
ADDRESS	PO Box 2010, New Bedford, MA 02741-2010, USA
PHONE	+1 508 992 4900
FAX	+1 508 984 7719
E-mail	swanzey@ultranet.com
Web	http://www..ernestina.org

Harvey Gamage

NATIONALITY	*USA*
HOME PORT	*New Hampshire*
SIZE OVERALL	*29 metres 95 feet*
PERMANENT CREW	*8*
INSTRUCTORS	*3*
PAYING SAIL TRAINEES	*69 (day) 27 (overnight)*

HISTORY
Harvey Gamage is a traditional schooner common in the US in the 19th and early 20th Centuries.

SAFETY CERTIFICATES AND INSURANCE
She is a registered as a Passenger Vessel (Subchapter T), indicating she is a small passenger vessel under 100 gross tons carrying passengers for hire, and required to pass regular US Coastguard inspections of the ship and her onboard equipment.

PROGRAMME
She sails the east coast of the USA down to the Caribbean, with trainees mainly from 13 to 17 years old, and she has on board many different types of school and groups. She combines sail training with history, science, and ecology.
In 1999 the Foundation ordered a new 100 foot three mast schooner, also for sail training, for 2000+.

CONTACT	Schooner Harvey Gamage Foundation Inc
ADDRESS	PO Box 60, Francestown,
	New Hampshire NH 03043
PHONE	+1 603 547 2702
FAX	+1 603 547 8802

Heritage of Miami II

NATIONALITY	USA
HOME PORT	Miami, Florida
SIZE OVERALL	26 metres 85 feet
PROFESSIONAL CREW	3
PAYING SAIL TRAINEES	49 (day) 18(overnight)

HISTORY

She is designed after the fast and seaworthy coastal schooners that sailed the waters of Florida's East Coast, the Bahamas and Florida Keys in the late 1800's. They were built of local hardwoods, and Heritage of Miami II's main difference is that she was built in
Cor-Ten steel under Subchapter T of the Coast Guard regulations for passenger carrying vessels.

ON BOARD

She is affiliated with the Boy Scouts of America, and operates from their High Adventure base in the Florida Keys. She also sail trains with the local school system in Miami. Students are from 13 to 21.

PROGRAMME

She makes passages to the Gulf of Mexico and the Bahamas on week long voyages. She also engages in a few public day sailings and private and corporate charters. Many of the American Sail Training professional crew have started their careers on this ship.
The cost is $500 a week, and she sails all year round.

CONTACT	Barbara Maggio
ADDRESS	Schooner Heritage of Miami, Inc, 3145 Virginia Street, Coconut Grove, Florida II. 33133
PHONE	+1 305 442 9697
FAX	+1 305 442 0119

Ji Fung

NATIONALITY	*Chinese*
HOME PORT	*Hong Kong*
SIZE OVERALL	*40.2 metres 132 feet*
PROFESSIONAL CREW	*10*
PAYING SAIL TRAINEES	*36-40*

HISTORY

The Outward Bound Trust is an international organisation with many programmes designed to stretch the young (and not so young), by climbing, walking, and other adventures, mostly on land. But the Trust also has one ship, the Ji Fung in Hong Kong, a gift from the Royal Hong Kong Jockey Club. Designed free of charge by John Brookes of New Zealand (he also designed that country's Spirit of Adventure), she was originally intended to be steel, but she ended up in wood, built by local Hong Kong craftsmen in the yard of Kong and Halvorsen. All paint was given free by Epiglass of New Zealand, which developed a special antifouling for her. Her masts were also from New Zealand, her engine was from England, and her generators from Japan. She launched in 1980 and on her maiden voyage took a group of senior executives to the Philippines and back, logging 1,250 nautical miles.

ON BOARD

Ji Fung is dedicated to serve the community by providing personal development courses to those as young as 12 years of age, and to groups with special needs, such as youth-at-risk, the physically or mentally handicapped, socially deprived, and ex-addicts undergoing rehabilitation. She also serves as a microcosm of an organisation, where companies can develop team work and team spirit. She also takes on board trainees from diverse cultural and economic backgrounds. One group had, for instance, climbed some of the highest peaks in south east Asia.

SAFETY CERTIFICATES AND INSURANCE

Ji Fung is 100A1 at Lloyds, and is inspected annually by Lloyds representatives. She is also inspected regularly by the Hong Kong Marine Department.

PROGRAMME

Courses are from 3 days to 18 days in length, and she frequently sails across the South China Sea to other Asian countries such as Japan, Malaysia and the Philippines. She has taken part in the China Sea Race, winning line honours in 1982. In the Osaka Quadricentennial Festival in 1983, she sailed with an all-girl crew. She took part in the San Fernando Race in 1987. She was the first tall ship to enter the Chinese port of Hainan, the first sailing ship to pass through Brunei River since 1911, and in 1987 she took part in the Sail Osaka event from Hong Kong to Okinawa, Kagoshima and Osaka. She won the award as the best sail training ship and the friendliest crew amongst the 40 participants. Under engine she can cruise 1,500 miles at 8 knots, but her real 'engine' is her 14 sails.

CONTACT	Gail Yuen
ADDRESS	Tai Mong Tsai, Sai Kung, New Territories, Kowloon, Hong Kong
PHONE	+852 279 13214 or +852 279 24333
FAX	+852 279 29877

Kaisei

NATIONALITY	Japanese
HOME PORT	Yokohama
SIZE OVERALL	43 metres 141 feet
PROFESSIONAL CREW	10
PAYING SAIL TRAINEES	32

HISTORY

Japan has taken to sail training with enthusiasm only recently, when the ocean racer of international fame, Kaoru Ogimi, inspired the foundation of STA Japan. An opportunity to buy a ship came in 1990 when Poland's financial plight, brought on by the changes to a market economy, led to the offer of Polish-built Zew. She was at the time in Antigua, West Indies. Her new Japanese owners decided to return her to Poland for a refit. She then sailed to Weymouth, England for rigging and her conversion from a topsail schooner to a brigantine. In 1992, she sailed for Cadiz, Spain, for the start of the voyage across the Atlantic to celebrate the 500th anniversary of the first voyage of Christopher Columbus. She had the privilege of being allowed to be the one ship to fly the United Nations flag. She then continued her way to Japan via the Panama Canal. Ever since, she has sailed Eastern waters, and welcomes fee paying trainees who join the mainly Japanese crew. Of Japan's sail training ships, Kaisei is the one which is most active in seeking international trainees who join from America, Australia, Asia and also Europe.

ON BOARD

Kaisei is available to anyone over the age of 15, She operates in Japanese waters for most of the year, and makes regular visits to Tokyo, Kobe, Fukuoka, and she spends the winter months in Okinawa. Regular voyages have also taken her to Pusan, Korea, and Hong Kong.

Accommodation is in six and eight berth cabins. There are hot showers, and some air conditioning.

SAFETY CERTIFICATES AND INSURANCE

She is certified as a special purpose sail training ship by the Japanese Ministry of Transport and complies with International Sail Training Association regulations.

PROGRAMME

Anyone 15 years of age and over can book to sail on Kaisei. Reasonable fitness is required, but no previous sailing experience is necessary. The cost covers all tuition, use of equipment, accommodation and meals on board. You don't need any wet weather gear as working clothes, safety harnesses and life jackets are provided. Travel to and from the port of departure is not included.

Five day, six day and longer cruises are available. Costs are subsidised for some voyages, so that you may pay as little as $60 a day, and this includes meals and insurance. It is recommended that you bring sheets and pillowcases, good deck shoes, toiletries and sailing gloves. Wet weather gear, safety harnesses, and helmets are provided. Smoking is permitted, but not in the living quarters.

CONTACT	Sail Training Association of Japan
ADDRESS	Nanyo-do Building, 2F 1-14-4 Hongo, Bunkyo-ku, Tokyo 113, Japan
PHONE	+81 3 3818 6273 FAX +81 3 3818 7816

Leeuwin

NATIONALITY	*Australian*
HOME PORT	*Fremantle, Western Australia*
SIZE OVERALL	*40 metres 131 feet*
PermAnEnt CREW	5
VOLUNTEER CREW	8
PAYING VOYAGE CREW	40

HISTORY

The dream for a Western Australian sail training ship started in 1974. The State Government gave ocean racer Alan Bond funds to help his defence of the America's Cup in Fremantle. So why not ask for funds for sail training? After all, the 150th Anniversary of the founding of Western Australia would be in 1979.

A dedicated group gained advice from the New Zealand's Spirit of Adventure Trust, who suggested a welded steel hull, and after further advice from the UK and The Netherlands, a new proposal was made to build a ship in time for Australia's bicentennial in 1988. With many enthusiastic helpers and sponsors (mainly Challenge Bank), the keel was laid in 1985, for a welded steel, teak decked three masted brigantine, not based on any previous vessel. She was designed specifically for local West Australian conditions. Her rig is quite typical of Australian vessels in the 1850's, and she was named Leeuwin (meaning Lioness) after the

Dutch ship which was first to round the south west tip of Australia in 1622.

To administer her, two organisations were established. First to come was the Sail Training Association of Western Australia in April 1984, founded to promote the concept of sail training in 'WA' and to support the operations of Leeuwin through a widely based membership. Then, in August 1984 came a Foundation, at first called the Leeuwin Sail Training Foundation, and now called the Leeuwin Ocean Adventure Foundation. It owns Leeuwin, employs all staff and operates the training programmes.

ON BOARD

Whilst the focus of Leeuwin has remained unchanged for ten

years of operation, two years ago the Foundation altered its name to remove the words 'Sail Training'. This was done to shake off the confusion associated with people wishing to obtain training in the sport of sailing, and to present a clearer, more attractive image to the Australian youth market. Leeuwin's main objective remains unquestionably Person Development through challenge and adventure, and hence the new words 'Ocean Adventure'.

The ship carries out a variety of tasks. In addition to the main market of senior high school pupils (aged 17-18), and a good relationship with those helping with the long term unemployed, there have been on occasion voyages for the disabled, when the crew mix is 26 trainees with physical and intellectual limitations, and 14 as trainees doubling as 'buddies'. Leeuwin's plan to enter other markets has led her to try and attract 'employed youth', those with four weeks paid holiday a year, and also older persons. Many of the voyages are for 10 days, with a strict Day 1. You must join at 0900, to learn safety procedures, use of safety harnesses, the rudiments of rope handling, bridge work, bracing the yards, and going aloft. Sailing at 1400, the ship tacks and wears, to teach working as a team. She anchors for the night, then begins a 24 hour watch system. Towards the voyage's end, on Days 8 and 9, watch leaders withdraw and the trainees elect their own leaders, and they have to reach the destination port, with the crew acting as safety cover. A test of trainee initiative indeed.

SAFETY AND INSURANCE

Leeuwin is built to Australian Maritime Safety Authority standards. The trainee fare covers normal public and indemnity insurance for accidents arising from negligence of the Foundation. However, should the individual wish to take out personal accident insurance to cover their own negligence, the Foundation has a policy available for the additional charge of $Au 1.50 to $Au 3.00 a day, depending on the rate which they care to purchase.

PROGRAMME

Leeuwin sails off Western Australia in the summer, and has now extended to the Northern Territories for the winter. The number of Ocean Adventure voyages, called 'Eco Adventure' voyages, focusing on ecology and the real wonders of the coastline, have been extended to 11 each year. Besides, Leeuwin is to take part in more special voyages further afield, following her success with Sail Indonesia in 1995 and in view of the Olympic Games in Sydney in 2000. To encourage South Africa's hope to embark on sail training, Leeuwin has been invited there.

Adventure holiday costs were recently Au$1250 (but Au$890 for students), including all meals and accommodation. Minimum age 16 (unless otherwise indicated).

Weekend trips are from Friday 6pm to Sunday 6pm, for Au$323 for two nights aboard, and all meals. The minimum age is 21. All must be in good health and reasonably fit. For the over 50s, a Foundation Medical Information Form must be signed by a doctor. All wet weather gear, harnesses and working smocks are provided.

CONTACT	Leeuwin Ocean Adventure Foundation
ADDRESS	PO Box 1100, Fremantle, WA 6160, Australia
PHONE	+61 9 430 4105
FAX	+61 9 430 4494

Lady Nelson

NATIONALITY	*Australian*
HOME PORT	*Hobart*
SIZE OVERALL	*14.8 metres 49 feet*
PAYING SAIL TRAINEES	*Day only 38*
	Overnight 10

disabled are charged the same rates as school groups, which are Au$225 for a half day and Au$375 a full day. Adult groups are charged Au$325 for a half day and Au$600 for a full day. Individual fares are, for a 1 hour plus cruise, Au$5.00, a half day cruise at Au$10.00, and a full day for Au$20.00. An overnight cruise is Au$80.00.

CONTACT	Lady Nelson Office
ADDRESS	GPO Box 1587, Hobart 7000, Tasmania, Australia
PHONE	+61 02 72 2823
FAX	+61 02 23 5959
	Dockhead Buildings, Franklin Wharf, Hobart 7000, Tasmania, Australia
PHONE	+61 3 62 34 3348

HISTORY

Operated by the Tasmanian Sail Training Association, the 50 tonne brig Lady Nelson undertakes cruises and excursions for the public, while handicapped and disabled people can go cruising in the harbour. She visits all accessible harbours in Tasmania at least once a year.

She is a full sized replica of the original Lady Nelson and her historical significance makes her an invaluable teaching aid and she is frequently used as such by schools.

The original was built at Deptford on the Thames in London in 1799 for service on that river. She was designed with sliding keels, precursors of the familiar centre-board. In 1800 she set sail under the command of Lieut. James Grant RN from London bound for the colony of New Holland as Australia was then known. Sailors nearby nicknamed her 'His Majesty's Tinderbox' because of her diminutive size. Indeed her freeboard amidships, owing to the heavy cargo, was only 2 foot 9 inches, hardly reassuring for skipper and crew contemplating a 12,000 mile voyage which included the infamous 'Roaring Forties'. But she made safe harbour at Port Jackson being the first ship to sail through the Bass Strait from west to east, arriving at the end of 1800. She had an adventurous 25 year life sailing around the eastern and northern seaboards of Australia and voyaging as far as New Zealand. Her end was as dramatic as the rest of her history. Searching for supplies she called at Baba Island where her crew were murdered and she was burned out by local natives.

PROGRAMME

Groups of handicapped and

"One & All"

NATIONALITY	Australian
HOME PORT	Adelaide
SIZE OVERALL	43 metres 141 feet
PROFESSIONAL CREW	9
PAYING SAIL TRAINEES	24

HISTORY

"One & All" is Australia's only wooden brigantine purpose-built to conduct sail and adventure training. Although this is primarily for young people between 16 and 25, there is in fact no upper age limit for most voyages. Since 1990 "One & All" has taken a much wider interstate role by providing a first class sailing facility for recreational, educational and leisure voyages for many different groups.

This gaff-rigged ship, carrying two square sails on the foremast, has taken part in many differing events which included participation in the Bi-Centennial First Fleet Re-Enactment from the UK to Australia when she joined the First Fleet at Rio de Janiero.

ON BOARD

She carries out a comprehensive programme of sail training voyages for school groups and the general public, and voyages sponsored by major companies. Eco-tourism voyages are made, for instance to tag and weigh sea turtles across the top of Australia. She also charts this lonely coastline which is only accessible from seaward. Further eco-tourist voyages to the Spice Islands of Indonesia and ornithological voyages to the Sir Joseph Banks Islands have been made. She has also undertaken adventure sailing voyages through the Great Barrier Reef and the Whitsunday Islands. "One & All" has also competed in the Darwin to Ambon race and acted as radio relay support vessel to the veteran and vintage fleet which took part in the 50th Sydney-Hobart race.

PROGRAMME

There is dormitory accommodation aboard for the voyage crew and trips are normally 5 to 10 days in duration at an average cost of Au$120 a day.

Currently she is based in Adelaide through the summer months, heading for North Queensland via Melbourne, Sydney and Brisbane for the winter.

CONTACT	"One & All"
ADDRESS	P O BOX 222, Port Adelaide SA 5015, Australia
PHONE	+61 8 8447 5144
FAX	+61 8 8341 0167

Pacific Swift

NATIONALITY	*Canadian*
HOME PORT	*Vancouver*
SIZE OVERALL	*33.8 metres 111 feet*
PROFESSIONAL CREW	*5*
PAYING SAIL TRAINEES	*30*

HISTORY

Modelled on the Swift of 1778, a fast brigantine, she was built at the Vancouver World's Fair of 1986, completing in 1988. Since then she has crossed the Pacific twice and the Atlantic twice, usually in winter, returning to the Pacific Canadian coastline in the summer months. She is operated by SALTS, the Sail and Life Training Society, who operate their own shipyard.

SAFETY CERTIFICATES AND INSURANCE

She is certified as a Candian passenger vessel, and as a sail training vessel under this certification

ON BOARD

Her programmes are designed to take 13 to 25 year olds of both sexes, using Christian values as a guideline, and instruction into maritime history and all nautical matters on an everyday basis.

PROGRAMME

Her usual voyage is over 10 day periods, though her longer distance voyages across oceans take crews up to a month of more. In 1998 the American Sail Training Association awarded her the year's Best Sail Training Programme.

CONTACT	SALT
ADDRESS	Box 5014, Station B, Victoria, British Columbia V8R 6N3, Canada
PHONE	+1 250 383 6811
FAX	+1 250 383 7781
E-MAIL	WEB http://www.

Pride of Baltimore II

NATIONALITY	*USA*
HOME PORT	*Baltimore*
SIZE OVERALL	*51.8 metres 170 feet*
PROFESSIONAL CREW	*12*
PAYING SAIL TRAINEES	*35 by day 6 overnight*

HISTORY

Baltimore Clippers were developed on Chesapeake Bay with enormous sail areas, with the object of out sailing British frigates in the 1812-1815 war. A replica of one of these Clippers, the first Pride of Baltimore, was built in 1979, and sank in a freak storm off San Juan, Puerto Rico, in 1986. Another replica was demanded by the public, and their subscriptions helped fund the new Pride of Baltimore II, designed to be even faster, with improved accommodation and safety equipment, to exceed Coast Guard specifications. 'Pride II' sails in USA waters, mainly off the coast of Maryland. She is also an important goodwill ambassador for her State, Port, and Tourism, and she travels far and wide - to Europe (North Sea, Channel, Mediterranean) in 1996, to the Far East (including Hong Kong and Japan) in 1998, and back to Europe in the Year 2000.

Pride of Baltimore II is owned by the citizens of the State of Maryland, and is operated by Pride of Baltimore Inc, a private, non profit making body, receiving funds through the State, the city, corporations, membership dues, and foundations.

SAFETY CERTIFICATES AND INSURANCE

She is a registered as a Passenger Vessel (Subchapter T), indicating she is a small passenger vessel under 100 gross tons carrying passengers for hire, and required to pass regular US Coastguard inspections of the ship and her onboard equipment.

ON BOARD

She has two alternating captains, 2 mates, an engineer, cook, boatswain, with six deckhands. Most crew members are professional sailors and are on board for six months. She also has 3 cabins with two berths in each, which are for paying 'guests' who can work the ship or not, depending on their choice. The cost is $150 a day with a minimum age limit of 18.

CONTACT	Pride of Baltimore Inc
ADDRESS	World Trade Center, 401 East Pratt Street, Suite 222, Baltimore MD 21202, USA
PHONE	+1 410 539 1151 FAX +1 410 539 1190
E-MAIL	pride2@pride2.org
WEB	http://www..pride2.ord

Shenandoah and Alabama

NATIONALITY	*USA*
HOME PORT	*Massachusetts*
SIZE OVERALL	*33 metres 108 feet*
PERMANENT CREW	*9*
PAYING SAIL TRAINEES	*35 (day) 30 (overnight)*

HISTORY

Shenandoah looks similar to the 1851 built Joe Lane, a Revenue Cutter, and to emphasise the point her original white hull is now in the black and white checkers of that service. She has been operated since 1964 by the Coastwide Packet Company, based in Vineyard Haven on the island of Martha's Vineyard, and in 1998 she was joined by the slightly smaller 90 foot ex-pilot schooner Alabama.

ON BOARD

Shenandoah (below) and Alabama (right) mainly sail with youngsters off the southern New England coast. Everyone gets involved washing down the vessel before breakfast, setting up for and cleaning up after meals, making one's bunk and keeping one's area neat, hoisting and stowing sails, steering, learning basic knots and understanding charts, swimming overside, jumping from the rigging, learning how to row and sail the vessels' four small boats, learning rope's names and location, with occasional hikes ashore.

SAFETY CERTIFICATES AND INSURANCE

She is a registered as a Passenger Vessel (Subchapter T), indicating she is a small passenger vessel under 100 gross tons carrying passengers for hire, and required to pass regular US Coast Guard inspections of the ship and her onboard equipment.

PROGRAMME

She has carried all the fifth grades of the Vineyard's schools for the past four years, and for several weeks each summer on each vessel, there are 'kid's cruises', lasting six days, with an age group between 11 and 14. The price per person is $600. Three chaperones are provided, and with the vessel's crew, adequate supervision is provided. School sponsored weeks cost $500 a person. With older people, she sails to whaling ports, and privateering ports in and near Massachusetts, taking paying people usually between 12 and 20 on week long voyages. She describes her activity as sail training, and windjammer cruises.

CONTACT	Coastwide Packet Co, Inc
ADDRESS	PO Box 429, Vineyard Haven, Massachusetts MA 02568
PHONE	+1 508 693 1699
FAX	+1 508 693 1881

Rose (HMS.)

NATIONALITY	American
HOME PORT	Bridgeport, Connecticut
SIZE OVERALL	54.6 metres 179 feet
PROFESSIONAL CREW	18
PAYING SAIL TRAINEES	80 (Day)
	31 (Overnight)

HISTORY

The original HMS Rose was a 24-gun English frigate, built in Hull in 1757 in anticipation of war with the reluctant 'colonials'. She saw action in the Seven Years War (called the Indian War in America), in which George Washington wore the uniform of a Redcoat officer. HMS Rose was then assigned to help keep law and order with the soon-to-be rebels. During the war that followed, she was scuttled in 1779 in the Savannah River's main channel, preventing the French from laying siege to the City. After the war she was destroyed to re-open the channel.

History books note that her activity, both in the Seven Years War and in the American Revolution, was a direct cause of the founding of the US Navy in 1775, as her threat posed an immediate American response.

Her original plans were held by the National Maritime Museum in the UK and they were used as the basis of the building of the present replica. She was ready in time for the celebrations for the American Bicentennial in 1976. She was usually berthed alongside on the waterfront at Newport, Rhode Island. In 1984 she was bought by her present owners who rebuilt her entirely to meet all safety requirements for a sailing vessel of her size, wishing to take paying people on board under sail.

ON BOARD

HMS Rose is a sail training ship, but she also takes part in films, festivals and promotions. Sometimes she agrees to one-day programmes for corporate, civic, religious and other groups.

When on voyages, she signs on trainees aged between 9 and 90, but usually she takes aboard those from school to adults, with the majority in their 30s.

Below decks, there are concessions to the modern day, most noticeably the original five feet of headroom is now nearer seven feet; and she has two powerful diesel engines. Accommodation is in 12 bunk co-ed cabins. Bunks are in threes, above each other, so no sitting up please. She's 'special' in many ways. 'Correct' is the right word, as

her sails are made from recycled material - from plastic soda bottles and from modern car fenders. Over 126,000 bottles collected from wastetips were used for her 17 sails.

SAFETY CERTIFICATES AND INSURANCE

She has a dual certificate as a Sailing School Vessel (Subchapter R) meaning she is registered as less than 500 tons, carrying more than six sailing school students or instructors, mainly under sail, operated by a non-profit making education body only for sail education, so she has to pass regular US Coast Guard inspections.

She is also listed as 'an Attraction Vessel'. She is the first and only Class A Tall Ship to be US Coast Guard certified as a Sailing School Vessel.

PROGRAMME

Her usual route is along the Eastern Seaboard of the USA, from May to the end of September, on cruises of three days to two weeks. In 1996 she came to Europe and hopes to be back, maybe sail training, soon. The kind of prices she charged on her European visit were for 6 days, $660.

CONTACT	Richard Bailey
ADDRESS	HMS Rose Foundation, 1 Bostwick Avenue, Bridgeport, Con. 06605, USA
PHONE	+1 203 335 1433 FAX +1 203 335 6793

Spirit of Massachusetts

NATIONALITY	*USA*
HOME PORT	*Massachusetts*
SIZE OVERALL	*31.4 metres 103 feet*
PERMANENT CREW	*7*
PAYING SAIL TRAINEES	*50 (day) 22 (overnight)*

HISTORY

Built in 1984, she is modelled on the fast 1889 schooner Fredonia, which used fish mainly off the Grand Banks off Newfoundland and the Georges Bank. Today she is operated by Schools for Children Inc, an independent non profit education organisation based in Arlington, Massachusetts.

ON BOARD

Schools for Children creates a broad range of high quality learning environments and alternative educational experiences to support the development of children, adolescents and young adults. This it has done since the early 1900s, combining exploration of new teaching techniques with a commitment to meet the individual needs of a wide range of students. In addition to their ship, School for Children administers diverse educational programmes including the Seaport Campus in Charlestown and Lesley Ellis School and Dearborn Academy. Programmes are made possible part through the support of the Massachusetts

Port Authority, Boston National Historic Park, Courageous Sailing Centre and Boston Redevelopment Authority.

SAFETY CERTIFICATES AND INSURANCE

'Spirit' is a Sailing School vessel (under Subchapter R), meaning she is registered as less than 500 tons, carrying more than six sailing school students or instructors, and operated by a non-profit making education body only for sail education. She has to pass regular US Coast Guard inspections.

PROGRAMME

All aboard learn the skills of the past. As well, each voyage has its own theme, be it environmental, historic, or involved with marine science, and marine literature. The lower age limit is 15. Schools and scouts are major participants. The cost is $100 a day for individuals, or for the whole ship, $2,500 for a day sail, and $2,000 a day for longer periods. Summer programmes are out of New England usually for three to six days at a time. In November and December she sails to the Caribbean, for 14 to 21 day programmes.

CONTACT	New England Historic Seaport
ADDRESS	197 Eighth Street, Charlestown Navy Yard, Boston, Mass 02129
PHONE	+1 617 242 1414
FAX	+1 617 242 4322 or +1 781 641 2713

Spirit of New Zealand

NATIONALITY	New Zealand
HOME PORT	Auckland
SIZE OVERALL	45 metres 148 feet
CREW	10 crew, 2 leading hands
TRAINEES	40

HISTORY

The Spirit of Adventure Trust is the only sail training organisation operating out of New Zealand. It started with Spirit of Adventure, gifted by Auckland businessman Lou Fisher in 1972. She gave 30,000 New Zealanders the opportunity to sail. In 1986 the larger Spirit of New Zealand was commissioned, with the support of New Zealanders from every walk of life. After a period when the two ran together, the original Spirit of Adventure was sold in 1997, and she continues sailing for the Captain Cook Cruise Company as a commercial venture sailing out of Nadi, Fiji. Spirit of New Zealand continues with the sail training activities of the Trust.

PROGRAMME

Spirit has a whole variety of programmes, including youth development (10 day programmes for 15 to 19 year olds), adult weekends of 2, 3 and 4 day voyages, sailings for the disabled, half day sails, day sails, and courses when she is alongside. 10 day voyages are slotted into the programme, and these run for eleven months of the year around the coast of New Zealand, from Hauraki Gulf to the Bay of Islands, from Marlborough Sound to Stewart Island. Berths are allocated annually to all New Zealand secondary schools who in turn nominate students who might benefit from the experience. Some berths are allocated to individual nominations from the Trust's supporters club and other youth organisations which include those disadvantaged or at risk.

CONTACT	John Lister
ADDRESS	Princes Wharf, Quay Street, P.O. Box 2276, Auckland, New Zealand
PHONE	+9 373 2060 FAX +9 379 5620

Svanen

NATIONALITY	*Australian*
HOME PORT	*Sydney*
SIZE OVERALL	*40 metres 131 feet*
PROFESSIONAL CREW	*6*
PAYING SAIL TRAINEES	*20*

HISTORY

Svanen was built in Denmark in 1922 and rigged as a 2 masted schooner. She was massively constructed of white oak with frames only 6 inches apart. Her hull was 12 inches thick, good protection for her cargo of grain which she carried between Greenland and Denmark for the Danish beer company, Tuborg. After surviving the Second World War she was fitted with an engine and continued trading in grain until 1969. As her last cargo was being unloaded in that year she was bought by a Canadian couple who signed ownership papers and for the next 10 years she stayed in Denmark, converted into a 3 masted barquentine. In 1979 she sailed from Denmark to her new home in Canada where she was quickly signed up by the Canadian Government to be used as a sail training vessel for the Royal Canadian Sea Cadets. She remained with the Sea Cadets until 1985 when she was sold to a group of Canadians who took her to England to take part in the First Fleet Re-enactment for Australia's Bicentennial celebrations. After her arrival in Australia she has

had two owners, and her name was reregistered as Svanen instead of Our Svanen. She has spent 4 years whale-watching around Frazer Island and currently sails the New South Wales coasts on sail training voyages and harbour day trips.

ON BOARD

She takes up to 80 passengers on day cruises and has accommodation for 20 trainees. Her short stable barquentine rig allows her to continue sailing in heavy weather. She has a large saloon and fully equipped galley. The crew include the ship's master, mate, and chef.

SAFETY CERTIFICATES AND INSURANCE

She is fully surveyed by the New South Wales Maritime Service Board in conjunction with the shipping laws of Australia. She is able to operate as a charter and sail training vessel in both coastal & inshore waters.

PROGRAMME

Svanen has a versatile programme, tailored to suit sail training, general charter, and harbour commitments.

CONTACT	Svanen Charters Pty Ltd
ADDRESS	P O Box 352, Alexandria, NSW 2015, 148-152 Regent Street, Redfern, NSW 2016, Australia
PHONE	+61 2 9698 4456
FAX	+61 2 9699 3392 or 9699 3399

Westward & Corwith Cramer

NATIONALITY	USA
HOME PORT	Woods Hole, Massachusetts
SIZE OVERALL	38/41 metres 125/134 feet
PROFESSIONAL CREW	11
PAYING SAIL TRAINEES	24/25

HISTORY

The Sea Education Programme (SEA) was founded in 1971 by a group led by Corwith 'Cory' Cramer, Jr. and Edward 'Sandy' MacArthur. With an eight acre campus in Woods Hole, SEA is part of the community of renowned research and teaching institutions that make up the oceanographic centre of eastern United States.

ON BOARD

Westward and Corwith Cramer, SEA's two ships, are similar (below). On board, the professional staff of eleven includes captain, chief scientist, three deck officers or mates, three assistant scientists, an engineer and a steward. A visiting scholar is frequently on board.

SAFETY CERTIFICATES AND INSURANCE PROGRAMME

Both ships are certificated by the US Coast Guard as Sailing Vessels. In fact, SEA was instrumental in working with the Coast Guard to create the Sailing School Vessel certification. Both ships meet or exceed all safety requirements in their class.

PROGRAMME

SEA operates all year round. Its sailing vessels routinely sail the waters of the Northern Atlantic Ocean and the Caribbean, as far north as Newfoundland and as far south as Venezuela. SEA Semester (12 weeks) or SEA Summer Session (8 weeks) students spend the first half of their semester at SEA's campus studying oceanography, nautical science and maritime studies. During the second half of the programme the students go to sea to put their knowledge into practice. Teaching is conducted in small groups on deck and in a laboratory while under sail. The consistent annual cruise tracks provide unparalleled opportunity to gather consistent data in the same regions every year. In addition SEA has programmes for high school age students and teachers in the summer.
A replacement for Westward is building for 2002.

CONTACT	Sea Education Association
ADDRESS	SEA PO Box 6 Woods Hole, MA 02540, USA
PHONE	+1 508 540 3954
FAX	+1 508 457 4673
E-MAIL	admission@sea.edu
WEB	http://www..sea.edu

Windeward Bound

NATIONALITY	Australian
HOME PORT	Hobart
SIZE OVERALL	33.5 metres 110 feet
PROFESSIONAL CREW	4
PAYING SAIL TRAINEES	12 at sea,
	55 for day trips

HISTORY

Windeward Bound is the replica of a schooner originally built at Boston, USA in 1848. Her lines have been slightly altered aft to accommodate an engine and propeller, and to provide more extensive accommodation to meet Australian survey standards. All the timber used in the hull, except the hull planking, has been re-cycled from demolished ships and old buildings, dismantled piecemeal by the voluntary building crew. She carries a traditional brigantine rig using blocks and tackles and 'heave-ho' instead of winches. Aloft she carries 4 square sails, 3 head sails, 3 staysails between the masts, a gaff main and gaff topsail.

ON BOARD

There is accommodation for up to 12 in addition to a crew of 4 and she is fitted with hot and cold fresh water showers plus a sea to fresh water maker, unusual for a ship of this type.

PROGRAMME

She undertakes sail training voyages, mainly in Tasmanian and Australian waters for those looking for adventure and of all ages.

SAFETY CERTIFICATES AND INSURANCE

Windeward Bound is fully insured and meets Australian Commonwealth survey and safety requirements.

CONTACT	'Windeward Bound'
ADDRESS	PO Box 196, Crows Nest, NSW 2065, Australia
PHONE	+61 3 6224 0205
MOBILE	+61 0418 120399
FAX	+61 3 6224 0519

Young Endeavour

NATIONALITY	*Australian*
HOME PORT	*Sydney*
SIZE OVERALL	*44 metres 144 feet*
PROFESSIONAL CREW	9
YOUTH CREW	24

HISTORY

Australia's national sail training ship Young Endeavour was a gift from the UK to the Government and people of Australia to mark the Bicentenary in 1988. She is designed by Colin Mudie and her brigantine rig drives her at up to 14 knots under full sail and a steady 10 knots from her twin Perkins diesel engines. Mudie's design retains all of the romance of the old sailing ships combined with the sophistication of modern navigation, communications and safety equipment. She sailed from Cowes, Isle of Wight in the UK in 1987 on her 'delivery voyage' to Australia. In addition to the professional crew, drawn from the Royal Australian Navy, were 12 young Australian trainees chosen from more than 7,000 applicants, and 12 young British trainees. In 1990 Young Endeavour made her first international voyage since delivery to take part in New Zealand's sesquicentennial celebrations and the opening there of the Commonwealth Games. Two years later she completed a circumnavigation which included commemorating the 500th anniversary of Columbus' original voyage of discovery towards America.

ON BOARD

Each year she conducts a programme of 10 day sail training voyages for young Australians aged between 16 to 23 and a series of half day cruises for young people with disabilities. She is open to the public at her various ports of call.

At sea the youth crew are divided into three watches, four hours on and eight off. They are involved in all aspects of sailing the ship. Each trainee has the opportunity to lead their watch and, on the final day of the voyage, command the ship. The crew elect their own command team and are responsible for sailing the ship with minimal supervision. Wherever possible an environmental or community aspect is included in the voyages, for example turtle-tagging, and seabird marking, in particular albatross chicks in the Bass

Strait, and she visits research stations on the Great Barrier Reef.

PROGRAMME

A typical 10 day programme might include voyages from Mackay to Cairns, or Cairns to Townsville, Townsville to Gladstone, Gladstone to Brisbane, Brisbane to Sydney, or out and back from Sydney.

CONTACT	The Secretary
ADDRESS	Young Endeavour Youth Scheme, P O Box 399 Potts Point, NSW 2011, Building 130, Garden Islands NSW 2000, Australia
PHONE	+61 2 9368 1800
	Toll free phone 1800 267 909
FAX	+61 2 9368 0183
E-MAIL	yngendvr@ozemail.com.au

Amerigo Vespucci (above)

Adventure (below)

List III is of service, government, or armed forces sail training ships.

ADVENTURE (JOINT SERVICES ADVENTUROUS SAILING CENTRE GREAT BRITAIN)

Rig Cutter
Length 16.8 metres 55 feet
Crew 12

Camper and Nicholsons of Gosport, south England, designed and built the first 'Nic 55' Lutine for Lloyds of London Yacht Club in 1970, and amongst a fleet of other 'Nic 55s', nine were built for the British services, of which this is one.

AMERIGO VESPUCCI (ITALIAN NAVY)

Rig Fully Rigged Ship
Length 100.5 metres 330 feet
Officers 240
Cadets 120

Whilst many organisations have recreated 19/20th century Clippers, the Italians looked back further and designed two ships based on Warships of the 18/19th century. The first, Christophoro Columbo was built in 1928, and went to the Soviet Union at the end of World War II as reparation for war damages. She sailed a few years in the Black Sea and later was broken up. Amerigo Vespucci was the second, built in 1931. She was named after Florence's navigator who sailed with Christopher Columbus between 1497 and 1502, sailing along the East coast of the New World. As a result of Amerigo's maps, the New Continent discovered by them was called America. To-day the ship bearing his name trains officers for Italy's Navy and is a welcome sight when she arrives in a port. She seldom races between ports, but she did in the Columbus Regatta in 1992 and in the 1996 Cutty Sark Tall Ships' Race in the Mediterranean.

ARUNG SAMUDERA (ROYAL MALAYSIAN NAVY)

Rig Schooner
Length 39.6 metres 130 feet
Crew and cadets 19

The 'Kri' that is usually put before her name is the same as Poland's ORP or the British HMS, indicating that she is a naval ship. Bought from the New Zealanders, she is her country's first sail training ship, and entered the Cutty Sark Tall Ships' Race in the Mediterranean in 1996.

ASTA (GERMAN NAVY)

Rig Sloop
Length 16.3 metres 53.5 feet
Crew and cadets 9

Asta was commissioned in 1972 for the German Navy, Flensburg, as a sail training and cruising yacht. In that year she participated in the Cutty Sark Tall Ships' Race and in 1992 she crossed the Atlantic in the Columbus Race.

BELLE POULE (FRENCH NAVY)

Rig Schooner
Length 30 metres 98 feet
Professional officers 1
Professional crew 15
Trainees 15

Belle Poule and Etoile are two sisterships owned by the French Navy. Based on fishing boats who fished the Grand Banks off Newfoundland, they really are 'twins' and quite apart from looking alike, they quite often manoeuvre together, even in port. They were built in 1932 at Chantiers de Normandie at Fecamp.

BLUENOSE II (CANADA)

Length 49 metres 161 feet
Rig Schooner
Professional crew 5 officers
Seamen 8 Cadets 4

The Bluenose Trust, based in Lunenburg, Nova Scotia, is a volunteeer organisation founded to preserve and operate Bluenose II at Lunenburg and Halifax

Arung Samudera (below)

Capitan Miranda

BROADSWORD (JOINT SERVICES ADVENTUROUS SAILING CENTRE GREAT BRITAIN)
Rig Cutter
Length 16.8 metres 55 feet
Crew 12
Camper and Nicholsons of Gosport, south England, designed and built the first 'Nic 55' Lutine for Lloyds of London Yacht Club in 1970, and amongst a fleet of other 'Nic 55s' nine were built for the British services of which this is one.

CAPRICIA (ITALIAN NAVY)
Rig Yawl
Length 22.5 metres 73.8 feet
Crew 5
Trainees 9
Designed by Sparkman and Stephens, she was built in Sweden and launched in 1963. A comfortable fast cruising yacht with distinctive varnished topsides, she made her debut in Cowes Week 1963 and gained line honours in the Fastnet Race which followed. Two years later the owner of Fiat, Giovanni Angelli, bought her, sailed her for 28 years, and then donated her to the Italian Navy in 1993. She is used by cadets and midshipmen of the Naval Academy of Livorno.

CAPITAN MIRANDA (URUGUAYAN NAVY)
Rig Schooner
Length 53 metres 174 feet
Crew 102
Built in 1920, this three masted schooner worked for forty years as a hydrographic vessel plotting the reefs and inlets of Uruguay. She was rescued from being broken up and is now a sail training vessel. When in European waters, she is a popular asset to any port - with a band able to bring a smile to all.

CAROLY (ITALIAN NAVY)
Rig Yawl
Length 23.7 metres 77.8 feet
Crew 6
Trainees 10
The first large yacht designed and built in Italy after the second world war, in 1947, she has a rather small draft and centreboard - her owner had extensive interests in Argentina, and the mouth of the River Plate is shallow. She crossed the Atlantic in 1948/9, sailing back to Italy in 1956. Sons of the owner, Riccardo Preve, presented her to the Italian Navy in 1982 as a sail training ship. She now sails from Livorno, used by Cadets of the Naval Academy in winter, and she cruises with Midshipmen in the Mediterranean in the summer.

CHASER (JOINT SERVICES ADVENTUROUS SAILING CENTRE GREAT BRITAIN)

Rig Cutter
length 16.8 metres 55 feet
Professional officers 2
Crew 12

Camper and Nicholsons of Gosport, South England, built a fleet of 'Nic 55s', nine of them for the British services of which this is one.

CISNE BRANCO (BRAZIL)

Rig Fully Rigged Ship
Length 78 metres 255.6 feet
Crew Over 90

Built by the year 2000, Cisne Branco (the White Swan) is a three mast sistership of Stad Amsterdam (see List 1), her hull the second of the two, but a speedier completion was intended to prepare her for the five hundredth anniversary of the European arrival in Brazil in 1500, with a commemorative voyage from Portugal to Recife.

CORSARO II (ITALIAN NAVY)

Rig Yawl
Length 20.9 metres 68.6 feet
Crew 5
Trainees 10

She was commissioned to develop a programme of advanced seamanship training for young officers after their basic training on board Amerigo Vespucci. Designed by Sparkman and Stephens and built in 1960, she completed 7 important cruises by 1967, racing in the Los Angeles-Honolulu Race (twice),the Newport to Bermuda, Transatlantic, Fastnet, Buenos Aires-Rio, and Sydney-Hobart. She has taken part in a number of Cutty Sark Tall Ships' Races. To-day she trains cadets of the Naval Academy at Livorno during the winter and cruises in the summer in the Mediterranean with a crew of young midshipmen.

Capricia (below)   Broadsword (bottom)

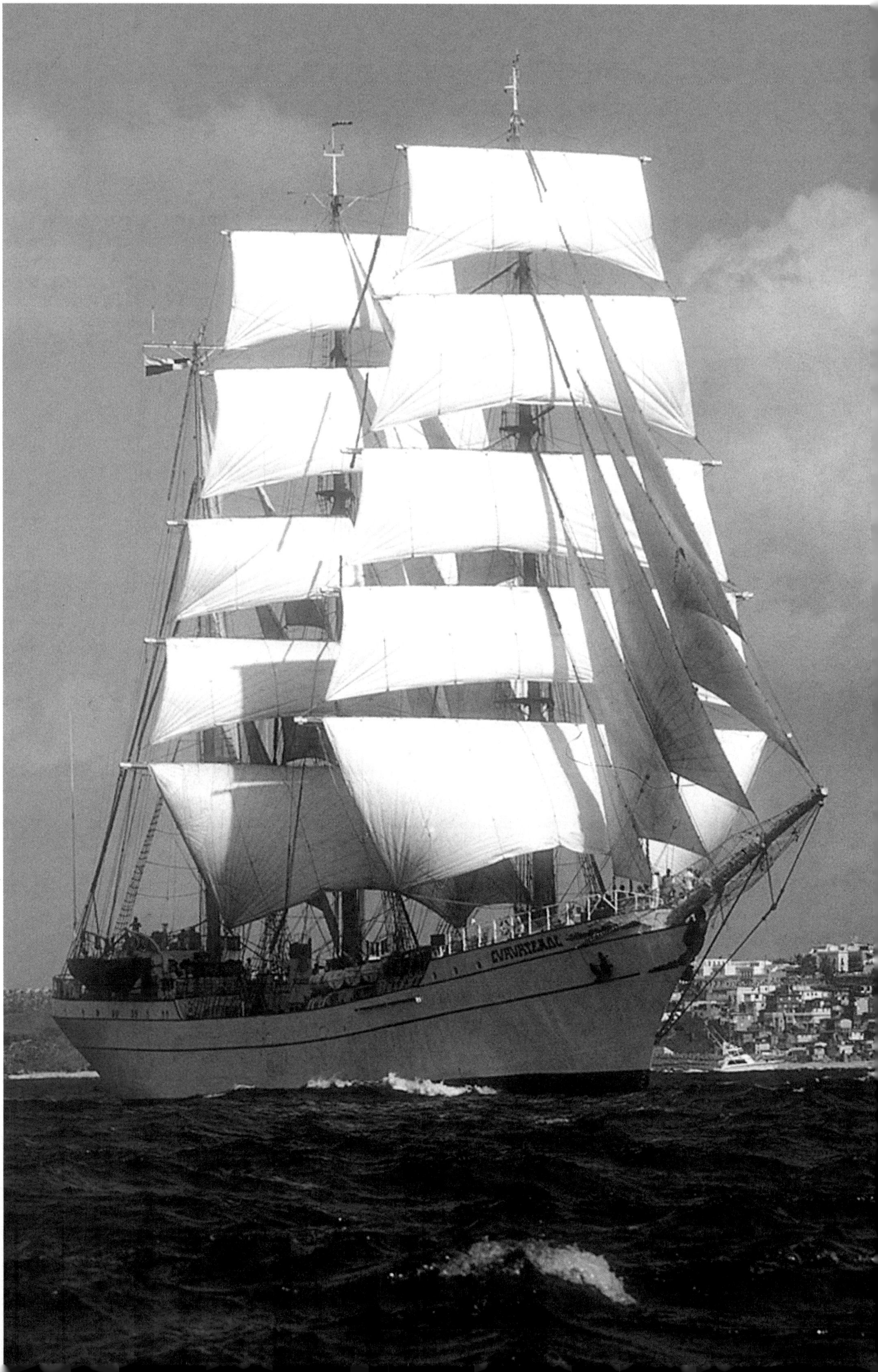

CUAUHTEMOC (MEXICAN NAVY)

Rig Barque
Length 92.4 metres 303 feet
Professional officers 164
Trainees 52

Four of the South American sail training ships were built at Bilbao Spain. They are Guayas, Gloria, Simon Bolivar and Cuauhtemoc. Cuauhtemoc was the son of the sun god, killed by the invading Spaniards under Cortes. A smart and popular visitor to Europe, she won the coveted Cutty Sark Trophy in 1998.

DANMARK (DENMARK)

Rig Fully Rigged Ship
Length 74 metres 243 feet
Professional officers 9
Professional crew 8
Trainees 80

Built in 1933, she has trained cadets all her life, even during World War II, in America, where she found herself at its outbreak. Returning to Danish control after the war, she continued sail training.

She does few long distance voyages these days, but on occasion enters Cutty Sark Tall Ships' Races.

DASHER (JOINT SERVICES ADVENTUROUS SAILING CENTRE GREAT BRITAIN)

Rig Cutter 12
Length 16.8 metres 55 feet
Crew 12

Camper and Nicholsons of Gosport, south England, designed and built a fleet of 'Nic 55s' nine were for the British services of which this is one.

DEWARUTJI (INDONESIAN NAVY)

Rig Barquentine
Length 58 metres191 ft
Crew 110 (including 78 midshipmen)

Dewarutji, god of courage, is an Indonesian Navy sail training ship. Building her started in 1932, but the war intervened and she took twenty years to complete. Her latest participation has been in 1997's Hong Kong to Osaka Race.

Cuauhtemoc (left)

Corsaro II

EAGLE (US COASTGUARD)
Rig Barque
Length 81 metres 266 feet
Crew and cadets 209
Built in Germany in 1936, she changed home in 1946 to become the US Coast Guard's sail training ship, and it is on her that young male and female trainees have their first taste of the sea. She is easily identified by the red stripe and the words Coast Guard in large letters down either side of her hull. She is one of five sisterships in this guide, the others are Mirces II, Sagres, Tovarisch, and Gorch Fock.

ESMERALDA (CHILEAN NAVY)
Rig Schooner-Barquentine
Length 93 metres 305 feet
Crew and cadets 328
This four master is a near sistership to Spain's Juan Sebastian de Elcano. Built in 1942, almost destroyed by fire, she was rescued and sold to the Chileans.

Caroly (below)   Dewarutji (above)   Danmark (right)

Eagle

Esmeralda

Georg Stage (above)

Guyas (below)

ETOILE (FRENCH NAVY)

Rig Schooner
Length 30 metres 98 feet
Professional officers 1
Professional crew 15
Trainees 15

The French navy have twins. The other is Belle Poule. Both ships are famous for their joint manoeuvres at sea and in harbour.

FALKEN (SWEDISH NAVY)

Rig Schooner
Length 34 metres 112 feet
Crew and cadets 48

Just as the French Navy has twins in Belle Poule and Etoile, so the Royal Swedish Navy has twins with Falken and Gladan, recognized by SO2 on Falken's sails, and SO1 on Gladan's. Naval Cadets usually have monthly stints on board. They were built in 1947 by the Naval Dockyard at Stockholm, and had major overhauls in 1986 to 1988 where all technical systems were updated or replaced.

Falken (below)   Etoile (above right)

GEORG STAGE (DENMARK)

Rig Fully Rigged Ship
Length 42 metres 138 feet
Permanent Crew 5
Voluntary professionals 10
Cadets 56

Young Danes between 16 and 20 years of age, and of good behaviour at school, can join her for a five month period of intensive training on all matters nautical, as well as other school subjects, from April to September. Her sponsors include the Danish Government, and companies, as well as trust funds.

GLADAN (SWEDISH NAVY)

Rig Schooner
Length 34 metres 112 feet
Crew and cadets 48

The French Navy has twins in Belle Poule and Etoile, so the Royal Swedish Navy has Falken and Gladan, and you can tell them apart from the SO2 on Falken's sails, and SO1 on Gladan's. Naval Cadets usually stay on board for a month at a time.

GLORIA (COLOMBIAN NAVY)

Rig Barque
Length 65 metres 213 feet
Crew and cadets 10 officers and 88 trainees

Commissioned in May 1969, she was built at Bilboa, Spain. She comes frequently to Europe, and sails into and out of harbour with cadets aloft manning her yards, whenever she can.

GORCH FOCK II (GERMAN NAVY)

Rig Barque
Length 81 metres 266 feet
Crew and cadets 269

With varnished topsides above her white hull, she is named after the famous German marine author Johann Kinau, who used the nom de plume Gorch Fock. You can recognise her from a horizontal strip of brown along the top of her white hull. She was commissioned in 1958 and entered her first Cutty Sark Tall Ships' Race in 1960.

Gorch Fock II

GUAYAS (ECUADOREAN NAVY)

Rig Barque
Length 65 metres 213 feet
Crew and cadets 180

Ecuador's Navy has its training school on the river Guayas, hence the name of their sail training ship. Commissioned in 1977, she was built in Spain at Bilbao.

ISKRA (POLISH NAVY)

Rig Barquentine
Length 49 metres 161 feet
Permanent Crew 18
Naval Academy Instructors 4
Trainees 45

The Polish Navy Academy of Gdynia owns her, and she trains cadets destined for the Polish Navy, students at the Westerplatte Heroes Naval Academy. Designed by Zygmunt Choren and built at the Gdansk Shipyard, sisterships include Pogoria and Kaliakra. She has taken part in numerous Cutty Sark Tall Ships' Races, and transatlantic voyages too. You may find her name in lists as ORP Iskra, the ORP prefix showing she is a naval ship, like 'HMS'.

Iskra was built in 1982 and until 1987 she made training cruises in the Baltic Sea and North Sea. In 1989 she was awarded the Cutty Sark Trophy. In 1990 she was invited by the UN Secretary General to visit UN Headquarters, and there she became the first Navy ship to be awarded the UN Peace Medal. In 1992 she took part in the Columbus Regatta from Europe to the Americas and back, and in 1995 she made a round the world cruise following the Clipper route.

On board, the 45 trainees are divided into three equal watches who do four hours on watch, and eight hours off.

JUAN SEBASTIAN DE ELCANO (SPANISH NAVY)

Rig Schooner
Length 93 metres 305 feet
Crew and cadets 163

In 1522 Juan Sebastian de Elcano was captain of the first ship to complete a circumnavigation of the world, in the five ship expedition during which the famous Magellan died. The ship that now bears Elcano's name trains Spanish cadets, and has made seven circumnavigations.

KAIWA MARU II (JAPAN)

Rig Barque
Length 110 metres 361 feet
Crew 317

Built in 1984, she incorporates lessons learnt from Japan's 1930 sisterships, Kaiwa Maru I and Nippon Maru 1, and she sails for the merchant marine. A sistership built five years later is Nippon Maru II.

KALIAKRA (BULGARIA'S NAVIGATION MARITIME BULGARE)

Rig Barquentine
Length 49 metres 161 feet
Permanent Crew 21
Cadets 30

Kaliakra is a close sistership to Poland's Iskra and Pogoria, and was built in 1984 at Gdansk, Poland. She bears the name of a legendary Bulgarian girl who preferred death to conversion during the Turkish conquest. It is also the name of the most impressive Cape on the Bulgarian Black Sea coast. Legend has it that from these heights Kaliakra and 40 other girls jumped into the stormy seas.

The ship is designed for the training of students from the Maritime Academy in Varna, their aim to become the future officers of the Bulgarian merchant fleet. Her trips are of 4-5 weeks in the area of the Black Sea and the Mediterranean, with some ventures further afield, thus to the 1992 Transatlantic Columbus Regatta. She took part in Cutty Sark Tall Ships' Races from 1996 to 1999.

Gloria

196

KUKRI (JOINT SERVICES ADVENTUROUS SAILING CENTRE GREAT BRITAIN)
Rig Cutter
Length 16.8 metres 55 feet
Crew 12
Camper and Nicholsons of Gosport, south England designed a fleet of nine 'Nic 55s' for the British services of which this is one.

LIBERTAD (ARGENTINE NAVY)
Rig Fully Rigged Ship
Length 91 metres 299 feet
*Crew and cadets 315*One of the largest sail training ships, with a figurehead showing 'Liberty', one of her fast runs was 8 days and a half, from Canada to the Channel. In 1998 she visited Dublin before sailing for Portsmouth at the invitation of the British Navy.

Kukri (above left)   Juan Sebastian de Elcano (below)

Iskra (above left)

Kaliakra (below left)

LORD PORTAL (JOINT SERVICES ADVENTUROUS SAILING CENTRE GREAT BRITAIN)
Rig Cutter
Length 16.8 metres 55 feet
Crew 12
Camper and Nicholsons of Gosport, south England, designed and built a fleet of nine 'Nic 55s' for the British services of which this is one.

Libertad (below)

Mircea II (above)

Mutin (below)

Nippon Maru II

MIRCEA II (ROMANIA)
Rig Barque
Length 74 metres 243 feet
Professional crew 83
Crew 65
Cadets 120

Five three masted barques were built in the late 1930's at Blohm and Voss, Hamburg, Germany. All are still around but after hectic lives, they are in contrasting condition. In good condition are Eagle the US Coast Guard ship, Gorch Fock II the pride of Germany, and Portugal's Sagres II, but recently Tovarisch and Mircea II almost slipped from sight. They became victims of the changes in East Europe and the Balkans over the past few years, with economies in massive turmoil in the switch from centrally controlled to open markets. Budgets for sail training ships were cut drastically. However, times are changing, and moves are afoot to get Tovarisch repaired up to international standards. There is also news from Mircea II, that she is gradually being repaired and restored, with a new deck for instance in 1996, with wood placed on top of her old steel deck. Her previous major overhaul was at Hamburg in 1966. To help pay her bills in future she may well to follow other East European giants, and instead of being used exclusively by her owners, the Romanian Nautical College at Constanta, for their students (half from the Navy and half from the Merchant Navy), she could well include berths for outside trainees and paying passengers.

MUTIN (FRENCH NAVY)
Rig Yawl
Crew About a dozen

Built as a yacht in 1927, she now sails with the French Navy. During the war she had a British crew and pretending to be a tuna fishing boat, landed personnel on the French coast.

NIPPON MARU II (JAPAN)
Rig Barque
Length 110 metres 361 feet
Crew 317

Built in 1989 for the Institute of Sea Training in Japan, she is a sistership of Kaiwo Maru II. Her forebear, Nippon Maru, is now a floating museum.

ORIOLE (CANADA)
Rig Yawl
Length 31 metres 101.7 feet
Crew (overnight) 22

Launched in 1921, she was willed to the Navy League of Canada in 1941, and in 1957 the Royal Canadian Navy bought her. She remains almost unaltered with no winches for sail handling. Based in Esquimalt, she trains Canadian forces in seamanship.

Pallada (above)

Tovarisch (below)

203

ORSA MAGGIORE (ITALIAN NAVY)
Rig Ketch
Length 28.3 metres 93 feet
Crew 8
Trainees 12

She is a recent addition to the Italian Navy. Launched in 1994, designed by Vallicelli and built in Venice, her role is to take cadets of the Italian Navy Academy of Leghorn, and petty officers of the Taranto school, for long training voyages across oceans. She takes her name from the constellation Orsa Maggiore (The Great Bear or Big Dipper). According to the Greeks the Big Dipper was the nymph Callisto, seduced by Zeus, and their offspring was Arcas. Zeus's wife was not pleased and transformed Callisto and her son into bears. The Greeks and Romans, the Arabs, and the Red Indian Irochesi tribe all believe these stars represent a bear.

PALINURO (ITALIAN NAVY)
Rig Barquentine
Length 68.9 metres 226 feet
Crew 65
Trainees 90

Built in Nantes, France, in 1933, she fished cod on the north western Atlantic banks. At first her name was Commandant Louis Richard and then Jean Marc Aline. She was bought by the Italian Navy in 1950 and renamed Palinuro after the Greek Prince of Troy, Enea (Aeneas). After Troy's destruction, Palinuro was lost overboard near the Italian coast while seeking for a new homeland. In 1955, the extensively restructured ship started her new life as a training ship for future petty officers of the able seaman branch. Her home port is La Maddalena in Sardinia, and she sails mainly in the Mediterranean. She raced for the first time in Cutty Sark Races in the Mediterranean in 1996 and for the first time outside the Mediterranean in the 1998 Cutty Sark Tall Ships' Races.

PALLADA (RUSSIA)
Rig Fully Rigged Ship
Length 108 metres 358 feet
Officers, crew and teachers 56
Cadets 143

One of the famous three masted sisterships, with Dar Mlodziezy, Mir, Druzhba, and others, she is based in Russia's far east port of Vladivostok. She ventures far afield, including to

the 1997 Hong Kong to Osaka Race, Europe's Columbus Regatta in 1992, to Europe in 1991, and to America's West Coast in 1991 and 1989. She offers joint training schemes to foreign marine college cadets, for 1.5 to 3.5 months. Her sides are easily recognisable with their distinctive 'false gunports'.

POLAR (PORTUGUESE NAVY)
Rig Schooner
Length 28.3 metres 92.8 feet
Crew 3
Cadets 12

A 70 ton schooner, Polar is owned by the Portuguese Navy and is based in Lisbon. She was built in 1977 as Anne Linden, and is a replica of the yacht America which won the the famous 1,000 Guinea Cup in 1851 off Cowes, England, the Cup which is known today as the America's Cup. Built in 1977 she chartered until 1982 and joined the Portuguese Navy in 1983. Today, she normally carries 12 cadets who learn practical seamanship and navigation whilst they are aboard. Although Navy ships are usually not able to take paying civilian sail trainees, they do carry cadets from other navies on exchange visits, and, on occasion young men and women from other uniformed forces.

Orsa Maggiore

Sagres II

Palinuro (below)   Shabab Oman (above)

RACER (JOINT SERVICES ADVENTUROUS SAILING CENTRE GREAT BRITAIN)
Rig Cutter
Length 16.8 metres 55 feet
Crew 12
Camper and Nicholsons of Gosport, south England, built a fleet of 'Nic 55s'. Nine were for the British services, and this is one.

SABRE (JOINT SERVICES ADVENTUROUS SAILING CENTRE GREAT BRITAIN)
Rig Cutter
Length 16.8 metres 55 feet
Crew 12
She is a sistership of Racer (above).

SAGRES II (PORTUGUESE NAVY)
Rig Barque
Length 82 metres 269 feet
Crew and cadets 224 - 10 officers, 18 petty officers 136 ratings and 60 cadets
Sagres is the point of land off south west Portugal where Prince Henry the Navigator lived in the 15th century, devoting his life to the study of navigation and to ships' construction. The red crosses on her sails are her distinctive feature. Built in the Blohm and Voss shipyards, Hamburg, in 1937-8, she was third of a series of ships - Eagle, Tovarisch, Gorch Foch II, and Mircea II. Damaged by a mine in the Baltic, she was handed over to the Brazilians post war, and bought by Portugal in 1962. Now, she takes midshipmen and cadets of the Portuguese Naval Academy on sail training voyages.

Stella Polare

SHABAB OMAN (ROYAL OMANI NAVY)

Rig Barquentine
Length 53.3 metres 175 feet
Crew 23
Cadets 31

Shabab Oman, meaning 'Youth of Oman' entered the service of the Sultan of Oman's Navy in 1979 for use as a sail training ship. She had been launched in 1971 as the Captain Scott and initially owned by the Loch Eil Trust of Scotland as a then experimental sailing

project to provide sea training opportunities for youngsters, modelled on the highly successful Outward Bound sea and adventure schools in the UK. She is built of Scots larch on oak frames with decks of Oregon pine. She is one of the largest sailing ships in the world made of wood, and thanks to the Sultan of Oman, His Majesty Sultan Qaboos bin Said, she is still very much in active service. Rigged as a 3 masted barquentine, the foremast is square-rigged and the others 'fore and aft'. She is easily recognisable by the red

Svanen (above)   Thyra (below)

'coat of arms' of the Sultanate on her foresails and gaff topsails. This
is made up of crossed scimitars with the 'Khunjar' - the Omani
ceremonial dagger - super-imposed at the centre. During her service
she has visited 17 countries, including a 7 month voyage to the USA
in 1986 to join the anniversary celebrations of the Statue of Liberty.
The following year she left for Australia to take part in the
Bicentenary there. She was also in the 1992 Columbus Regatta.
Oman has a tradition of seafaring. Navigators and seamen sailed
their 'dhows' and 'booms' pioneering trade routes to India and in
particular down the east coast of Africa, hundreds of years ago.
Today aboard Shabab Oman, Omani cadets learn the habits and
disciplines of those long ocean voyages, just as their forefathers did.

SIMON BOLIVAR (VENEZUELAN NAVY)
Rig Barque
Length 86.3 metres 283 feet
Crew 96
Cadets 108
A traditionally rigged 3 masted barque, she was built in Spain and
launched in 1979. Her design may go back a century, but her interior
fittings and navigational aids are modern. Her designers have
created a sea-kindly hull with a clipper bow and a 'deck sheer' which

ends in a fine counter stern. She has black false gunports on her
white hull, painted to discourage pirates. She is named after General
Simon Bolivar, 'El Liberator', who assisted Venezuela and other
South American countries to 19th century independence.

ST BARBARA V (UK ROYAL ARTILLERY)
Rig Cutter or sloop
Length 12.8 metres 42 feet
Crew 2 permanant, 7 others
The famous St Barbara name will be carried through the millenium
by a new Rustler 42, replacing a Nicholson 40. Besides training the
Royal Artillery, she is available for weekend charters, Cutty Sark
Races, and cruises to the Canaries.

Polar (above)   Racer (below)

STELLA POLARE (ITALIAN NAVY)

Rig Yawl
Length 21.5 metres 70.5 feet
Crew 5
Trainees 10

After the success of Corsaro II, the Italian Navy decided to add another similar vessel to its sail training fleet. Designed by the same US firm of Sparkman and Stephens, Stella Polare was built by the Sangermani yard and launched in 1966. In her first oceanic cruise she won the Transatlantic Race (1968) and in the following years she raced in several Cutty Sark Tall Ships' Races in the Atlantic Ocean and in the North and Baltic Seas. Her home port is Livorno at the Naval Academy, and she day sails with cadets in the winter and cruises with midshipmen in the summer.

SVANEN and THYRA (DANISH NAVY)

Rig Yawl
Length 21 metres 69 feet
Professional crew 1
Cadets 12

These are two Danish Navy sail training ships, similar in size and built in 1961.

TARANGINI (INDIAN NAVY)

Rig Barque
Professional crew 22
Cadets 30

A close relative of Lord Nelson, to look at, except she has a normal bowsprit and open bridge, she is the Indian Navy's first sail training ship. To Colin Mudie's design, she came on active service after sail trials in the spring of 1998.

TOVARISCH (UKRAINE)

Rig Barque
Length 82.1 metres 269.4 feet
Crew 51
Cadets 134

Tovarisch suffered in the transition of Eastern Europe to an open market economy, when funding dried up for her as with others - Mircea II and Kaliakra

Zenobe Gramme (above)

Urania (below)

for instance. But Kaliakra (Bulgaria) started racing again in 1996, and Mircea II (Romania) is repaired. Tovarisch had to stay in Newcastle as her safety certificates had not been renewed and she needed repairs to bring her up to standard. In 1997 she moved to Teesside., then in 1999 to Wilhelmshaven, where Tall Ship Friends are raising funds to complete her restoration, and she should sail again, but not before 2002..

TUNAS SAMUDERA (ROYAL MALAYSIAN NAVY)

Rig Brigantine
Length 35 metres 115 feet
Crew and cadets 37

Sistership to Australia's Young Endeavour, both were given by the British to their countries. A wide variety of young people from Malaysia are eligible to sail on board her, usually on ten day voyages.

URANIA (THE ROYAL NETHERLANDS NAVY)

Rig Ketch
Length 23.7 metres 77.9 feet
Crew and cadets 17

Since 1830 the Royal Netherlands Navy has operated a sail training ship named Urania. In Greek mythology Urania is the muse of astronomy, and this ships' crest and spinnaker represent this by showing the celestial sphere and zodiac. Her motto 'Caveo non timeo' means 'Vigilant without fear'. The present Urania is the fourth with this name, built in 1928 by Haarlemse Scheepsbouw Maatschappig as a private yacht called Tromp. In 1938 she joined the Navy and changed her name to Urania, and her rig from a schooner with wishbone rigging, to her present bermudian ketch rig. On board accommodation is for three officers, two petty officers and twelve trainees. Most of the trainees are midshipmen from the Royal Netherlands Navy College, but they can also be other personnel under training. One good reason to get trainees on board is to confront them with sea and weather, basic to their future job. For this reason, Urania makes many trips from Den Helder every year between March and November to many European countries, and she takes part in Cutty Sark Tall Ships' Races, when she can.

VEGA (PORTUGUESE NAVY)

Rig Sloop
Length 21.6 metres 71 feet
Crew 3
Cadets 10

An attractive white hulled sloop she is nearly 50 years old but still much involved with the Portuguese Navy's sail training programmes for young naval cadets. She carries 3 officers and 10 cadets in her roomy 40 ton hull. Her sailing is mostly in the eastern Atlantic and the western Mediterranean coasts.

Vega

ZENOBE GRAMME (BELGIAN NAVY)

Length 28.1 metres 92 feet
Rig Ketch
Crew 2 officers 2 under-officers and 11 trainees

Zenobe Gramme is the pride of the Belgian Navy. She is used as a military sail training ship, and for the first time in 1996 young civilian marine cadets and students of the merchant navy took part in training cruises. She sails to many European events, for instance in 1997 to Den Helder for the feeder race to the Cutty Sark Tall Ships' Races, from Aberdeen to Trondheim in July, before an August and September visit to the Mediterranean, for the 700th Anniversary of the founding of the Grimaldi dynasty of Monaco, with stops in Marin, Lisbon, Malaga, Ibiza and Oporto.

Dark Horse (below)   Lowaci (above)

ARTICA 11 (ITALIAN NAVY SAILING ASSOCIATION)

Rig Yawl
Length 13.2 metres 43.3 feet
Crew 3
Trainees 4

Designed by John Illingworth as a development of Mouse of Malham, she launched in 1956. Extremely light and innovative in construction, she did well in ocean races in many Mediterranean competitions, under the Royal Ocean Racing Club's rules. She also took part in the Cutty Sark Tall Ships' Races of 1956 and 1958, from Torbay to Lisbon, and Brest to Tenerife in the Canary Islands. She left the racing world as newer designs and rule changes made her less competitive, but after a 1987 refit, she still takes part in races and vintage yacht rallies in Italy and France.

BARCELONA (NAUTICAL SCHOOL SPAIN)

Rig Ketch
Length 12 metres 40 feet
Professional officers 1
Students 7

There are seven yachts in Spain involved in merchant marine sail training, Barcelona, Marineda, Tenerife, Tartessos, and Saltillo, with two more smaller yachts that belong to the Escuela Superior de la Marina Civil of Gijón. The first four are sisterships from the board of Peter Ibold. They are of the Belliure 40 class, built in Calpe, Alicante. Usually this type are sloops, but the school wished for two masted ships, with four berths up front, 3 in the stern, and 2 in the centre, though the usual compliment is smaller. Barcelona is owned by Facultat de Nautical de Barcelona (Nautical Faculty of Barcelona) Universitat Politecnica de Catlunya, and was launched in 1985. She sails for about one and a half months in the year, and at weekends. She mainly sails in the Mediterranean (Malta, Turkey, Corscia, etc) and has sailed further to join Cutty Sark Tall Ships' Races.

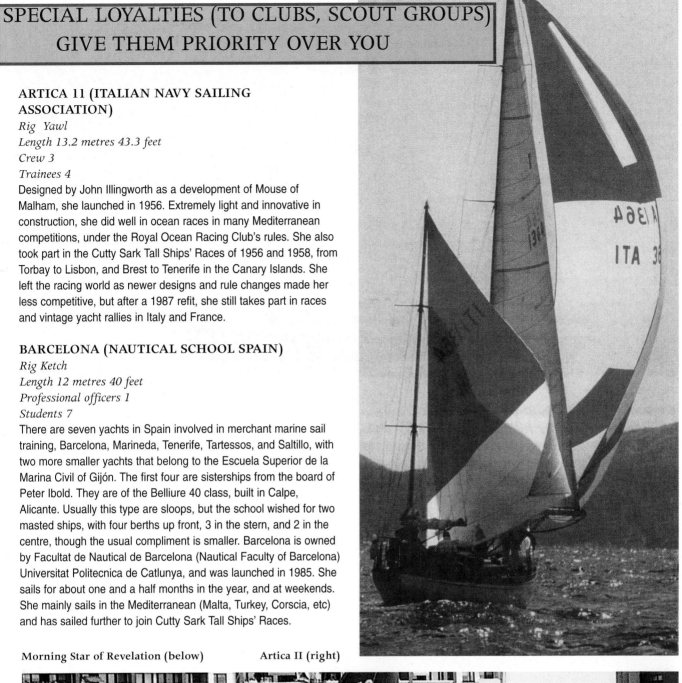

Morning Star of Revelation (below)   Artica II (right)

Return of Marco Polo (above)   Right top Barcelona (four other Spanish sisters of the same class are in the following five pages)

DARK HORSE (A UK Bank)

Rig Schooner
Length 17 metres 56 feet
Professional officer 4
Trainees 9

The symbol of this bank, Lloyds, is - you've guessed - a black (dark) horse - and her role is to help anyone who works for the bank and wishes to learn about the sea. As a regular in Cutty Sark Tall Ships' Races, she represents the modern concept of sail training. She was built in 1979 with a glassfibre hull and of the 'Ocean 60' class, dividing her sail area between two masts, to make it easier for novices to handle as each sail is smaller, and more fun as each sail has to be dealt with separately so there is more work to do.

LOWACKI (POLAND)

Rig Brigantine
Length 24 metres 79 feet

When the Poles took over this engine-only 1944 built patrol vessel, they first named her Henryk Rutkowski. In 1951 sails were added to make her a gaff ketch. After a period when she required finance to refit, she re-emerged in 1986 as a brigantine. Since 1989 she has entered more Cutty Sark Tall Ships' Races than she has missed, engaging in friendly rivalry with the UK's Royalist and Ireland's Asgard II.

On occasion, she has carried disabled crews on board.

Ocean Scout (below)   Royalist (facing page below)

Sofia

MARINEDA (NAUTICAL SCHOOL SPAIN)

Rig Ketch
Length 12 metres 40 feet
Professional officers 1
Students 7

Marineda is owned by Escula Superior de la Marina Civil de La Coruña (Superior Nautical School of La Coruña) Universidade da Coruña, and is of the Belliure 40 class, built in Calpe, Alicante in 1986. Usually this type are sloops, but the school wished for two masted ships, with four berths up front, 3 in the stern, and 2 in the

centre, though the usual compliment is smaller. She usually sails around the Andalucia coast and in the Strait of Gibraltar. As well as a sail training ship, she is used in research projects. She has joined Cutty Sark Tall Ships' Races.

MONSUN (MARINESCHULE MURWIK GERMANY)

Rig Yawl
Length 17.4 metres 57 feet
Professional officers 2
Trainees 6

Launched in 1948, she has taken part in Cutty Sark Tall Ships' Races.

MORNING STAR OF REVELATION (CHRISTIAN TRUST UK)

Rig Ketch
Length 19 metres 62 feet

Based in Kent, south east England, she is run by Christians, believing that sailing can be challenging to a person's character and to their christian faith, though views are forced on no one. Groups from churches, youth clubs and disadvantaged groups, and from outside organisations, take part. Morning Star usually cruises in the southern North Sea, ports in Belgium, Holland and France, and sometimes as far afield as Portugal or the Baltic. Also owned by the Trust is the 27 foot Eagles Wings.

Ocean Spirit of Moray

Valborg (above)

OCEAN SCOUT (SCOUTS OFFSHORE UK)
Rig Ketch
Length 15 metres 50 feet
Crew Professional 2 crew 8
The Scout Association has, through Scouts Offshore, two yachts which are identical, both built by Oyster Marine of Ipswich, and the two are based in east England's Colchester. Ocean Scout was first of the two, launched in 1994, and in 1997 and 1999 she sailed in the Cutty Sark Tall Ships' Race, together with her sistership Offshore Scout. Her usual voyages last between 2 and 14 days, with a crew of 14 year olds and upwards. Crews are mixed, and the cost is from £25 a day including food.
CONTACT 'Tolken', The Lane, West Mersea, Colchester, Essex CO5 8NT PHONE +44 1206 385071.

OCEAN SPIRIT OF MORAY (SCHOOL UK)
Rig Ketch
Length 24.4 metres 80 feet
Staff 5
Crew 16
The first owners were Ocean Youth Club (now Ocean Youth Trust) who claim the largest youth sailing fleet in Europe. They have seven yachts between 20 and 24 metres long, most with a crew of 12. Team Spirit of Wight (now Ocean Spirit of Moray) was their first 80 footer, the latest and largest yacht.. Designed and built by Oyster Marine Ltd she has a standard 'Oyster 80' hull but fitted out to OYC's exacting specifications for sail training. However, in 1998 there was a change of policy. She seemed too big for personal contact with new crews, who came on board not knowing each other, and so a more suitable home was required. Gordonstoun

School was the answer, as school members would know each other well before even coming on board, so the larger number of crew would be no problem.

OFFSHORE SCOUT (SCOUTS OFFSHORE UK)
Rig Ketch
Length 15 metres 50 feet
Crew Professional 2 crew 8
The Scout Association (see above, Ocean Scout) has, through Scouts Offshore, two yachts which are identical, both built by Oyster Marine of Ipswich, and the two are based in east England's Colchester. Offshore Scout only recently launched in 1996, and in 1997 she sailed with her sistership in the Cutty Sark Tall Ships' Race. Her voyages are similar to her sistership's.
CONTACT 'Tolken', The Lane, West Mersea, Colchester, Essex CO5 8NT. PHONE +44 1206 385071.

RETURN OF MARCO POLO (SCHOOL OF WINESTEAD UK)
Rig Schooner
Length 36.3 metres 119 feet
Crew Professional officers 1
professional crew 7
trainees 12.
The Small School of Winestead is in England's north east, and is for disadvantaged youth who might benefit from a controlled environment. Part of their activities can - if a student wishes - be aboard one of the school's ships. Return of Marco Polo is a three master built in 1907 as a lightship, and a sistership to Denmark's Den Store Bjorn.

ROYALIST (SEA CADETS UK)

Rig Brig
Base Gosport
Size 28.1 metres 92.2 feet
Professional Crew 6
Paying Sail Trainees 24

Although she does not look her age, Royalist is nearing 30 years old. She was built at Groves and Gutteridge in Cowes, Isle of Wight, in 1971 to a design by Colin Mudie. She is constructed in steel with aluminum masts. She is owned and operated by the British Sea Cadet Association and recently has undergone a major mid-life refit to extend her future active service by another 20 years at least. Although she is partially supported by the Navy, the expenses of running the ship falls largely on the Sea Cadet Association, a UK registered charity, which subsidises sea cadets' passage costs aboard by about one third. Each year Royalist provides 800 cadet berths.

Royalist usually runs weekly cruises, except when taking part in Tall Ships' races, such as the Cutty Sark event. Each week 24 members of the UK Sea Cadet corps, aged between 13 and 18, or of other uniformed youth organisations, plus 3 adult volunteers, set sail. Work aboard is guided by 6 permanent crew. The captain and his sailing master are qualified Merchant Navy Officers. Accommodation is comfortable but 'cosy' - each cadet being allocated a bunk and a small clothes locker - much in the way that ratings were accommodated in 19th century sailing ships. These simple living conditions are buttressed by excellent bathroom facilities, separate for boys and girls. TS Royalist's cruising pattern takes in the south coast of England, south west England, south Wales, the Irish Sea. Longer voyages take her to Scotland and the North Sea.
CONTACT Offshore Commander
'TS ROYALIST', HMS DOLPHIN, Gosport, Hants, PO12 2AB.
PHONE +44 1705 765888
FAX +44 1705 527224

SALTILLO (NAUTICAL SCHOOL SPAIN)

Rig Ketch
Length 12 metres 40 feet
Professional officers 1
Students 7

Saltillo is owned by Escula Superior de la Marina Civil de Bilboa (High School of the merchant marine of Bilbao) Universidad del Pais Vasco, and was the first of the seven Spanish ships in List IV to be involved in sail training.

SOFIA (ADMIRAL MAKAROV ACADEMY CADETS RUSSIA)

Rig Sloop
Length 10.8 metres 36 feet
Crew 2
Cadets 5

Built in 1992 at St. Petersburg and owned by the Admiral Makarov State Maritime Academy she is primarily used to train cadets from the navigational department of the Academy. In 1997 Sofia entered the Cutty Sark Tall Ships' Races with a crew of cadets from the Frunze Naval Academy, the oldest and most famous Russian Naval College, founded by Peter the Great in 1701

STORYLINE (DOCKLANDS SCOUT PROJECT UK)

Rig Sloop
Length 11 metres 36 feet
Crew 9

The Project, in London's Dockland's, has a 36 foot yacht which is usually at sea for between 2 and 14 days, exclusively on the South Coast of England. People 12 years old and upwards are accepted, either as individuals or groups. The cost is from £15 a day. Other organisations outside the Docklands may also join, and she usually sails with 3 professionals and six crew. A new yacht is also planned.

TARTESSOS (NAUTICAL SCHOOL SPAIN)

Rig Ketch
Length 12 metres 40 feet
Professional officers 1
Students 7

Owned by Facultat de Ciencias Nauticas de Cadiz (Faculty of Nautical Sciences of Cadiz) Universidad de Cadiz, she is of the Belliure 40 class, built in Calpe, Alicante, in 1986. Usually this type are sloops, but the school wished for a two masted ship, with four berths up front, 3 in the stern, and 2 in the centre, though the usual compliment is smaller. She usually sails around the Andalucia coast and in the Strait of Gibraltar and is used for sail training and in research projects.

TENERIFE (NAUTICAL SCHOSPAIN)

Rig Ketch
Length 12 metres 40 feet
Professional officers 1
Students 7

Tenerife is owned by Centro Superior de Nautica y Estudios del Mar de Tenerife (High School of Nautical and Sea Studies of Tenerife) Universidad de la Laguna, and is of the Belliure 40 class, built in Calpe, Alicante in 1986. Usually this type are sloops, but the school wished for two masted ships, with four berths up front, 3 in the stern, and 2 in the centre, though the usual compliment is smaller. She usually sails around the Canary Islands, and as well as sail training, she is used in investigation projects.

VALBORG (SCOUTS FINLAND)

Rig Ketch
Length 36.6 metres 120 feet
Professional officers 1
Professional crew 9
Trainees 50

Finland's Scout's have a number of sailing ships and power boats, and Valborg is the largest.

VARUNA (SEA CADET CORPS INDIA)

Rig Brig
Length 28 metres 92 feet

A sistership to the Colin Mudie design Royalist, you can easily spot the difference: Royalist has a black hull with a white horizontal stripe carrying gun ports painted on it: Varuna is the reverse, with a white painted hull, and a dark stripe.

ZAWISZA CZARNY (PATHFINDER SCOUTS POLAND)

Rig Schooner
Length 36 metres 118 feet
Professional Officers 8
Trainees 38

She is entered regularly in Cutty Sark Tall Ships' Races, by her owners the Centrum Wychowania Morskiego ZHP (the Pathfinder Scouts). She was named after the famous hero who in the key battle of 1410, Grunwald, helped the Poles defeat the Teutonic Knights who had become so powerful in the north. The Scouts help preserve past Polish culture especially by song and dance, and performances ashore in ports.

The ship is noted as one of the few 'wishbone' schooners around, with the high up 'wishbones' controlling how far the main sails are let out, rather than low down booms as on most of the ships with 'fore and aft' rigs.

Zawiszy Czarny (below)

Ariel (above)   Akela (above right)

Bylina (below)   Antica (below right)

List V. Smaller and occasional sail training ships, a list which grows each year, and more of them can be found in our Index at the back of this Guide

221

AKELA (Russia)

Rig Yawl
Length 14 metres 46 feet
Crew 12 including 8 cadets

Built in 1985 in Poland, she belongs to the St. Petersburg University of Water Communications (Leningrad Water Transport Institute). She has taken part in many regattas, including Cutty Sark Tall Ships' Races six times. In 1992 she was first in Class C in the Race from Tallin to Gdynia. Those who wish to sail on her should contact her captain

CONTACT Anexy Chegurnov. 129/3-146 Engelsa av, St. Petersburg, Russia
PHONE +7 812 5980651
FAX +7 812 2510114/2170682

"ALAND ISLANDS SHIP" (FINLAND)

Length 18.3 metres 60 feet.

The Maritime Museum of the Åland Islands have in hand a replica of a 17th Century freightship, with square sails on two masts, and a small lateen sail on the aft mast. She will both charter and sail train.

ALBATROS (RUSSIA)

Rig Sloop
Length 13.2 metres 43 feet
Crew 10 including 5 cadets

She is a sail training ship and so half her crew are cadets, from the Admiral Makarov State Maritime Academy. However, she invites outsiders, maybe 2 or 3 each year, to join as trainees.

Built in 1974 in Poland, she has a mahogany hull. For years owned by the Baltic Shipping Company, she is now in private hands, registered at St. Petersburg. She was champion of the annual Baltic Cup, many times. Since 1989 she has participated in Cutty Sark Tall Ships' Races, and awarded a number of prizes.

CONTACT Radmir Leontiev, Korablestroiteley st, 29/5-138, St. Petersburg, Russia
PHONE I +7 812 3128143
FAX +7 812 3127732/2170682

ANTICA (POLAND)

Rig. Cutter
Length 16.7 metres 55 feet
Trainees 4

Built in 1953 in Ustaka, Poland, as a fishing boat, to a Danish design, she was rebuilt between 1980 and 1990 as a sailing boat, a gaff ketch, taking part in the Columbus Regatta from Genoa to New York in 1992. From then until 1997 she sailed round the world, covering 60,840 miles and she visited 36 countries. In 1998 she entered the Cutty Sark Tall Ships' Races as an occasional sail training ship, and after a stay in Lisbon, she took off for a voyage through Cape Horn to Alaska. After Tall Ships 2000 from Bermuda to Amsterdam she sailed home. Her owner is a member of the Academic Sailing Club of Gdansk.

CONTACT Jerzy Wasowicz, Piastowska 80/20, 80-363 Gdansk, Poland.
PHONE +48 58 553 27 83
E-MAIL wasowicz@gd.onet.pl

ARIEL (RUSSIA)

Rig Sloop
Length13.6 metres 45 feet
Crew 11 including 7 trainees

She was built in 1981 in Gdansk, Poland to a design by American Doug Peterson. She belongs to the watersport facility owned by Kyrolvsky, Russia's largest tractor plant. Her home base is on the Bay of Finland, 20 km from St. Petersburg and near the famous palace of the Russian Tsars, Petrodvoretz. She has done well in national and international regattas. In 1990 she took part in the classic Sydney-Hobart in Australia but lost her mast. In 1966 she entered the Cutty Sark Tall Ships' Races for the first time, and won the second race, in her class and overall.

CONTACT Anatoly Konovalov, 25 Pristanskaya st, Petrodvorzetz 5, St Petersburg, 198903, Russia
PHONE +7 812 4211167
FAX +7 812 4214040/2170682

Flora

Aurora (below)

Athena (above)

Binda of Western Port (below)

Forward (above)   Colin Archer (above)   Eda Frandsen (below)

AURORA (RUSSIA)

Rig Sloop
Length 16.6 metres 54 feet
Crew 5
Trainees 7 includes 3 paying
Owned by the St. Petersburg
University of Maritime Technology
(Shipbuilding Institute) Yacht Club,
Aurora was built in 1977 in Gdansk
(Poland) to a design by Richard
Langer as a cruiser/racer. For the most
part she is crewed by teachers and
students from the University, but she
does offer paying places aboard to
foreign trainees, in particular during
Cutty Sark Tall Ships' Races in which
she has participated since 1990. Each
year 3-4 foreign sail trainees sail on
board her, and her modern navigation
and safety equipment is suitable for
young sea enthusiasts. She has taken
part in many events in the Baltic, North
Sea, and Biscay, sailing about 3,000
miles each year.

BINDA OF WESTERN PORT (BELGIUM)

Rig Cutter
Length 11 metres 36 feet
Crew 4
In 1998 she took part in her fourth
Cutty Sark Tall Ships' Races. Built in
Sydney, Australia, in 1978, her name
means 'deep water' in the Aboriginal
language. She came to Europe in
1994, and in 1998, after visiting
Dublin, she sailed back to Australia
with a two person crew.

BYLINA (RUSSIAN NAVY CLUB)

Rig. Sloop
Length 12.4 metres 41 feet
Crew 3
Cadets 5

This wooden hulled yacht was built in Leningrad (now St. Petersburg) in 1975 and belongs to the Russian Navy Yacht Club. In the late 1970s and throughout most of the 1980s she was used for sail training in the Baltic. In 1991 she entered the Cutty Sark Tall Ships' Races, the first time that a Russian Naval sailing yacht with navy cadets and officers had participated. In 1991/92 she was renovated and refitted, with the help of sponsors, to become a well equipped and seaworthy sail training yacht. In 1998 she trained naval cadets in the Baltic and participated in local maritime festivals.
CONTACT Andrey Berezkin, Admiral Makarov State Maritime Academy, 15a, Kosaya Linia, St. Petersburg, 199026, Russia.
PHONE +7 812 3566069
FAX +7 812 2170682
PHONE/FAX +7 812 2723663

COLIN ARCHER (NORWAY)

Rig Ketch
Length 13.9 metres 46 feet

Colin Archer was a Scot whose family had emigrated to Norway. He first built sturdy pilot boats. As Norway developed the idea of a lifeboat organisation, he was asked for a new design, which was accepted, and in all 52 such boats - larger than the pilot boats - were built. Named after him, Colin Archer was built in 1893. Renovated, she still sails on many Cutty Sark Tall Ships' Races with a dedication to train young Norwegians.

Sparta (below)

Helena Cristtina (above)

EDA FRANDSEN (SCOTLAND)

Rig Cutter
Length 16.2 metres 54 feet
Professional crew 4
Guest crew and trainees 8

Eda was built in Denmark in 1939 as a fishing boat and originally carried a ketch rig with a single cylinder engine. After decommissioning she was bought, in a semi derelict state, by her present owners and was rebuilt with traditional rig, including an 18 foot bowsprit. She has sailed regularly in Cutty Sark Tall Ships' Races. Her home ground is the west of Scotland and the islands of the Hebrides, where she offers charter holidays, corporate entertainment, and management team building as well as sail training. Numbers of guests and crew vary, with a maximum of 14 persons on board.
CONTACT Doune Marine, Knoydart, by Mallaig, PH41 4PU, Scotland
PHONE +44 1687 462667

FLORA (RUSSIA)

Rig Yawl
Length 14 metres 45 feet
Crew 8 including 4 cadets

For many years she was owned by the Baltic Shipping Company, but now she is in private hands. She is also registered as a Children's Sail Training School, and every year she sails with 14-20 year olds. She was built in 1979 in Poland. A graceful wooden hulled yacht, she is the most regular of Russia's fleet in Cutty Sark Tall Ships' Races. She took part for the first time in 1982.
CONTACT Captain of Flora, Martynova emb 92, St Petersburg 197042, Russia
PHONE +7 812 2170682
FAX +7 812 2307585

FORWARD (RUSSIA)

Rig Sloop
Length 11.1 metres 37 feet
Crew 2
Cadets 5

She was owned by the Baltic Shipping Company's yacht club, and is now privately owned. She was built in Leningrad (now St. Petersburg) in 1983, of wood, and is designed especially for longer distance races. She takes 5 trainees and has participated in six Cutty Sark Tall Ships' Races between 1987 and 1996, winning prizes in most of them, and in 1989 she was first overall in Class CIII in both races. In 1997 she sailed in the Baltic, participating in races and local maritime festivals.
CONTACT Boris Khriachtchev, Zhukova st 30/2-64, St. Petersburg 198303, Russia
PHONE +7 812 1585189
FAX +7 812 3252136
E-MAIL ppmilakh@dux.ru.//

GRENADA (ESTONIA)

Rig Sloop
Length 12.2 metres

Owned by Baltsail, she entered the 1981 Cutty Sark Tall Ships' Race

HEBE II (CZECH)

Rig Sloop
Length 11.6 metres 40 feet

Built in 1995 she is a welcome first entry from Czechoslovakia in Cutty Sark Tall Ships' Races.

HELENA CRISTINA (NETHERLANDS)

Rig Ketch
Length 14.3 metres 47 feet
Crew 2
Cadets 8

Launched in 1985, Helena Cristina set sail with AAD Twigt, Hella, and their two children Agnita and Alies, sailing round the world rounding both Cape Horn and the Cape of Good Hope from East to West, a voyage that lasted until 1990. Following her return to Holland she is used as a sail training ship, participating in the Cutty Sark Tall Ships' Races of 1995, 1997 and 1998. She is built in steel, and sails as well in light airs as in gale force winds.
CONTACT AAD Twigt
PHONE +31 181 324838

KENYA JACARANDA (UK)

Rig Ketch
Length 23.5 metres 77 feet

A 1923 built Brixham sailing trawler, based on the Thames Estuary and run by enthusiasts, she has been as far as the Channel Islands and France. She takes a mixed crew for a day to a week, from £30 per weekend including food.

LIV (NORWAY)

Rig Ketch
Length 16.2 metres 53 feet
Crew 7 including 4 trainees

Following the 1893 success of Colin Archer's RV1 (Rescue Vessel 1) in Norway, in the following years other such ships were built, in similar style. RV5 was Liv, designed by Christian Stevansen, with modification by Colin Archer. She is now converted to a private yacht, but takes part in Cutty Sark Tall Ships' Races.

Liv (above)   Moonduster (below)

Stephani

LIVELY LADY (UK)
Rig Ketch
Length 11.6 metres 38 feet
Run by the Meridian Trust Association from Portsmouth, she aims
to help youngsters who have 'got into trouble' or are in danger of
doing so. The Association also works with RYA Sailability to equip
yachts to allow the blind to go sailing. Another yacht, Richard
Langhorn, is also run by the Association.

MAIT II (ITALY)
Rig Yawl
Length 19 metres 62.3 feet
Professional officers 3
Trainees 5
Designed by Sparkman and Stephens, she was launched in 1957,
and became the first Italian entry in the Fastnet race (from Cowes
England to the Fastnet Rock, south Ireland, and back to Plymouth)
in 1959, and in the Buenos Aires to Rio race in 1962. In the
Mediterranean she won three times the classic Giraglia Race in
1962, 1963 and 1971. Her owner presented her to the Yacht Club
Italiano, based in Genova, for sail training. She has had several
owners since, she still participates in vintage yacht races and rallies
including the Mediterranean Cutty Sark Tall Ships' Race in 1996.

MIR (RUSSIA)
Rig Sloop
Length 13.6 metres 45 feet
Crew 10 including 5 cadets
Built in 1983 in Poland for racing, she has turned to sail training
since 1986. Awarded many prizes, she was given a special one in
1996 for seaworthiness. She has taken part in many other regattas
such as the Kotka International Regatta, Kiel Woche, and the St.
Petersburg Championship, with good results. Nowadays she is in
private hands, and sails in local races, sail training events and ports'
events in the Baltic.
CONTACT Alexander Kulikov,
PHONE +7 812 261064 FAX +7 812 2355846 +7 812 2170682

MOONDUSTER (IRELAND)
Rig Sloop
Length 17.4 metres 57 feet
Crew 14
Here is a famous ocean racer in which Denis Doyle from Cork,
south of Ireland, has taken part in many worldwide competitions,
bringing young and experienced to enjoy the sea. Moonduster

entered the Cutty Sark Tall Ships' Race of 1998.

RUS (RUSSIA)
Rig Sloop
Length 13.2 metres 43 feet
Crew 4
Trainees 6
Rus was built in 1973 in Poland, and has taken part in Cutty Sark
Tall Ships' Races since 1988. Her young trainees are cadets from
the Admiral Makarov State Maritime Academy and the Military
Medical Academy. For most cadets the races are the best chance of
getting training in real seamanship and sailing.
CONTACT Andrej Anrejainen 196247 St. Petersburg,
Post Office Box 316, Russia
PHONE +7 812 3279566.
FAX +7 812 3279484/ 217068

SPARTA (LATVIA)
Rig Sloop
Length 16.7 metres 55 feet
Owned by the Latvian Shipping Company, she was built in 1971 and
entered a Cutty Sark Tall Ships' Race in 1995.

"STAVANGER MUSEUM" (NORWAY)
The museum's two ships are Wyvern/ Anna af Sand
Rig ketch/ sloop
Length 18.2 metres 60 feet/ 15.8 metres 52 feet
Crew 12/ 6
Wyvern and Anna of Sand are owned by the Stavanger Maritime
Museum, and are run for the benefit of the museum, the town of
Stavanger and its county Rogaland. Wyvern has taken part in a
Cutty Sark Tall Ships' Race with trainees on board. Wyvern is
derived from old English fairy tales, the name of an evil winged-
dragon. Launched in 1897, she is the largest of designer Colin
Archer's 'double enders' (with canoe shaped stern). Anna af Sand is
probably the oldest seaworthy vessel in Norway built probably in
1848. Her type carried cargo along the fjords and coast of Norway,
and herring as far as St. Petersburg, returning with grain, timber and
hemp.

STEPHANI (GERMANY)
Rig Cutter
Length 13.2 metres 43.3 feet
Crew 5/7
Stephani and Vegewind (see list 1) are from the fleet of the

European foundation, EUROCO, based in Bremen and founded in 1986 to encourage educational youth exchanges and sail training. Stephani is a Colin Archer design, built by Aucoop so that she would have no limit for extended blue water sailing with young people on board. The North Sea and Baltic between Dublin and Gdansk are the waters she cruises for most of the year.

CONTACT NAME Capt Klaus Tietze-Scheer
ADDRESS AUCOOP-Bootswerkstatt Bremen, Schulkenstr. Tor Fahr, 28755 Bremen, Germany
PHONE +49 421 66 30 69 / 60
FAX +49 421 66 30 67
ADDRESS Navigator sail training e.V. Wilmannsberg 21, 28757 Bremen
PHONE +49 421 65 63 19
FAX +49 421 65 64 78

STOUTHEART (UK)
Rig Ketch
Length 13 metres 43 feet
Crew 3
Trainees 7

Designed by Bruce Roberts and launched in 1990, she is a steel ketch built specifically for sail training by owners Kath and Dave Broatch. She entered the Cutty Sark Tall Ship Races in 1991 and now intends to take part in further races from 1998 on a regular basis. Based in the Menai Straits, north west Wales, her usual voyages are from 2 to 14 days, with trainees of 14 or older. She is fitted with comfort, nautical atmosphere, and instructional facilities in mind.
CONTACT West Coast Maritime, Cae Gwydryn, Llanddeiniolen, Caernarfon, Gwynedd LL55 3AL
PHONE +44 1248 671291

THALATTA (UK)
Rig Spritsail
Length 30.5 metres 100 feet

Based on Maldon, East England, Thalatta is a Thames barge which usually has five day cruises along the East Anglian coastline, with a crew of up to 12 youngsters, sleeping in hammocks.

Trapageer

Stavanger Museum's Wyvern

TRAPEGEER (BELGIUM)
Rig Sloop
Length 13.4 metres 44 feet
Crew 8 including 6 trainees

Built in Boom (near Antwerp) as a cruising yacht in 1982, of the type Kalik 44, she's been many times to Greece, Spain, Portugal, France, Holland and Denmark, and she organises regular sail training weekends from 1st April, with England a favourite destination. Now owned by Geert Vandendriessche, with Jef Leyer and others from Belgium and Spain on board, she entered the Cutty Sark Tall Ships' Race for the fourth time in 1999. She has proved an excellent sea-boat in heavy weather, and she and her crew "especially like spinnaker-time when the skipper is cooking pancakes below".

ZVEZDA (RUSSIA)
Rig Sloop
Length 16.8 metres 55.1 feet
Total crew 10

Zvezda (meaning Star) was built in Germany at the shipyard Abeking and Rasmussen, near Bremen, in 1934. At first, her name was Stella Polaris. She came to St Petersburg when the German fleet was divided, post war, and since then she has belonged to the St. Petersburg Yacht Club of Trade Unions. Every year young sailors join the ship so she has become a real sail training school for many in St. Petersburg. In 1991 enthusiasts refitted and repaired the yacht, renewing her hull plating underwater.
CONTACT Igor Dementiev, Captain St. Petersburg River Yacht Club, 7, Petrovskaya kosa, St Petersburg 194111, Russia.
FAX +7 812 272 3663

List VI is of cruise ships that use sail rather than power, and recreate for us ships of yesterday. Passengers can take part in manoeuvres, and learn about the sea.

La France

NATIONALITY	French
HOME PORT	Cherbourg
SIZE OVERALL	170 metres 558 feet
PROFESSIONAL CREW	90
PAYING PASSENGERS	200
ACADEMY MEMBERS	50
SAIL TRAINEES	50

History

By 1911, sailing ships were finding it hard to compete against steam, especially with the Suez Canal completed. But Prentout Armaments took a gamble, and built France II as the largest sailing ship in the world, larger than existing ships at 150 metres long. France would be, with bowsprit, 170 metres. From 1913, she brought to Europe nickel from New Caledonia - the island north east of Australia, for use in composite metals. The public of the time fell in love with ocean cruises, so Prentout put in a grand piano, library, dark room, and Thalassotherapy (sea water therapy) equipment, for up to 50 passengers. In the First World War she was armed with two cannons and patrolled the three infamous Capes, Cape Horn, Cape of Good Hope, and Cape Leewin. After Prentout's death in 1916, her engines and propellers were removed. With sails alone, on a calm day in 1922, she ran aground on the Ouano reefs off New Caledonia. For twenty years she was a familiar site as a wreck, until 1944 when American bombers blew her up.

The new ship will have the precise measurements of France II

On Board

Maquette Gilbert Carrouget

.About 90 crew will run the ship. There will also be 100 cabins with two berths in each, all of the same class, for 'cruise' members, paying for the voyage. And there will be people training for future work. At the moment, France has no ship to provide on-board facilities for the shore-based Naval Academy of Marine Trade, which trains those seeking jobs in sea-cruising and maritime tourism This limits the numbers presently accepted by the Academy. La France hopes to help. Entrants will be taught on land, and then sail on board .So far the Academy claims total success with placing those who train with it, and waiting lists are large. There will also be room on La France for those engaged in sail training.

After the award of contracts for building La France, soon, completion is expected by 2001. The picture below is of a model of the new ship.

Safety Certificates and Insurance

She will be constructed under the classification of a passenger liner exceeding 500 tons.

Programme

Her usual voyages will take her round the world, via the Panama Canal and Suez Canal.

CONTACT	Association France II Renaissance
ADDRESS	95100 Argenteuil, France
PHONE/FAX	+33 130 25 35 35
E-MAIL	France@grand-voilier.com
WEB	http://www.grand-voilier.com/english.htm

Lili Marleen

NATIONALITY	German
HOME PORT	Neustadt, in the Baltic
SIZE OVERALL	76 metres 249 feet
PROFESSIONAL CREW	25
PAYING PASSENGERS	50

History
Lili Marleen is a three masted barquentine, built in 1994 in Elsfleth on the river Weser for Peter Deilmann Reederei.

On Board
Lili Marleen recalls the romance of old windjammers, but provides the security of latest navigational aids and the comforts of a modern, luxurious cruise ship, which boasts a fine cuisine. She has 25 fully air conditioned outside cabins with private shower/WC, with two bars and a library. Passengers may participate in sailing manoeuvres according to their capabilities, and there are daily lectures on nautical subjects given by the captain and the officers.

SAFETY CERTIFICATES AND INSURANCE
Lili Marleen complies with SBG and SOLAS; she has certificates for the Suez and Panama Canals, and conforms with US Coast Guard and US Public Health regulations for foreign flag ships.

She is classified under Germanischer Lloyd as a +100A5 Sailing Yacht, and as a passenger ship.

Programme
Lili Marleen has sailed transatlantic, but her present programme is in the Mediterranean and Canary Islands, with 7 day voyages, made from Las Palmas around the Canary Islands (November to March), from Nice along the Cote d'Azur and the Rivieras (April and June), from Piraeus or Antalya through the Aegean Islands (July to September), and from Palma de Mallorca around the Balearics (September to October). Fares start from £1380 per person, sharing a double outside cabin, including return flights from London, transfers and comprehensive travel insurance.

CONTACT	Peter Deilmann Ocean Cruises Ltd
ADDRESS	324/326 Regent Street, Suite 404, London W1R 5AA, UK
PHONE	+44 171 436 2931
FAX	+44 171 436 2607
E-MAIL	gv13@dial.pipex.com
ADDRESS	Am Hafensteig 17-19, Newstadt in Holstein, D-23730, Germany
PHONE	+49 4561 61060
FAX	+49 4561 8207

Star Clipper & Star Flyer

NATIONALITY	*Luxembourg*
MAIN PORTS	*Cannes Antigua Kusadasi Singapore*
	Phuket
SIZE OVERALL	*110 metres 360 feet*
CREW	*70*
PAYING PASSENGERS	*170*

History

Two identical luxury sisterships were built in 1991 and 1992 at Belgian Shipbuilders Corporation, Ghent, Belgium. They are operated and owned by Star Clippers Ltd with head offices in Miami and Monaco. The company is owned by its founder, Swedish ship owner Mikael Krafft. He was born and raised in Saltsjobaden at the seaside of Stockholm and for him, as for most boys in this village, sailing and the sea became a passion from early childhood. From the age of 10 he started to sneak away across the 20 miles of open sea singlehanded on his 16 foot open sailing boat, and a tent, to the Åland Islands, where he played on the former Gustav Erikson owned 4 mast barque Pommern. Since those days it was his dream to put commercial square riggers back into use. His Star Clipper ships concentrate as much as possible on sailing and lectures around sailing, the history of sail and navigation, where interested passengers can participate. The bridge is always open. In the early days quite a few captains had to leave the company as they were not using the sails enough.

On Board

On deck you'll think you are on any of the large sailing ships of yesterday. The fore and aft sails can be handled by the crew, and passengers may join in the fun. The top square sails are furled automatically, but the lower yards can be dealt with by hand. Throughout a cruise, sailing is dominant. The ships try to leave harbour with sails set (and engine running, rather like a Parade of Sail under the Cutty Sark Tall Ships' Races). At sea, they try to use sails as much as possible, certainly after dark where engine noise can be annoying. If you wish to climb the foremast, to the first crows nest, then you are welcome. On Star Clipper a 90 year old did so, unaided, except helped by two ropes and a piece of safety equipment adapted from mountain climbing practice which means you can only fall a short way. On board there is constant chat from a skipper familiar with the sea. There is teaching of knots, of sailing, and in small pools on board, you may learn how to scuba dive, when between ports. And when you go ashore maybe to a sandy beach, you can dive with skilled supervisors. The ships are unique as they are fully registered PADI Dive Resorts. Windsurfing, waterskiing, snorkelling are part of the on-beach diet.

Usually, you anchor or come alongside in the morning, depart at night time, and arrive the next morning (or the morning after that) at the next destination, then take off again after a day of watersports or excursions exploring historic and scenic sites.

SAFETY CERTIFICATES AND INSURANCE

The ships are classified by Lloyd's Register, Luxembourg, rated +100 A1, making them the first true sailing ships to be given this high classification since the early days of this century. The vessels also fully comply with all existing safety rules by US Coast Guard, US Public Health, Marpol, and can thus, unlike most other sailing cruise ships, visit any port in the world.

Programme

The two ships follow quite different schedules. Star Clipper spends her summer in the western Mediterranean, with maybe 7 or 14 day voyages to and from Cannes, which alternate between a 'Tyrrhenian' and a 'Ligurian' route, the former including Corsica, Elba, Sardinia, Italy, Monaco and France, and the later including Corsica, Sardinia, Italy, Monaco and France. A 7 day trip (no flights) to Calvi, Bonifacio, Sardinia, Elba, Italy and France, or to Corsica, Portofino, St Tropez costs from £780 a person (in a twin cabin).

On the way to winter in the Caribbean, maybe the voyage will be a 28 day cruise from the Cote d'Azur. She may call at Marseille, Barcelona, Malaga, or take a more southerly route via the Balearics (Palma, maybe Menorca, Ibiza and Formentera) to Malaga, before heading for the Canaries and the West Indies (Antigua). Such a cruise costs from £2,500 a person in a twin cabin. This includes air travel to and from Europe, with full board, port taxes, transfers. Not included are travel insurance, shore excursions, airport tax and gratuities.

In the West Indies there are 7 and 14 day voyages based on Antigua, with a 7 day route down to the best of the Grenadines, and another 7 days via the Leeward Islands to the Treasure Islands or the British Virgin Islands. If you take two full weeks you will thus cover all the very best of the Caribbean. You will visit many 'sailor's hidden paradises' where cruise ships and mass tourism will not bother you. The costs for 14 nights per person in a twin are from £2,110 (with air flights included).

Meantime Star Flyer's summer is in the Eastern Mediterranean, including Turkey's Bodrum, Kekova, Kusadasi, and Greece's Karpathos, Kos, Patmos, Samos, Santorini, Mykonos and Rhodes. The Turkey and Dodecanese trip takes in four Turkish and three Greek ports. The Cyclades route takes in six Greek and one Turkish port. For 7 nights, the cost could be from £700 a person in a twin cabin (with no airflights).

Then she travels through the Suez Canal, to the Far East, arriving in Thailand and Singapore. From November to early April she sails in Thailand and Malaysia between Phuket and Singapore. During this period the weather is stable and excellent. Nature in Thailand and North Malaysia is unique with fantastic rock formations, remote white sand beaches, coral reefs and the clean warm ocean.

A Singapore to Singapore voyage could include stopping at such as Pangkor, Butang Islands, Phi Phi Islands, areas such as the strange Pang Nga archipelago, Ko Dam Hok, Simian islands, Surin Islands (on the border with Burma), the Phi Phi Islands, the national part of Langkawi, Pankor and historically interesting Malacca. On her trip back from Singapore to the Aegean via the Andaman Island, Sri Lanka, Cochin, Goa, Aden, Egypt, the Suez Canal to Rhodes is from £3,340 in a twin (with airflights, full board, port taxes, transfers, and excluding travel insurance, shore excursions and gratuities).

CONTACT	Star Clippers Monaco
ADDRESS	27, boulevard Albert 1er, MC 98000, Monaco
PHONE	+377 93 50 50 00
FAX	+377 93 50 80 80
CONTACT	Star Clippers Miami
ADDRESS	4101 Salzedo Street, Coral Gables, Florida, USA
PHONE	+1 305 442 0550
FAX	+1 305 529 2490

Sea Cloud

NATIONALITY	*Maltese*
HOME PORT	*Valetta, Malta*
SIZE OVERALL	*96 metres 315 feet*
CREW	*60*
PAYING PASSENGERS	*69*

History

She launched as Hussar at Germania, Kiel, in 1931 for Edward F. Hutton, one of Wall Street's most successful investment brokers. He had her built for his wife Marjorie Merryweather Post. Marjorie, heiress to one of America's largest fortunes turned her into a glamourous meeting place for royalty, heads of state and society. She was renamed Sea Cloud by Marjorie on her separation from her husband.

Marjorie's third husband was a diplomat and confidante of the President Franklin D.Roosevelt. He, Joseph Davies, was appointed US Ambassador to Russia, and he turned the ship into a floating Embassy moored in Leningrad (now St. Petersburg). In the Second World War, she had her masts removed, and as IX-99, became a weather ship in the North Atlantic, with a navy grey coat of paint. She was leased to the government for only $1. After the war the US Coast Guard returned her to Marjorie who had her rerigged and renovated. Sailing under three succeeding new names, she was finally mothballed in Colon, Panama. There a group of German businessmen, looking for her, found her by chance and returned her to Hamburg in 1978 and to Kiel in 1979, where her second transformation turned her into a luxury cruise ship, with all the benefits of traditional style, and modern living conditions, communications and facilities. Her name Sea Cloud has returned to her.

On Board

When she arrives at a destination, watersports are given a priority, and snorkelling, windsurfing and waterskiing are priorities. Zodiac inflatables and tender boats take passengers every half an hour to beaches or the port, and instructors are available to encourage you to take on a new interest in the sea.

Programme

Her summertime destination is the Mediterranean, and for her it is the Caribbean in the winter. A typical Caribbean programme day by day might be as follows: arrive by air at Antigua, day at sea, Bequia, Grenada, Carriacou, St Lucia, Iles des Saints, Antigua,and then for a second cruise, Antigua, Virgin Gorda, Joost Van Dyke, St Martin, St Barts, St Kitts, Antigua. Usually there are 7 night cruises at approximately £2000 without airfare. A sample itinerary in the Mediterranean might include Istanbul, Canakkale, Mithimna/Lesbos, Delos, Mykonos, Patmos, Fethiye, and Kusadasi.

Sea Cloud II, owned by the same company, is soon to launch.

ADDRESS	Sea Cloud Cruises GmbH, Ballindamm17, D-20095 Hamburg, Germany
PHONE	+49 40 30 95920
FAX	+49 40 30 959222
E-MAIL	info@seacloud.com
WEB	http://www.seacloud.com

Royal Clipper

NATIONALITY	Luxembourg
HOME PORT	Barbados
SIZE OVERALL	133 8 metres 439 feet
CREW	90
PAYING PASSENGERS	228

HISTORY

In 1902 the world's then largest sailing ship at that time, Preussen, was launched. She was built for the famous Flying P line, whose fleet included Padua (now Kruzenshtern, and still sailing), Peking (now a museum ship at South Street Museum, New York), Passat (alongside without sails in Travemunde, but there are plans to bring her back to sail), Pommern (a longside in Mariehamn), and Pamir (sinking with the loss of 80 lives off the Azores). Most had four masts, and were barque rigged (with square sails, but with fore and aft sails on their last mast, to help them to get out of trouble with the wind ahead).

Preussen was different. She was larger than them all. She had five masts, and square sails on all of them. She had no engine, and so she had to be towed through the dangerous Straits of Dover, as far as south west England and Start Point. On a fateful voyage in 1910 she dropped her tow too soon after Dover, met adverse winds, and had to seek help from two tugs. Alas, their tows snapped before she could be brought into Dover. The remains of her hull still can be seen, sometimes, beneath the White Cliffs.

Comes on the scene Swedish businessman Mikael Krafft, owner of Star Clipper and Star Flyer (see a page on from this). What more famous ship to recreate than Preussen, who with the wind favourable could make well over 20 knots. Add an engine to help Royal Clipper in adverse conditions, and you have the new ship, her hull built in Poland by 1999, towed to western Europe to fit out, and ready for March 2000 to begin her life as a luxury replica ship. Mikael's passion for the sea has ensured that she is no cruise ship with a gesture of a sailplan. And (as on his other ships) there are - if you wish - lectures once or twice a day on the waters you sail through, the history of the sea and of traditional ships, and navigation. Watersports are taught on deck, the library is stocked with nautical books, you can climb a mast, and help with her sailing. Her hull has a sizeable glass enclosed atrium, through which to study fish and the seabed, and a marina platform drops from her stern, to help sports activities, and make it easy to get ashore, using fast motor boats. Her state of the art stabilising devices are a blessing in heavy weather.

PROGRAMME

At first she sails from Barbados on 7 and 14 day voyage to the lower Windward Islands and the Grenadines, in the winters, and then to Cannes and the Mediterranean in the summers. Her prices are in the luxury category.

CONTACT	Star Clippers Monaco
ADDRESS	27, boulevard Albert 1er, MC 98000, Monaco
PHONE	+377 93 50 50 00
FAX	+377 93 50 80 80
CONTACT	Star Clippers Miami
ADDRESS	4101 Salzedo Street, Coral Gables, Florida, USA
PHONE	+1 305 442 0550 FAX +1 305 529 2490

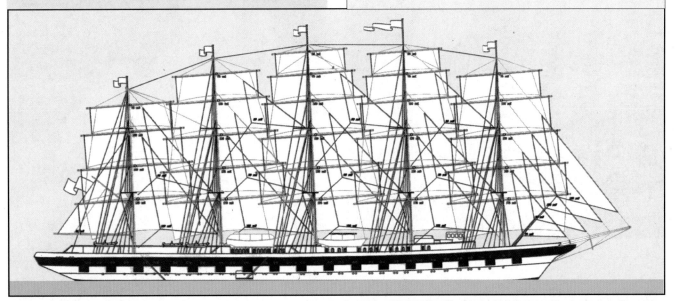

Sea Cloud II

NATIONALITY	Maltese
SIZE OVERALL	117 m 384ft
CREW	60
PAYING PASSENGERS	96

Larger than Sea Cloud (see over), with the same owners, she will be ready in late 2000.

She will sail the Caribbean, Gulf of Mexico, Aegean, Western Mediterranean, Canary Islands, and the historic ports of the Black Sea. Her builder is Astilleros Gondan S.A. in Figueras, North Spain.

Windjammer Barefoot Cruises

Offering you the West Indies, with experts on board to help show you the ropes, with scuba diving and watersports, is Windjammer Barefoot Cruises. The group claims to have the largest 'clipper' fleet in the world with five sailing ships, and a motorship. The ships are all registered in Equatorial Guinea. The company notes: it ships comply with all international safety standards, except 1966 fire safety standards, and are compliant with US Coast Guard safety standards.

COSTS Six day cruises start at $675 to $1500 per person, based on double occupancy. Port charges are about $100 extra. Ships sail the British, Spanish and American Virgin Islands, the Windward and Leeward Islands, the French West Indies and St. Vincent and the Grenadines. 13 day cruises on Mandalay start at $1500 to $2200.

CONTACT Windjammer Barefoot Cruises Ltd,
ADDRESS P.O. Box 190-120 Miami Beach, Fl 33119-0120
PHONE +1 305 672 6453
FAX +1 305 674 1219
E-MAIL windbc@windjammer.com WEB
http://www.windjammer.com

Polynesia

SIZE OVERALL 76 m 248 ft
CREW 45
PAYING PASSENGERS 126

Polynesia was built in Holland in 1938. Originally named Argus, she was the most profitable of the Portuguese' Grand Banks cod fishing fleet. She was bought in 1975 and renamed Polynesia. Her near sistership Creoula (also in our Guide) has also been converted to sail train.

Legacy

SIZE OVERALL 90m 294 ft
CREW 43
PAYING PASSENGERS 122

Originally France II, built in 1959 at Forges et al Mediterranée of Le Havre, she was a meteorological research and exploration vessel of the French government, before her acquisition in 1989 by Windjammer who converted her into a traditional tall ship.

Mandalay

SIZE OVERALL	72 m	236 ft
CREW		28
PAYING PASSENGERS		72

Cox and Stephens designed her in 1923 for financier E.F.Hutton and his wife, who named her their first Hussar. Shipping magnate Georges Vettlesen renamed her Vema in the 1930s, and by 1953 she was a floating laboratory for Columbia University's Lamont-Doherty Geological Observatory. It is said that nearly half of the existing knowledge of the ocean floor was gathered by the vessel. In 1982 she joined the Windjammer fleet.

Yankee Clipper

SIZE OVERALL 60 m 197 ft
CREW 24
PAYING PASSENGERS 64

One of a few armour plated private yachts in the world, Cressida (now Yankee Clipper) was built in Kiel in 1927 for German industrialist Alfred Krupp. After the war she was confiscated by the US Coast Guard as a warprize. Acquired by the Vanderbilts she was renamed Pioneer, and raced off Newport Beach, California. Acquired by Windjammer in 1965, she had a $4 million refurbishment in 1984, completed in 1987.

Flying Cloud

SIZE OVERALL	63 m	208 ft
CREW		28
PAYING PASSENGERS		66

Originally a French cadet training ship, named Oisseau Des Isles, she was built in Nantes, France in 1935 and sailed the French Polynesian Islands in the war as a decoy and spy ship. General de Gaulle decorated her for help in sinking two Japanese submarines. Used as a Mexican cargo ship after the war, she was acquired by Windjammer in 1968.

Circling the World Adventures

Once upon a time races round the world were dominated by sailors of experience, usually sailing in state-of-the-art yachts built to varied designs, using exotic materials and equipment. Times change, and now three groups offer sturdy yachts, all built the same for their race, high-tech but not the

highest, suitable even for a crew of newcomers. They offer different dates and courses. You pay a fee, you are taught pre-race, you are given the best heavy weather clothes, and off you go, under one expert as skipper. We outline the three races, the ultimate for those who wish to "Sail to Adventure".

SIR CHAY BLYTH'S GLOBAL CHALLENGE (2000-2001 BT TITLE SPONSORSHIP)

START AND FINISH	Southampton
LENGTH OF YACHT	22 metres 72 feet
PROFESSIONAL SKIPPER	1
PAYING CREW	17

Chay pioneered paying round the world races. He chose an arduous course, down to the Roaring Forties, sailing against the wind east to west, around Cape Horn and the Cape of Good Hope, through icebergs and snow. His next races Round the World start in September 2000 and September 2004, and take 10 months, in 12 new yachts of 72 feet. The Global course is to Boston, Buenos Aires, Australia, New Zealand, Cape Town, and back, for £24,850. Each of six legs costs about £8.000. Recently Chay has acquired other race-events, so a whole package of routes and dates are now on offer, All 14 of his early 67 foot Classic yachts are still around, for these and other events, such as one from San Francisco to Japan.

CONTACT The Challenge Business
ADDRESS The Box Office, Box, Minchinghampton, Glos GL6 9HA.
PHONE +44 1453 836333
FAX +44 1453 836943
WEB http://www.challengebusiness.com

SIR ROBIN KNOX JOHNSTON'S CLIPPER VENTURES

START AND FINISH 2000/2003	PORTSMOUTH
LENGTH OF YACHT	18 metres 60 feet
PROFESSIONAL SKIPPER	1
PAYING CREW	14

Robin's different idea, of a warm water race through the tropics, uses more stop-over ports to keep racing tight. The seven yachts in 1998-9 finished 12 minutes apart from Cuba to Panama. The 11 month race of 1998-9 is followed by The Times Clipper races in 2000-2001, and 2002-3 with six legs and 16 stops; from Portsmouth to the Canaries and Cuba; to Panama the Galapagos and Hawaii; to

Japan, Shanghai and Hong Kong; to Singapore and Mauritius; to Cape Town and Brazil; and to the USA, Europe and Portsmouth. Legs costs £6,500 to £6,950 and the whole costs £23,500. Robin's fleet, now eight ships strong, could grow to a dozen for the Times Clipper 2000.

CONTACT Clipper Ventures Plc
ADDRESS Incon House, 10 Stilebrook Road, Olney, Bucks MK46 5EA
PHONE +44 1234 711 550   FAX +44 1234 711 250
WEB http://www.clipper-ventures.com
E-MAIL HQ@clipper-ventures.com

THE MILLENIUM ROUND THE WORLD RACE

START AND FINISH	Portsmouth
LENGTH OF YACHT	20 metres 65 feet
PROFESSIONAL SKIPPER	1
PAYING CREW	14

Ten new yachts are to be completed for the second 2003 race, with most available for the first race starting October 1999, in an eleven month voyage to even more ports than the other two races. There are 39 ports, and the event is grouped into six Phases. Phase I from Portsmouth to the Canaries, Lanzarote, Antiga, Guadeloupe, Martinique, St Lucia, St Vincent, the Grenadines, and Grenada to Trinidad & Tobago (74 days). Phase 2 ports are Aruba, Panama Canal, Galapagos, Marquesas, and Tahiti (51 days). Phase 3 sails to Tonga, Fiji, Auckland and Sydney (37 days). Phase 4 heads for Cairns, Darwin, Christmas Island, Maldives, and Mauritius (61 days). Phase 5 is to Durban, Cape Town, to Recife in Brazil (41 days), and Phase 6 is to the Azores, France, and back to Portsmouth (34 days).
Costs are from £6,500 for a Phase, to £29,500 the whole trip.

CONTACT   Millenium Yachting International Ltd
ADDRESS   Deepdale Close, Hartington Park, Staveley, Chesterfield, S43 3YF
PHONE/ FAX   +00 44 1246 477377
E-MAIL info@millenium-rtw.co.uk
WEB http://www millenium-rtw.co.uk

Yachts from (above) Clipper Ventures, and (below) Millenium.

Lists I covers ships which offer sail training and adventure voyages, with (paying, sometimes subsidised) berths available, which are more usually found in European waters, in the Canaries, Mediterranean, and Caribbean. Descriptions of these ships and their programmes make up the major part of this guide. Most of them in this list have places for 10 or more trainees, so enabling groups to join them, though some ships prefer to take only individuals. We include a few ships which are from charter organisations, from time to time booked by sail training organisations and school groups, especially in Cutty Sark Tall Ships' Races.

List II Ships where you can get berths on board, but which are seldom seen in European waters but which have their base in THE FAR EAST, (Japan, Hong Kong, Australasia), or THE AMERICAS and could be of interest to the more adventurous.

LIST III Ships that are Government owned, owned by military services or civilian services. You'll find it difficult or impossible to get a berth (unless you 'join up' first). Many of them will take people from OTHER similar services.

LIST IV Ships owned by dedicated organisations (sailing clubs, scout groups, etc) where availability to get on board may be limited, as no doubt, 'club' members will have first claim on places aboard.

LIST V Others involved from time to time, and who have joined in Cutty Sark Tall Ships' Races. We include smaller yachts who have room for less than 10 trainees on board.

List VI Luxury cruise ships usually built as near replicas of the clipper ships of times past, where paying passengers can play a role, if they wish, in the running of the ship, the handling of the sails, etc, and where the sensation of SAIL is paramount to that of MOTOR.

List VII Three Round the World Races See pages 236-237.

Photographers

The main photographs have been provided by each ship, and we thank them for their care. We now list these photographs (where they have names attached), and others that have been selected from a large number of excellent slides and prints, with the main ones from Beken of Cowes.

Other German Ships

Besides those listed in detail in this Guide, there are a large number of other German sail training ships who are members of STAG (Sail Training Association Germany). Full details of these can be found in an 112 page A5 hardback book (half the page size of our Guide) called Mitsegeln auf Sail-Training-Schiffen by Monika Kludas . In German, it has either colour or black and white photos of ships listed. The book can be obtained from NWD-Verlag, Haven Strasse 142, D-27576, Bremerhaven, Germany at 29.80DM. It includes the German ships in this Guide, and most of the following which are presently sailing under the STAG flag.

Mitsegeln auf Sail-Training-Schiffen

Ein praktisches Handbuch der S.T.A.G. mit Schiffsportraits von Monika Kludas

NWD-VERLAG

Ship/ Home base/ length overall
Aglaia/ Kiel/ 15 metres
Astarte/ Bremerhaven/ 28.8 metres
Athena/ Bremen/ 18 metres
Carola/ Kiel// 25 meters
Cloud Clipper/ Hamburg/ 15 metres
Colomba/ St. Goar/ 29 metres
Diana/ Ditzum/ 17 metres
Fritiden/ Hooksiel/ 12 metres
Fulvia af Anholt/ Hamburg/ 22 metres
Geo/ Emden/ 12 metres
Gesine von Papenburg/ Papenburg/ 18 metres
Godeke Michels/ Bremen/ 23 metres
Greif/ Greifswald/ 41 metres
Grete/ Høruphav/ 13 metres
Grönland/ Bremerhaven/ 29 metres
Hanse-Kogge/ Kiel/ 24 metres
Kathrin/ Bremerhaven/ 12 metres
Korsar/ Lübeck/ 12 metres
Mutsch/ Kiel/ 11 metres
Olifant/ Wedel/Holstein/ 16 metres
Peter von Danzig (II) Kiel/ 17 metres
Regina-Germania/ Frankfurt am Main/ 15 metres
Swantje/ Emden/ 18 metres
Symbiose/ Braunschweig/ 12 metres
Ubena/ Bremen/ 23 metres
Walross III/ Berlin/ 16 metres
Wappen von Bremen II/ Bremen/ 17 metres

Other French Ships

There are a large number of French ships, some sail training ships, or attraction ships, or those which you can book for a day trip or more, in addition to those in our Guide. Full details of these can be found in a 274 page book (each page 40% of the size of a page in this book) called partir sur les grands voiliers. It is in French, with colour photos of each ship. The book can be obtained from Guide Balland, 33, rue Saint-Andre-des-Arts 75006 Paris, France at 170 francs (including postage). It includes all the French ships in this Guide, plus the following (and it also includes 59 other international sailing ships), with details how to get on board.

Ship/ Home Port/ Length in metres
Alliance/ Marseille/ 27
Amadeus/ Port Camargue/ 47
L'Audiernais/ Le Plan-Medoc/ 27
La Belle Étoile / Camaret/ 24
Andre-Yvette/ Etel/ 27
L'Audiernais/ Le Plan-Medoc/ 27
La Belle Angèle/ Pont-Aven/ 24
Cap Sizun/ Audierne/ 21
Corentin/ Quimper/ 32
Dahl Mad/ Quimper/ 17
Escamouche/ Marseille/ 23
Fleur de Lampaul/ Île d'Yeu/ 30
Hoedic/ Le Lavandou/ 27
La Cancalaise/ Cancale/ 31
La Dame de Canton/ Paris/ 28
La Granvillaise/ Granville/ 32
Le Nebuleuse/ Lannebert/ 32
L'Émigrant/ La Rochelle/ 25
Le Grand Lejon/ Plerin Lejon/ 20.7
Le Renard/ Saint-Malo/ 30
Lys Noir/ Granville/ 24
Marie-Fernand/ Le Havre/ 23.5
Maria-Gilberte/ Mediterranean/ 25
Marie Madeleine/ Saint-Hilaire-Petitville/ 21
Michel Daniele/ Les Sables-d"Olonne/ 30
Neire Maove/ Barneville-Carteret/ 23
Noctilio/ Cassis/ 31
Notre Dame de Rumengol/ L'Hopital-Camfrout/ 28
Popoff/ Saint-Malo/ 21
Rara Avis/ Paris HQ/ 38
Saint C'hireg/ Tregastel/ 24
Saint-Jeanne/ Erquy/ 24
Soliman/ Montpellier/ 21
Solveig/ Douarnenez/ 19
Vieux Copain/ Paimpol/ 29

Others from the Americas

Besides those ships from the Americas which are in our guide, there are many others, ships used for sail training, attraction ships, historic ships, ones you can sail on for a day, or more, and they are listed below. Full details of these can be found in a 312 page A5 sized book (half the page size of our guide) It is called Sail Tall Ships!. In English, with black and white photos, it includes all ships from the Americas in this Guide, plus the following listed here. To buy, write to The American Sail Training Association, PO Box 1459, Newport, Rhode Island, 02840, USA at $15 plus $3 postage

Ship/ State	
A.J.Meerwald/ New Jersey	American Rover/ Virginia
Adirondack/ Rhode Is	Amistad/ Connecticut
Adventure/ Massachusetts	Appledore II// Maine
Adveturess/ Washington	Appledore IV/ Michigan
Alaska Eagle/ California	Argus/ California
Alcyone/ Washington	Aurora/ Rhode Island
Alma/ California	Bagheera/ California
Alvei/ USA	Balclutha/ California
Amara Zee/ Ontario Canada	Bee (HMS)/ Ontario Canada
America/ Maryland	Bill of Rights/ California
American Eagle/ Rhode Island	Black Jack/ Ontario Canada
	Black Pearl/ Connecticut

Sail Tall Ships!®

A Directory of Sail Training and Adventure at Sea

ASTA
American Sail Training Association

Bluenose II/ Nova Scotia Canada	Imagine...!/ Maryland
Bounty/ Massachusetts	Inland Seas/ Michigan
Bowdoin/ Maine	Intrepid/ Rhode Island
C.A. Thayer/ California	Irving Johnson/ California
Californian/ California	Isabelle/ Rhode Is
Challenge/ Ontario Canada	John E.Pfriem/ Connecticut
Chance/ Maine	Jolly II Rover/ Pennsylvania
Clearwater/ New York	Joseph Conrad/ Connecticut
Clipper City/ Maryland	Kaliulani/ California
Columbia/ Rhode Island	Kalmar Nyckel/ Delaware
Compass Rose/ Florida	Lady Maryland/ Maryland
Constellation (USS)/ Maryland	Lady Washington/ Washington
Constitution (USS)/ Massachusetts	Larinda/ Massachusetts
Coronet/ Rhode Island	Lark/ Massachusetts
Corsair/ California	Lettie G.Howard/ New York
Corwith Cramer/ Massachusetts	Liberty/ Massachusetts
Cutty Sark/ Washington	Liberty Clipper/ Massachusetts
Daniel Webster Clements/ Florida	Lisa/ Delaware
Dariabar/ California	Mabel Stevens/ Washington D.C.
Distant Star/ California	Madeline/ Michigan
Dorothea/ Nova Scotia Canada	Maine/ Maine
Ebb Tide/ Massachusetts	Malabar/ Michigani
Edna Berry/ Maine	Manitou/ Michigan
Elissa/ Texas	Margaret Todd/ Maine
Elizabeth II/ North Carolina	Mary Day/ Maine
Endeavour/ Rhode Island	Mary Harrigan/ Virginia
Endeavour/ Australia	Mike Sekul/ Mississippi
Esperanza/ Argentina	Minnie V/ Maryland
Europa/ The Netherlands	Misty Isles/ Florida
Exy Johnson/ California	Mystic Whaler/ Connecticut
Fari Jeanne/ Ontario Canada	Neferiti/ Rhode Island
Fantasy/ St. Lucia	Nehemiah/ California
Federalist/ Virginia	Niagara/ Pennsylvania
Fridhem/ Georgia	Nina/ Texas
Friendship/ Massachusetts	Norseman/ Delaware
Frydraca/ Maryland	North Star of Herschel Island/ British Columbia Canada
Gazela of Phiadelphia/ Pennsylvania	Northern Light/ Rhode Island
Geronimo/ Rhode Island	Odyssey/ Florida
Gleam/ Rhode Island	OMF Ontario/ New York
Glenn L.Swetman/ Mississippi	Pacific Grace/ British Columbia Canada
Governor Stone/ Florida	Palawan/ Maine
Gyrfalcon/ Maryland	Pathfinder/ Ontario Canada
Half Moon/ New York	Peking/ New York
Hawaiian Chieftain/ California	Phoenix/ New York
Heritage/ Rhode Island	Picara/ Massachusetts
Hewitt R. Jackson/ Washington	Picton Castle/ Cook Islands
	Pilgrim/ California
	Pilgrim/ New York